T0301831

Fiscal Policy in a Turbulent Era

IN A TURBULENT ERA SERIES

These are turbulent and changing times. The longer-term effects of phenomena such as pandemics, the climate crisis, disruptive technologies, war, rising inequality, and shifts in global influence and power, on business, the economy and geo-politics are still unknown. Given these rapidly changing economic and social norms, businesses, organisations and institutions must be nimble to thrive. Focusing on one area at a time, this series seeks to investigate best practice, cutting-edge research and new ways of operating in this turbulent era.

For a full list of Edward Elgar published titles, including the titles in this series, visit our website at www.e-elgar.com.

Fiscal Policy in a Turbulent Era

Tectonic Shifts

Edited by

Enrique Alberola

Adviser, Banco de España, Spain; former Chief of the BIS Americas Office, Mexico

IN A TURBULENT ERA SERIES

Edward Elgar
PUBLISHING

Cheltenham, UK • Northampton, MA, USA

© The Editor and Contributors Severally 2024

Cover image: Josep Castells on Unsplash.

All rights reserved. No part of this publication may be reproduced, stored in a retrieval system or transmitted in any form or by any means, electronic, mechanical or photocopying, recording, or otherwise without the prior permission of the publisher.

Published by
Edward Elgar Publishing Limited
The Lypiatts
11 Lansdown Road
Cheltenham
Glos GL50 2JA
UK

Edward Elgar Publishing, Inc.
William Pratt House
9 Dewey Court
Northampton
Massachusetts 01060
USA

A catalogue record for this book
is available from the British Library

Library of Congress Control Number: 2023951006

This book is available electronically in the **Elgar**online
Economics subject collection
http://dx.doi.org/10.4337/9781035300563

ISBN 978 1 0353 0055 6 (cased)
ISBN 978 1 0353 0056 3 (eBook)

Printed and bound by CPI Group (UK) Ltd, Croydon, CR0 4YY

Contents

Figures

Tables

Contributors

Enrique Alberola is currently Adviser at Banco de España and Editor of its blog. Previously, he has worked at the Bank for International Settlements (BIS) from 2014 to 2022, first as Chief of the Americas Office in Mexico and then as Adviser at the headquarters in Basel. His professional career started at Banco de España, where he reached a senior management position in the International Department. He has lectured in several universities in Spain and Mexico. His research has often appeared in top field journals. A graduate of Valencia University, he received his PhD in Economics in 1995 from the European University Institute in Florence.

Javier Andrés is a Professor of Economics at the University of Valencia since 1991 and holds a Master of Science in Economics from the London School of Economics, where he was visiting researcher at the Center for Economic Performance. He is a research consultant at the Bank of Spain and member of the Advisory Board of the Independent Authority for Fiscal Responsibility. His research interests include economic growth, fiscal and monetary policies, and the effect of financial frictions on macroeconomic stability.

Martín Ardanaz is Senior Fiscal Specialist at the Fiscal Management Division of the Inter-American Development Bank. His research interests are in public economics and political economy with a focus on the working of fiscal policy in developing countries. His research has been published in journals such as *World Development*, *Journal of International Money and Finance*, and *Journal of Comparative Economics*. He received a PhD in Political Science from Columbia University and a BA from Universidad de San Andrés (UdeSA), Argentina.

Claudio Borio was appointed Head of the Monetary and Economic Department (MED) of the Bank for International Settlements (BIS) on 18 November 2013. At the BIS since 1987, Mr Borio has held various positions in MED. From 1985 to 1987, he was an economist at the OECD. Prior to that, he was Lecturer and Research Fellow at Brasenose College, Oxford University. He holds a DPhil and an MPhil in Economics and a BA in Politics, Philosophy and Economics from the same university.

Aida Caldera is Head of Division at the OECD. In this capacity she leads an international team of economists covering nine European and Latin American countries, doing macroeconomic and structural policy surveillance, preparing regular economic reviews of OECD member and non-member economies, doing forecasts and giving policy advice to governments. Before joining the OECD, she worked for the European Investment Bank, France's Central Bank, and the think tank, Bruegel. Aida holds a PhD in Economics from the Université Libre de Bruxelles.

Eduardo Cavallo is Principal Economist at the Research Department of the Inter-American Development Bank (IDB) and Adjunct Professor at SAIS, Johns Hopkins University in Washington, DC. Before, he was a Vice-President and Senior Latin American Economist for Goldman Sachs in New York. He holds a PhD in Public Policy and an MPP from Harvard University, and a BA in Economics from Universidad de San Andrés (UdeSA) in Buenos Aires, Argentina.

Benedict Clements is Visiting Professor of Economics at the Universidad de las Américas in Ecuador. Prior to his retirement from the International Monetary Fund (IMF) in 2020, he was an Assistant Director in the African Department and Division Chief in the IMF's Fiscal Affairs Department. Mr Clements earned his PhD in Economics from the University of Notre Dame and has published widely on fiscal policy, macroeconomics, and inequality in both journals and books.

Aitor Erce is an independent advisor on sovereign debt policy issues with over 15 years of experience. Most recently, Aitor has been supporting the African Development Bank in the design of an African Financial Stability Mechanism. He is currently research fellow at CERDi in France. Prior to this, Aitor has advised the Independent Evaluation Office of the IMF, The World Bank and The Inter-American Development Bank and the European Stability Mechanism on issues related to sovereign debt restructuring and official lending. Aitor holds an MSc in Finance from CEMFI in Madrid and a PhD in Economics from the European University Institute.

Marc Farag is a Senior Member of the Basel Committee on Banking Supervision Secretariat. In that capacity, he supports the analytical, policy and supervisory work of the Committee and advises the Chair. Marc previously worked at the Bank of England, where he was involved in a range of financial stability initiatives. Marc received a bachelor's degree in Economics from the London School of Economics. He went on to receive a Master's degree from the University of Cambridge.

Lorenzo Forni is Professor at the University of Padua's Department of Economic and Business 'Marco Fanno'. He has been the Head of Prometeia Associazione, an economic think tank within the Prometeia Group in Bologna, since 2017. Prior to his current positions, Forni worked at the IMF in Washington, DC from 2010 to 2016 and at the Bank of Italy's Research Department in Rome from 1999 to 2010. He has published extensively in international economic journals, including the *American Economic Review* and the *Journal of Public Economics*, and has contributed book chapters and numerous working papers. His book *The Magic Money Tree and Other Economic Tales* was selected as one of the *Financial Times'* best books in economics in 2021. Forni holds a Master's and PhD in Economics from Boston University, and was a visiting scholar at Harvard University in 2005–2006.

Vitor Gaspar is Director of the Fiscal Affairs Department of the International Monetary Fund. Prior to joining the IMF, he held a variety of senior policy positions in Banco de Portugal, including Head of Research and Statistics. He served as Minister of State and Finance of Portugal during 2011–2013. He was head of the European Commission's Bureau of European Policy Advisers during 2007–2010 and director-general of research at the European Central Bank during 1998–2004. Mr Gaspar holds a PhD and a post-doctoral agregado in Economics from Universidade Nova de Lisboa; he also studied at Universidade Católica Portuguesa.

Sanjeev Gupta is Senior Policy Fellow at the Center for Global Development in Washington, DC. Previously, he was deputy director at the IMF. Prior to joining the IMF, Gupta was a fellow of the Kiel Institute of World Economics, Germany; Professor in the Administrative Staff College of India, Hyderabad; and Secretary of the Federation of Indian Chambers of Commerce and Industry. Gupta has authored/coauthored over 200 papers, many of which are published in well-known academic journals, and has authored/coauthored/ coedited 13 books.

Shafik Hebous is a Deputy Division Chief in the IMF's Fiscal Affairs Department. His research is mainly in the area of public finance, including topics such as wealth inequality and the taxation of multinationals. Shafik has provided extensive tax policy advice and capacity development in countries in Asia, Africa, Europe, and the Middle East. Shafik was Adjunct Professor in Oslo Fiscal Studies at the University of Oslo and Assistant Professor in the Economics Department at Goethe University Frankfurt, where he obtained his PhD in Economics.

Pablo Hernández de Cos is Governor of the Banco de España and member of the Governing Council of the ECB. He is Chair of the Basel Committee for Banking Supervision and of the Advisory Technical Committee of the

European Single Resolution Board. He is a member of various European and International Committees related to central banking and finance. He is also Vice-Chairman of the Board of the Spanish Macroprudential Authority. He holds a PhD in Economics (Complutense University, Madrid), a degree in Economics and Business Studies (CUNEF, Madrid) and a degree in Law (UNED).

Alejandro Izquierdo is Deputy Director of the Research Department of the Inter-American Development Bank (IDB); previously he was Chief Economist (ad interim) of the IDB, as well as Regional Economic Advisor for Mexico and Central America at the IDB. He has also worked in the Economic Policy Department of the World Bank. He holds a PhD in Macroeconomics and International Finance from the University of Maryland, and a MA in Macroeconomics from Instituto Di Tella, Argentina.

Enisse Kharroubi is an Economist in the Macroeconomic Analysis division at the BIS. Prior to that, he served as an economist in the Monetary Policy Unit at the BIS. Enisse Kharroubi holds a PhD from the Paris School of Economics and started his career as an economist at the Banque de France. His main areas of research are Macroeconomics, Growth, and Fiscal and Monetary Policy.

Sandra Lizarazo is the Assistant to the Director of the Fiscal Affairs Department at the IMF. She joined in 2014. Before joining the IMF, she held positions as Assistant Professor of Economics in ITAM and Carlos III, and she worked as an Economist in the Banco de la Republica in Colombia. Sandra's research focuses on sovereign debt, financial crisis, contagion, and income distribution. Sandra holds a PhD in Economics from Duke University; she has a BA from Universidad de los Andes in Colombia.

Benoit Mojon was appointed Head of Economic Analysis at the Bank of International Settlements (BIS) on 1 September 2018. Before joining the BIS, he worked at the Bank of France. He was Head of the Monetary Policy Division from 2008 until 2011. He then became Director of Monetary and Financial Studies and a member of the Eurosystem Monetary Policy Committee. Previously, he held research positions at the Federal Reserve Bank of Chicago (2007–2008) and the European Central Bank (1998–2006). He holds a PhD in Economics from the University of Paris Nanterre. He taught at the University of Aix-Marseille (2004–2006) and Sciences Po (2008–2010) and was an adjunct professor at Ecole Polytechnique (2011–2018) and INSEAD (2018).

Ugo Panizza is Professor of Economics and Pictet Chair in Finance and Development at the Graduate Institute of International and Development Studies in Geneva. He is also the Director of the International Centre for Monetary and Banking Studies, a Vice President of CEPR, Fellow of the

Fondazione Luigi Einaudi, and Editor of *Oxford Open Economics and International Development Policy*. Previously he was the Chief of the Debt and Finance Analysis Unit at UNCTAD and a Senior Economist at the Inter-American Development Bank.

Adrián Peralta-Alva is Deputy Division Chief in the Research Department of the IMF. Prior to joining the IMF, Mr Peralta-Alva was Professor of Economics in the University of Miami, Senior Economist in the Federal Reserve Bank of St. Louis and Adjunct Faculty for PhD students in the Department of Economics of Washington University in Saint Louis. Mr Peralta-Alva has published extensively in top peer-reviewed economics journals. His areas of research include computational economics, monetary economics, macro finan-cial linkages and macro distributional issues. Mr Peralta-Alva holds a PhD in Economics from the University of Minnesota.

Luiz Pereira da Silva became Deputy General Manager of the Bank of International Settlements (BIS) on 1 October 2015. Before joining the BIS, Mr Pereira da Silva, a Brazilian national, had been Deputy Governor of the Central Bank of Brazil since 2010. Prior to that, he worked in various positions for the World Bank in Washington DC, Tokyo and southern Africa. He also served as Chief Economist for the Brazilian Ministry of Budget and Planning, and as Brazil's Deputy Finance Minister in charge of international affairs.

Mattia Picarelli is an Economist at the European Stability Mechanism. His research and policy work focuses on sovereign debt and financial stability. Before joining the ESM, Mattia worked for the European Investment Bank and the European Parliament. He holds a PhD in Economics from Sapienza University of Rome and an MSc in Economics and Finance from LUISS Guido Carli.

Andrew Powell is at the Research Department (RES) of the Inter-American Development Bank (IDB) and has a PhD from Oxford University. He has been Research Fellow at Nuffield College and Professor at Queen Mary's College, London, Warwick and Torcuato di Tella. He worked at the Central Bank of Argentina as Chief Economist from 1996 to 2001. He joined the IDB in 2005, where he has occupied several positions, the most recent as RES Principal Advisor. Andrew has published many papers in highly rated academic journals on commodity markets, regulation, capital flows, banking, emerging market crises, the role of international financial institutions, natural disasters, and monetary and fiscal policy among other topics. He has edited several books on commodity taxation and urban quality of life and has been in charge of several of IDB's flagship and macroeconomic reports. Current projects include how Multilateral Development Banks can shift risk from their balance sheets, the changing nature of capital flows, the syndicated loan market network, the impacts of regulatory forbearance and debt restructuring.

Dorothée Rouzet is Chief Economist of the French Treasury. Prior to joining Citi in 2022, she was an advisor at the French Ministry of Economy and Finance. Previously, she spent eight years at the OECD as a senior economist and advisor to the Chief economist. Dorothée holds a PhD in Economics from Harvard University and is a graduate from Ecole Normale Supérieure and ENSAE in Paris.

Niels Thygesen (b. 1934) is Professor (emer.) of International Economics at the University of Copenhagen. He trained at Copenhagen and Harvard Universities, worked for the Danish and Swedish Governments, Harvard Development Advisory Service (in Malaysia) and the OECD, and taught at Copenhagen University until 2005. His main research is in monetary economics with a focus on European integration; he served as an independent member of the Delors Committee on EMU 1988–1989. He evaluated the efficiency of IMF surveillance 1998–1999, and chaired the Economic Development and Review Committee of the OECD 2000–2008. In 2016, he became the first Chair of the European Fiscal Board, an independent body advising the European Commission.

João Tovar Jalles is Associate Professor of Economics at the University of Lisbon. Previously, he was senior economist at the Portuguese Fiscal Council and before that staff economist at the IMF, OECD and ECB. He taught at Sciences Po, University of Aberdeen, University of Cambridge and Universidade Nova de Lisboa, and has written more than 130 articles published in peer-reviewed scientific journals. He has a PhD in Economics from the University of Cambridge.

Fabrizio Zampolli is the Head of Emerging Markets at the Bank for International Settlements (BIS). Before his current position, he was Head of Economics for Latin America and the Caribbean (2018–2022), Head of Macroeconomic Analysis (2015–2016), principal economist at the Representative Office for Asia & the Pacific in Hong Kong SAR (2014–2015) and a senior economist (2009–2014). He holds a PhD from the University of Warwick and a Laurea in Economia e Commercio from the Catholic University of Milan.

Foreword

Pablo Hernández de Cos

At a particularly challenging juncture for economic authorities worldwide, this book offers highly relevant insights for policymaking. We are in one of those periods in which history accelerates and we must constantly adapt our policy tools to the evolving needs of society, both from a theoretical and a practical perspective.

The decades of relative stability and prosperity, characterized by the waves of globalization and the rise of new economic powers such as China and other emerging market economies, were abruptly interrupted by the Global Financial Crisis, a severe endogenous shock that triggered the current *era of economic turbulence*. The legacy of that crisis was very persistent, and we were still grappling with its consequences at the policy level – particularly in the monetary and financial areas – when the COVID-19 crisis struck. The pandemic is now over, but new shocks have emerged: a war in Europe and a rise in inflation after it had been dormant for decades. Nor does it seem that we can count on a prompt end to this phase of turbulence. Indeed, since the beginning of this century we have been experiencing an extraordinary period of economic and financial earthquakes that are reshaping our way of thinking about the economy and the optimal policy response.

Certainly, we have witnessed forceful – and on many occasions urgent and dramatic – policy responses to many of these shocks. Disaster has been averted, but the scars and costs for the economy and society are still apparent. Long gone are the times when economic debates revolved around tenths of a percentage point of GDP, inflation or interest rates. As policymakers we have had to adapt our understanding, behaviour and tools to a new and more complex reality. It has been a rollercoaster of learning by doing. The social demands to central bankers, finance ministries and international financial leaders have multiplied, while the risks of making mistakes have grown commensurately, in a new and uncertain environment.

The situation has been evolving so intensely, and remains so demanding, that we have still to assess the magnitude and significance of these tectonic shifts. In particular, there is a pressing need to reassess the capacity, limits and interactions of monetary, financial and fiscal policies designed to stabilize economies. But before a fully integrated framework can be established, some groundwork is needed to grasp the full implications of the recent transformations in each of these policy areas. Some of the book's chapters also deal with the complexities of the policy interactions, leading the way for future work on this front.

As for fiscal policy, the book offers a much needed solid theoretical and practical base. It provides a thorough analysis and assessment of how all of these changes have impacted fiscal policy: how it is conducted and how it should be conducted. The value of *Fiscal Policy in a Turbulent Era: Tectonic Shifts* is that it sets out the magnitude and breadth of the changes which, taken together, represent a paradigm shift in fiscal policy.

For such an ambitious goal, the book brings together an impressive team of authors who provide mutually complementary, valuable and insightful contributions. Each chapter may be read separately, while the different contributions shape a coherent story of how fiscal policy has changed and developed. The book also describes the challenges and risks that lie ahead, and offers guidance for policymakers, summed up in the introductory chapter.

As involved as I currently am, as a central bank Governor and Chair of the Basel Committee on Banking Supervision, in pressing monetary and financial challenges, the imprint on my mind of my early days as a researcher in fiscal policy has resurfaced vividly as I have read this book; a very gratifying experience I must confess. Moreover, I am particularly pleased to have been asked to write this foreword, not only because of the book's importance, but also because of my close and long-standing professional relationship with the editor, Enrique Alberola. We shared an office together at the Banco de España when we started work there as junior economists, in what now, in view of all the changes witnessed since, seems to be the distant past. In a twist of fate, Enrique was more interested in monetary and financial policy back then, but now he is editing a book on fiscal policy. A switch of roles, or perhaps merely a mutually enriching intellectual journey.

Some of the authors have been known to me for some time and I have long admired their work in their roles as leading academics or policy officials. Some are responsible for policy work that has enriched, and continues to enrich, our views on fiscal policy from their respective institutions (the IMF, OECD, BIS and IDB), while others have produced valuable research in different aspects of public finance from which we have all benefited. I also wish to acknowledge their contributions here.

All in all, the book is a valuable guide to fiscal policy changes, challenges and options in the turbulent era. I can but recommend it as an indispensable volume on the subject and for anyone seeking to learn how policymaking can provide better answers to society's most profound economic demands.

Preface and acknowledgments

The origin of this book is the proposal I received in early 2022 from Stephanie Hartley, supervising editor at Edward Elgar Publishers. They were launching the series '*In a Turbulent Era*' in Economics and Finance and contacted me to write the volume on fiscal policy.

Initially, I was reluctant. Writing a book from scratch is no minor endeavor. I am not an expert in all areas of fiscal policy and I do not follow closely academic and policy developments in the field. But fiscal policy has always attracted me and the combination of the fiscal policy and the outcomes in 'turbulent era' was inspiring. Somewhat unconsciously, I started to ponder the possibility of writing the book.

I found myself reflecting on how the turbulent era – the period since the Global Financial Crisis starting in 2007 – has reshaped fiscal policy. The outcome of this brainstorming turned out to be surprisingly rich. The views on fiscal policy have undergone dramatic changes: the tectonic shifts in the title of this volume. I listed the areas of public finance where the changes were most evident. The structure and ideas for a book were suddenly in front of me and I felt it was worth it.

Yet I felt unfit to develop the specific contents with enough depth and breadth. Before returning to the publisher, I prepared another list: the names of candidates to write each chapter. Some were experts I know well and with whom I have interacted in my career; even in the distant past such as my former professor in Valencia or an author that impressed me during my degree. I knew less well other reputed experts, but I was eager to have them onboard. To my surprise and delight they agreed to participate. I did not know others, in areas further from my expertise, but their response was also positive. The project was taking shape. Before the line-up of contributors was completed, I returned to the publisher with a counterproposal: I would lead and coordinate the book that would be mostly written by a team of experts. The proposal was duly accepted. The making of the book had started.

The outcome is in your hands or on your screen: a collection of contributions in different areas where the views on fiscal policy and public finance have changed in the last decades. The overview is not complete. Developments in taxation, cyclicality or the size of government are not covered in detail. In the introductory chapter, I use the contributions to compose a structured picture of the changes and fill these gaps. The conclusion is that the changes are deep and consequential. Whether they represent a change of the fiscal policy paradigm is merely a semantic question.

The contributors to this book are a mix of policymakers, academics and officials in top international financial organizations and academics. And I feel privileged that they have offered their knowledge and time for this book. They also agreed to review and comment on the other chapters. This peer review has facilitated the revision of the book and added relevant insights and cross-references to the chapters. The process has been smooth; the authors have provided the drafts timely and have duly replied to my requests. So, my first thanks go to the devoted contributors. I would also like to thank David López and Roberto Ramos, fiscal experts at Banco de España, who completed the list of reviewers.

This book started when I was working at the Bank for International Settlements (BIS) in Basel and was completed after my return to Banco de España in Madrid. My line managers Benoit Mojon in Basel and Javier Pérez in Madrid have allowed me to devote enough time to the project. My thanks go to both of them. Mercedes García Escribano suggested names for some of the chapters. Gema Pérez, who formatted and polished the chapters, has been of great help in the final phase of production. And finally, to Eva, who is always supportive in my professional adventures.

Enrique Alberola
Valencia, May 2023

1. Introduction: the transformation of fiscal policy in the turbulent era

Enrique Alberola

1.1 INTRODUCTION

The global economy has gone through the two biggest recessions since the Second World War in the last two decades: The Global Financial Crisis (GFC) of 2007–08 and the Pandemic Crisis of 2020. The recovery from the pandemic reawakened inflation, dormant for several decades. An old-fashioned type of war in Europe triggered an energy crisis that entrenched inflation and clouded global economic perspectives.

We are indeed living in a turbulent era for the global economy and, by extension, for fiscal policy. This book focuses on this period and gazes into the future. We argue that these economic earthquakes are catalysing a profound change in fiscal policy along multiple dimensions.

Paradigms in economic thinking usually brew and develop in academic circles, rise to the policy sphere and, eventually, dominate policymaking. Established views that look solid fall out of favour when they fail to explain new realities, to fulfil their promises or to successfully face new economic challenges. Fiscal policy is no exception.

The Keynesian revolution in economics was a response to the Great Depression. The laissez-faire, liberal paradigm of the time became unfit to overcome the crisis (Jacobs and Laybourn-Langton, 2018). The basic principles of the Keynesian paradigm were the conviction in the stabilizing role of proactive fiscal policies and the central role of the state in allocating and redistributing economic resources. The rise of Keynesianism facilitated the economic recovery in the 1930s and the reconstruction after the Second World War. However, its glow faded in the 1960s as deficits and inflation surged. It was progressively abandoned in the 1970s, with the demise of the Bretton Woods regime of fixed exchange rates and the surge in inflation and deficits (Furman, 2016). A parallel political shift consolidated the swing in the late 1970s and 1980s. Free enterprise, trade and markets and lower state intervention in the economy were the trademarks of the new political economy climate.

The new paradigm favoured rules over discretion in fiscal policy and questioned its stabilizing role. Monetary policy came to the fore as an independent policy focused on achieving price stability; one that could be effective in stabilizing the economy through the cycle, too. The shift gave place to a neo-classical synthesis, in the Hegelian sense, that partially restored the classical paradigm of the first decades of the twentieth century and combined it with Keynesian elements.

The neo-classical paradigm – dubbed by critics as neo-liberal – had a good start. The global economy enjoyed a prolonged phase of solid global growth, opening and deepening of global markets and price and macroeconomic stability, known as the Great Moderation (Stock and Watson, 2002). This period welcomed countries that had failed under alternative economic systems to the global market: China and the Soviet bloc. An expanded group of emerging markets and developing economies (EMDEs) also enjoyed the benefits of globalization and made substantial economic and social progress

But this expansionary phase ended up in a sequence of financial crises. The crises started in EMDEs in the 1980s and became recurrent in the 1990s. The opening of the EMDEs' capital accounts favoured market excesses, fiscal laxity and the accumulation of financial imbalances. Later, these fragilities extended to advanced economies (AEs): light financial regulation and the overconfidence in – and of – central banks to overcome periods of financial stress undermined the stability of the system and culminated in the GFC. The era of turbulence, in which we still are, had started.

The response to the GFC and beyond has reshaped the role of fiscal policy and prompted a deep change in thinking. In parallel, structural economic and social changes have shifted policy preferences that have a large imprint on public finances. The coincidence of these developments is transforming fiscal policy and challenging some of its basic principles.

The pendulum is swinging back: the proactive role of fiscal policy and of the state in the economy is in vogue again. The change has great significance. The economists contributing to this book – outstanding academics and officials in policy institutions – have grown up and developed their academic and professional careers – almost without exception[1] – under the neo-classical paradigm. The conjunction of this change of views on fiscal policy with recurrent economic turbulences and the higher uncertainty that marks this period entails daunting intellectual and policy challenges.

It is not clear whether we are undergoing a paradigm shift in fiscal policy or just a transitory reassessment of its role due to the changes in environment. In any case, the change is profound, lasting and consequential. It is timely and useful to take stock of the tectonic shifts that the turbulent era has brought to fiscal policy and to reflect on what lies ahead. This is the goal of this book.

1.2   ROADMAP TO THE BOOK AND SUMMARY OF THE CHAPTERS

The myriad changes in fiscal policy during this turbulence call for some structure, which is depicted in Figure 1.1 as a roadmap to this book. The terms in brackets refer to the chapter numbers.

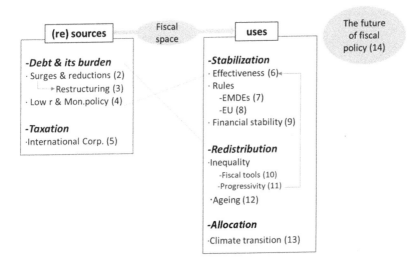

Figure 1.1   Roadmap to the book

We adopt in this book a broad concept of fiscal policy. Following the classical definition of Musgrave (1959), fiscal policy goes beyond stabilizing the economy; it also conveys the redistribution of income and the allocation of scarce resources in the economy. A proper analysis of fiscal policy requires considering all the financing sources, i.e. including debt along with revenues. The availability of resources for government, its conditions and costs determine the fiscal space; and the lack of fiscal space constrains fiscal policy.

The first part of the book analyses the resources that underpin fiscal policy. We focus on debt and how low interest rates and monetary policy have reduced its burden, opening space for fiscal policy. The other key source is government revenues. Taxes is a very broad area; we address just one specific aspect that has gained relevance recently: international taxation.

We then consider the uses of fiscal policy. The second part of the book focuses on the stabilizing role of fiscal policy. The aspects we consider are its effectiveness, the role of rules and the link between fiscal policy and financial stability. The third part covers the other two functions of fiscal policy: redistribution and reallocation, where priorities are shifting. The main theme regarding redistribution is inequality and the fiscal tools to mitigate it, but we will also address how redistribution impacts fiscal outcomes. The ageing of our societies dominates the intergenerational dimension of redistribution. Regarding reallocation, we focus on the rise of climate change as a key theme for fiscal policy. The concluding chapter of the book looks into the future of fiscal policy.

1.2.1 Part I. Fiscal Resources and the Fiscal Space

One of the most relevant developments for fiscal policy in the turbulent era has been the dramatic surge in public debt. The GFC and then the pandemic implied a large leap in debt that has reached all-time highs in many countries.

Chapter 2 by Panizza and Powell analyses debt surges and reductions with a particular focus on EMDEs. The ratio of debt to GDP is generally lower in this group of economies compared with advanced economies (AEs) and it has increased less in the turbulent era: from 36 per cent to 64 per cent in EMDEs compared with a leap from 71 per cent to 104 per cent in AEs.

Despite their lower debt ratios, concerns over debt sustainability arise more often in EMDEs. One main reason is the quality of institutions. Despite good progress in most EMDEs, institutional development remains work in progress. The weakness of institutions hampers the debt-carrying capacity and biases debt towards external sources and in foreign currency. Debt service and the ability to satisfy it becomes more uncertain and volatile, as it hinges on the market mood. As a consequence, the main drivers of debt surges in EMDEs are the spikes in interest payments and valuation effects – largely determined by exchange rate evolutions that impact on external debt. Inflation, which deflates the stock of debt, is the main driver of debt reduction episodes. High growth and low interest rates are other relevant drivers and they can be a powerful combination to reduce debt or keep it sustainable, as we note below.

High levels of debt may be difficult to reverse and risk becoming unsustainable when circumstances worsen. The evidence shows that sovereign defaults and debt restructuring play a central role in reducing public debt overhangs. Aitor Erce and Mattia Picarelli in Chapter 3 reviews the evolution and challenges of debt restructuring mechanisms. When a sovereign defaults, the resolution process tends to be lengthy and messy. Effective restructuring mechanisms could have eased the process, mitigated the costs of default and facilitated swifter economic recoveries, but they were lacking. The financial opening of EMDEs since the 1990s led to a larger private component in debt, which complicated resolution further. The proposals to improve restructuring processes at the beginning of the century were not successful.

Sustainability concerns came again to the fore with the GFC, when access to external financing was cut off for high-debt countries. This sudden stop also affected the economies in the euro area with weak fiscal fundamentals, underscoring that AEs were not immune to the debt crisis. Debt trends have been pointing upwards in a majority of countries even before the pandemic and only a few enjoyed substantial debt reductions in the 2010s. With the COVID-19 shock, the debt situation became desperate in some EMDEs. The G20 and the multilaterals relieved debt service for the most vulnerable. They have also designed a new mechanism for ordered restructuring: the G20 Common Framework for Debt Treatments, although it has limitations and it is not accepted by all stakeholders.

In spite of the surge in debt, defaults have not increased proportionally and they have remained far from the level of the 1980s, although they have recently spiked. Why has ever higher debt not led to serial sovereign defaults around the world? The short answer is that, in spite of ever higher debt, the cost of public debt has been declining in the last decades, particularly in AEs.

In Chapter 4, we look into the secular decline in the interest rates and the evolving role in monetary policy. Both have relieved the fiscal burden for the sovereign and mitigated debt sustainability concerns. Equilibrium or natural interest rates have dropped from around 5 per cent in the 1980s to around zero or even negative values, in real terms. A key arithmetic equation dominates debt dynamics: the difference between the real interest rate paid on debt and the growth rate of the economy: $r–g$. When the effective cost of debt is lower than growth ($r–g<0$) the dynamics of debt are benign for the sovereign: the debt-to-GDP ratio decreases with a balanced budget and even with sizable fiscal deficits.

Why have interest rates fallen so much? Because the natural or equilibrium interest rate (r^*) has plummeted. The factors that drive r^* are related to the saving–investment balance: ageing that reduces demand for capital and increases saving; higher inequality that also tends to increase savings; lower productivity and potential growth that diminishes the attraction to invest. The higher uncertainty in the turbulent era is an additional element. It has increased the demand for safe assets, and public debt is the epitome of this kind of asset, in particular for countries with good fundamentals. All these elements more than offset the upward pressure on sovereign yields from higher public debt.

The role of monetary policy in the fall of the natural interest rate is more contentious. The orthodox view maintains that only real factors can determine r^*, while monetary policy only affects nominal variables and is neutral in the long run. In any case, it is widely accepted that the evolution of monetary policy has reinforced the role of fiscal policy.

The conquest of inflation by central banks in the final decade of the last century enabled more accommodative monetary policies and looser financing conditions, also for governments. Then, the GFC turned conventional monetary policy largely inoperative as inflation dropped and interest rates clashed with the zero or effective lower bound (ZLB). New policy tools were adopted to face the crisis and bring inflation back to the target. They included huge liquidity to the banking sector, using public paper as collateral, and purchases of public debt. Both reduced further the financing cost for the government and facilitated a strong fiscal response. The lack of monetary tightening at the ZLB also implied a more powerful fiscal policy and fiscal expansions helped central banks to attain the inflation target. Through these channels both have got closely intertwined in the turbulent era.

The increasing debt and its importance in fiscal planning reflects the limits of revenue collection relative to increasing expenditure pressures. Taxation and, in general, fiscal revenues are the main source to fund fiscal policy, but its limits have become evident in the last decades. One of the main challenges to taxation is the transnational leakage of taxes through borders, in particular in the corporate sector.

In Chapter 5, Shafik Hebous analyses the challenge of taxing multinationals and assesses the 2021 Inclusive Framework agreement on international corporate tax reform. The rise of the global firm with a sophisticated cross-border organization, the digitalization of the economy, and the increased importance of intangible assets (know-how assets) constrain the ability of national jurisdictions to tax multinationals properly. Cross-border spillovers on tax rates and bases generate tax competition (to the bottom) between countries, and multinationals exploit international differences in corporate tax rules to shift profit from high- to low-tax jurisdictions.

The agreement is a step in the right direction. The two-pillar reform limits tax competition and profit shifting with somewhat positive effects on revenue. The first pillar redistributes the corporate taxes, shifting a portion of the tax base from low-tax jurisdictions to market countries. The second pillar aims at levelling the playing field by introducing a minimum effective tax of 15 per cent. The expected impact on revenue is positive but modest. The first pillar is mandatory but it only covers large multinationals; it is expected to reallocate only 2 per cent of the multinational's profits, so its revenue impact is small. The second pillar has more revenue potential – between 5 and 8 per cent of global corporate tax or 0.15–0.25 per cent of global GDP; but the second pillar is optional and has not been approved by important national constituencies yet. On top of the pending ratification, there are other layers of uncertainty, such as compliance, effective coordination and practical consequences in terms of relocation of headquarters, etc. The reform is not a panacea, but it is a breakthrough on tax coordination at the global level. It has required bringing many countries on board, including small jurisdictions that play an important role in hosting global income. Not a minor achievement.

1.2.2 Part II. Uses of Fiscal Policy: The Stabilization Role of Fiscal Policy

The second part of the book focuses on fiscal policy and stability, both economic and financial. In these areas, the views on fiscal policy have deeply changed in the turbulent era too.

In Chapter 6, Javier Andrés analyses the effectiveness of fiscal policy. Before the GFC, the conventional view – supported by the empirical evidence – was that discretionary fiscal policy was hardly effective. The underlying view was Ricardian: firms and consumers understand that fiscal expansions have to be repaid with future taxes; this expectation favours saving and reduces the impact of the expansion or multiplier.

The deep recession in the aftermath of the GFC required decisive fiscal support and it proved effective. The economic environment had also changed: at the ZLB, fiscal stimuli are more powerful, as noted above. Fiscal policy contributed to containing the damage and relieved the pressure on financially constrained households and corporates. The previous view of fiscal expansions impacting negatively on expectations and weakening fiscal policy, proved wrong this time. The fiscal response stabilized expectations and reinforced the impact of the fiscal expansion. The fiscal multipliers increased, as these factors more than offset the decreasing effect of higher public debt. Capitalizing on the experience of the GFC, the fiscal response to the pandemic was even faster and stronger. It contributed to buffering the economic and financial shock and facilitated a fast economic recovery.

The recent economic circumstances and policy experiences have established a more benign and proactive view of fiscal policy among academics and policymakers. Along with easy financing conditions, this view can lead to complacency and hamper fiscal discipline efforts at a time when debt is much higher.

How to promote fiscal discipline is a long-standing policy question. The political process surrounding fiscal policy tends to generate a deficit bias in the public accounts. Strong fiscal institutions and conviction is required to rein in the bias. Too often, financial markets force fiscal discipline upon governments through sudden stops of capital inflows and sharp increases in the credit risk, particularly in EMDEs. The neo-classical paradigm favoured rules over policy discretion. Fiscal rules have become the institutional mechanism to achieve fiscal discipline and they have become widespread. The idea is that fiscal rules that limit discretion can help fiscal policy to fulfil its countercyclical role and contain debt. In Chapter 7, Martín Ardanaz, Eduardo Cavallo and Alejandro Izquierdo review how fiscal rules have performed.

Despite their popularity, fiscal rules are not a panacea: their mere adoption is insufficient to prevent debt accumulation. Their performance depends on their quality, design and enforcement. The authors identify the key elements for effective rules: a design that anchors debt, e.g. through debt thresholds that feed-back on the rules; mechanisms to improve compliance, such as well-equipped fiscal councils and credible medium-term fiscal frameworks; and flexibility provisions to safeguard growth-friendly expenditure, such as productive public investment.

One conspicuous example where fiscal rules were insufficient to prevent a fiscal crisis was Europe in the years after the GFC. Niels Thygesen evaluates in Chapter 8 the evolution of fiscal integration in the European Union (EU).

The complexity of rules design multiplies in a supranational entity. The ░░░░░░░░ ░░░░░░ and close linkages in the EU would call for a strong central fiscal capacity in conjunction with fiscal rule. But monetary fiscal sovereignty has always been a sensitive issue. The reluctance of member countries explains the tiny size of the EU central budget (around 1 per cent of its GDP) and the limited scope of the fiscal rules embodied in the Stability and Growth Pact (SGP). As a result, the aim of the common fiscal framework in Europe has been limited to preventing excessive debt accumulation and bad spillovers or contagion. The SGP constrained to some extent the former, but not the latter. EU fiscal rules did not facilitate a countercyclical fiscal policy, nor improve the quality of public finance. Moreover, compliance was low.

A much-needed reform of the EU fiscal framework was underway when the pandemic hit. The reform was then framed in a quite different context. The policy response in the EU included a large centralized fiscal package (of around 10 points of GDP spread over several years and financed with common debt) that constituted a historical breakthrough in EU history. Posterior events, like the energy crisis following the Russian invasion of Ukraine or the higher priority given to the green transition (see Chapter 13) have strengthened the views in favour of a strong central fiscal capacity.

The reform proposal goes in the right direction, but not much beyond SGP. There are some improvements in the fiscal rules by looking more into the medium term, allowing for flexibility and interaction. Remarkably, it misses the elephant in the room: the issue of the central fiscal capacity is absent, as political resistance to it lingers. The proposal also omits any reference to interactions with monetary policy (the ECB in this case) that have also been nurtured in the turbulent era, as noted in Chapter 4.

The financial crisis highlighted the close nexus between fiscal policy and financial stability, an issue overlooked before the turbulent era. In Chapter 9, Claudio Borio, Marc Farag and Fabrizio Zampolli review the linkages, which are mutually reinforcing. Fiscal fragility weakens the financial system; either directly, through the reduced value of sovereign assets in times of stress, or indirectly, for instance through lower activity. Financial fragility may require the need of fiscal support, sometimes massively. These vicious circles can end in financial and sovereign crises that have a deep and lasting impact on the economies.

How to break these vicious cycles or 'doom loops'? Incorporating financial stability into the fiscal policy process would help. There are several mechanisms: (i) assessing the eventual costs of banking crises, taking these contingent costs into the assessment of the fiscal space and generating the adequate buffers; (ii) considering the impact of the financial cycle on fiscal balances, which are flattered by financial booms and expose fiscal vulnerabilities at the busts; (iii) reducing the bias towards debt in tax-subsidy regimes that would favour less exposure of banks to sovereign debt. Related to the latter, the authors raise a particularly contentious issue: whether prudential regulation should abandon the current favourable treatment that public debt enjoys in the in assessment of banks' risk.

1.2.3   Part III. Uses of Fiscal Policy: Redistribution, Allocation and Emerging Demands

The turbulent era is also having a deep impact on the social compact and preferences. The deep scars of the crisis explain the evolving concerns in the case of inequality; in others, the influence is more indirect. Population ageing is a long-term trend but it is gaining more and more relevance as its impact on public finances increases. Climate change is a long-standing concern that has climbed to a top policy issue; the transition to a greener economy requires public engagement and fiscal resources.

Inequality is addressed from different perspectives in the two following chapters.

In Chapter 10, Benedict Clements, Sanjeev Gupta and João Tovar Jalles examine the redistributive role of fiscal policy and the fiscal reforms to achieve better redistribution. Inequality has been decreasing at the global level, but increasing within countries, as measured by the Gini index. In AEs, higher income inequality is a consistent trend, while in EMDEs it has decreased in recent decades, until the pandemic.

Both groups have converged to a similar market Gini, but fiscal policy makes a big difference, as reflected in the Gini based on disposable income. In AEs, fiscal policy is three times more redistributive than in EMDEs. As a result, inequality in disposable income is much higher in EMDEs. Social protection in developing economies is lower and more ineffective; pensions and expenditure in health and education is also lower and biased towards middle and high income population. The pandemic underscored the differences: AEs provided strong support to the vulnerable, while EMDEs were more constrained.

Addressing inequality through fiscal policy is limited by high debt. Fiscal consolidation would open up some fiscal space but it could have negative redistribution effects if it dampens economic activity. AEs do not have much room to increase taxation but they could change its composition. Higher taxes on wealth, income and property, as well as a minimum corporate tax could help to reduce inequality. EMDEs have scope to increase taxes on income and VAT, together with strengthening fiscal practices: improving tax compliance and the efficiency of spending, redirecting and making more effective the expenditure on the poor or investing in universal health and education.

These reforms to address inequality would run counter to recent fiscal trends. Fiscal reforms, at least in AEs have decreased fiscal progressivity: marginal taxes have been lowered and the unemployment benefits have been shortened and reduced. The implications go beyond redistribution. Less progressivity reduces the stabilization role of fiscal policy and increases public debt. Enisse Kharroubi, Benoit Mojon and Luiz Pereira da Silva explore in Chapter 11 these implications.

The combination of deep recessions and standard expansions during the turbulent era have had a ratchet effect on inequality, the fiscal deficits and debt. Weaker automatic stabilizers mitigate the deficit rise in recessions, but also the improvement of the fiscal balances in expansions. Large recessions have made debt jump, while it is not reduced substantially in expansions, introducing an upward drift on debt. The corollary is counterintuitive: less fiscal redistribution leads to higher, not lower debt. Another interesting conclusion is that the weakening of the automatic stabilizers demands a bigger role of discretionary policy.

To improve redistribution and the effectiveness of fiscal policies in these circumstances, the authors propose better targeting and more resources to the more vulnerable population, and taking advantage of digital technologies.

The world is ageing. AEs are more advanced in the process, but EMDEs are quickly catching up. Aida Caldera and Dorothée Rouzet provide, in Chapter 12, an overview of the impact of ageing on public finances. The impact is not only direct, through higher expenditure, but also indirect, as ageing makes the economy less dynamic and more unequal. Ageing increases expenditure in three main areas: pensions, health and long-term care. Moreover, the increase in dependency ratios (the share of retired people over working population) reduces revenues. The widening gap between spending and revenues threatens fiscal sustainability in most AEs. The authors estimate a substantial increase in expenditure over GDP and – what is more challenging – revenues. Tax revenue would need to increase between 4.5 and 11.5 percentage points of GDP by 2060 to keep public debt ratios at current levels.

Strong and decisive action is required. The reform of pensions to make them sustainable is a priority. Raising the retirement age – linking it to life expectancy – higher contributions, lower pensions and encouraging older workers to work longer are the main instruments. In truth, there has been no shortage of reforms in recent times around the world. In most cases, they have fallen short of what is needed. The increasing share of votes of the elderly is a formidable political obstacle.

The rise in demand for health care is not only due to ageing but also to medical advances; beneficial for extending and improving the quality of lives, such advances also add to the costs. There is room for improvement in organization, cost management and the use of technology. Prevention of sickness and healthier life at advanced ages could also help, but not enough to reduce the bill. Cuts in health care provision is an avenue for savings that would face strong resistance in an ageing society. Long-term care at advanced ages is also in great demand. Its public funding is limited so far, raising additional concerns on future expenditure pressures. All in all, even with the right reforms, public finances will feel the heat from ageing in the next decades.

Lorenzo Forni explores the implications of the climate transition for fiscal policies in Chapter 13. The rise of climate change to a top policy priority has been protracted since the 1990s, but has accelerated in the last few years as temperatures increase and extreme climatic events have multiplied. The pandemic has accelerated the rise – perhaps because it has exacerbated our perception of vulnerability as a global community – and commitments have become bigger, engaging an increasing number of countries, led by Europe.

Even with firm commitments, fulfilling them is complex; it entails a careful strategy encompassing multiple sectors. The cost of policies for the affected sectors in the transition raises political sensitivities and erodes political determination. Moreover, the recent energy emergency has interrupted the push for a cleaner energy. This is a reminder of how political will may waver, not to mention the swings in views and commitments due to changes in governments. This uncertainty is deleterious for a strategy that requires decisive steps in energy development and very long-term planning.

The fiscal dimension is a big consideration. Coming out of the pandemic, the urgency to cut emissions has increased, but the debt is higher and the fiscal space is getting tighter. The carbon tax on emissions is still the preferred option to achieve the goal. But views are evolving. The rigidity of energy demand implies that substitution is limited and the lack of alternatives imposes higher costs, a sensitive issue in times of increasing inflation. The limitations of the carbon tax imply that a more proactive fiscal approach is needed. More public investment and incentives for private investment and adaptation are required; fiscal policy may need to buffer the possibly negative redistributive impact and sustain activity, as specific sectors will shrink in the transition. The magnitude of this fiscal effort is uncertain. Whether it would be enough to support a successful transition is also uncertain. The premise is that the role of the state and the fiscal resources to support the green transition will grow over time, placing additional demands on stretched public finances.

The concluding chapter of the book hosts the contribution of Vitor Gaspar, Sandra Lizarazo and Adrián Peralta-Alva, who reflect on the future of fiscal policy. They note the depth of the fiscal changes in the turbulent era. The dominant negative view on fiscal policy (crowding out investment, reducing growth and generating excessive debt) has given way to a more favourable view.

Low financing costs re-established the paradox of thrift, as low rates dissipate concerns about debt sustainability and their negative impact on growth: spending rather than saving can support growth, a U-turn on the previous view. What has not changed is that too expansive policies increase debt anyway and crowd out investment, diminishing growth potential. The large positive wedge between the return on capital and that on debt underscores the detraction of potential production from high debt.

As noted above, low interest rates have also changed the nexus between fiscal and monetary policy and their respective scope. However, the basic principles of separation remain. Monetary policy concentrates on price stability and financial stability, while the focus of fiscal policy is growth, distribution, efficiency, and sustainability. The practical challenge is how to make all the pieces fit together and readjust them when circumstances evolve. This is the case now with the rise of inflation and interest rates.

The turbulent times have also underscored the political nature of fiscal policy and its deep imbrication with the private sector (markets, households, etc.). After all, fiscal policy is the financial nexus between the state and the society. One of the challenges for the profession going forward is to overcome the political cycle in fiscal policy: how should the rules of the political and policy games be designed so that policies are conducted over time in such a way as to promote stable, inclusive, sustainable, and resilient growth? Another area that merits more attention from researchers is to understand better the reaction of stakeholders to policy actions. This would help to design policy rules, procedures and frameworks so that the behaviour of the private sector contributes to the achievement of policy objectives.

1.3   HOW HAS THE TURBULENT ERA CHANGED FISCAL POLICY? TAKEAWAYS

A review of the contributions to the book reveals the deep transformation of fiscal policy, the various risks and challenges for the future and some policy lessons. In this final section, we sum up our findings in 20 takeaways.

1.3.1 The Current Status of Fiscal Policy

(1) Fiscal policy has gained relevance across multiple dimensions...
For fiscal policy, the outcome of the turbulent era is more importance and better consideration in policy and academic circles. The economic environment, dominated by two big recessions and very low interest rates and inflation, has demanded a strong fiscal policy response and has also enabled making it more effective. Economic and social dynamics are expanding the demands on fiscal policy and the state at large. The turbulent era has also consolidated a shift in economic thinking that has placed fiscal policy and the role of the state under a more benign light.

(2) ...in spite of historical highs in public debt
Public debt has surged globally as a consequence of the economic crises and the required fiscal support to overcome them. A much larger supply of debt should have pushed up the financing costs and the debt service for governments. Had debt sustainability risks arisen, credit risk would have raised the sovereign yield further. The fiscal space would have shrunk, heavily constraining fiscal policy. But this has not been the case... so far: the fiscal space has been wider than could have been expected even before the increase in debt.

(3) Low interest rates explain the puzzle, as they widen the fiscal space
The main reason is that the natural or equilibrium interest rate (r^*) has been on a declining trend for 40 years, due to structural factors (ageing, low productivity growth, preference for safe assets). The reduction of the natural rate has lowered the whole structure of interest rates in the economy – including those of sovereign debt – both in nominal and real terms. The secular reduction in r^* has more than offset the upward pressure that higher public debt exerts on sovereign yields. Low for long interest rates paved the way for a more active fiscal policy, as government financing remained cheap.

(4) Monetary policy has empowered fiscal policy and these policies have become more interconnected
Inflation below target and very low natural rates after the GFC kept policy interest rates close to zero, even in expansions. In this environment fiscal policy is more powerful. The zero lower bound renders conventional monetary policy non-operative and triggered the use of unconventional monetary policy, such as asset purchases by central banks. These tools eased financing costs at longer horizons. And monetary operations and financial regulation further increased the demand for public securities. Through these multiple channels, monetary policy has supported fiscal policy in the turbulent era.

In the opposite direction, fiscal policy expansions help to push inflation back to target, helping central banks to fulfil their mandate. The two-way interaction implies that the nexus between monetary and fiscal policy has strengthened.

(5) Discretionary fiscal policy has become more effective...
The very low interest rates, coupled with inflation below target also implied that central banks did not hike interest rates in economic expansions, strengthening the impact of fiscal stimuli. Moreover, fiscal policy has proved to be more effective in large recessions. In this context, academic research has reassessed fiscal multipliers under the new environment. They are generally higher than previously thought in AEs; for EMDEs there is not much evidence so far.

(6) ...but automatic stabilizers have weakened
The tax structure and some types of expenditures buffer the cyclical fluctuations of the economy, enhancing the stabilizing role of fiscal policy. Fiscal stabilizers are typically less strong in EMDEs, due to the belated development of the welfare state and less developed or effective tax structures. On the contrary, they are powerful in AEs. However, fiscal reforms in the turbulent era have reduced marginal tax rates on income and unemployment benefits in AEs. The decrease in fiscal progressivity erodes the stabilizing role of automatic stabilizers and, by extension, of fiscal policy.

(7) The promise of fiscal rules to discipline fiscal policy has not been fulfilled
The widespread adoption of fiscal rules in the last decades to constrain the deficit bias in governments has been only partially successful. Fiscal rules generate procedures that tend to constrain the budget and also a certain discipline in fiscal accounts. However, there are large differences among rules with respect to their coverage, loopholes and their degree of compliance and enforcement. These elements, that is, the quality of the fiscal rules and their implementation, have determined their capacity to rein in fiscal accounts, as empirical evidence shows. Only high-quality rules have limited debt accumulation, while many of them have not passed the bar in EMDEs.

(8) The demands on fiscal policy have expanded...
Several factors explain the increasing demands that fiscal policy has experienced in the last decades. One has been the need to respond to severe economic crisis, as noted above. The others derive from structural economic and social changes: ageing requires increasing fiscal resources through pensions, health and long-term care; increasing inequality, which feeds social discontent and polarization, is also demanding more decisive fiscal actions; the fight against climate change has a strong fiscal component, encompassing public invest-

ment, subsidies to the private sector and compensations to the losers; the role of fiscal policy and the size of the required support to the financial system was tested in the GFC. More recently, deep geopolitical shifts are demanding higher public expenditure in defence, and also in initiatives that strengthen strategic autonomy.

The increased demands on fiscal policy find echo within the current fiscal mood, favourable to fiscal activism and state engagement. Some of the ideas now in vogue, such as the contribution of fiscal policy to growth, would have been out of tune some years ago.

(9) …and have gained regional and global scope
Global or regional challenges and issues such as international leakages in corporate taxation, climate change, infrastructure networks or strategic autonomy have enhanced the relevance of international coordination and cooperation in the fiscal sphere. The agreement on international corporate taxation has been an achievement on global coordination that can inspire cooperation in other areas. The limited scope and revenue impact of the agreement underscores the difficulties of the global advances.

The European Union is a special case where the pandemic has triggered a substantial fiscal response at the central level. This development may be – or not – the harbinger of a permanent central fiscal capacity in Europe.

1.3.2   Prospects and Risks

(10) Fiscal policy to lose effectiveness in the evolving economic environment…
The recent awakening of inflation portends a different economic landscape going forward. Higher interest rates and tighter and more reactive monetary policy implies a reduction of fiscal multipliers, that is, of the effectiveness of fiscal policy. The surge in debt also tends to reduce fiscal multipliers as agents are more financially constrained. Finally, a return to more normal business cycles would also make fiscal policy less effective.

(11) …albeit interest rates are still expected to remain low in the long run
Will this new environment herald an era of higher interest rates and inflation, where monetary policy reacts more and fiscal policy loses traction? It is uncertain how persistent high inflation will be. Putting the inflation genie back into the bottle can take a long time and be painful. A protracted phase of monetary tightening could keep interest rates and financing costs well above r^* for a long period. A comforting factor is that r^* is expected to remain low

in the medium to long run because the underlying real factors behind its fall continue to operate.

(12) Public finances are overstretched and the scope for increasing fiscal revenues is limited

Recent fiscal activism and increasing demands on governments have overstretched fiscal policy. Spending pressures are expected to remain and funding needs will remain high, or may even increase going forward. The revenue collection capacity in AEs is close to the limit; there is little room for increasing tax rates. The reduction of the labour share in the distribution of the GDP in favour of the capital share is another challenge to increase taxation revenues, as the capital tax base is more mobile across borders. In EMDEs, the scope for broadening and improving taxation in EMDEs is generally larger, but so are the demands for expanding given the insufficiencies of the welfare state (pension systems, health and education).

New sources of revenue are appearing – such as climate-related instruments (carbon emission rights, climate taxes). The agreement on international corporate taxation can provide a fairer allocation of taxes on profits and capital. However, it is doubtful that this progress is enough to finance the expanding fiscal needs.

(13) Higher discretion in fiscal policy risks making it less efficient

The scope for discretionary fiscal policy has increased for good reasons, such as the need to support the economy in deep recessions, its higher perceived effectiveness and expanded demands. The weakening of automatic stabilizers also increases the relevance of discretion. The problem is that discretionary fiscal policy measures are subject to the complexities of the political process, including long implementation lags. Discretionary tools may be considered more effective now than in the past, but they are less efficient than automatic stabilizers, at least to dampen the cycle. Thus, the increased importance of discretionary policy can reduce the overall efficiency of fiscal policy.

(14) Debt has reached dangerous levels and debt service is bound to increase

The economic recovery after the pandemic and the spike in inflation have reduced debt ratios from the record levels of 2020. But the ratios are still much higher than pre-pandemic and further reductions will be slow. The situation looks critical in several EMDEs, with an increasing number of countries in debt distress. The pandemic-related relief is over and sovereign defaults or stress are on the rise. The pitfalls in the restructuring mechanism augur painful consequences for defaulting debtors.

A higher debt plateau combined with an increase in interest rates point to a higher cost of financing and debt service for governments in the next years. The situation may appear under control, but can change rapidly if confidence in the sustainability of debt falters and financing is cut. The increase in the number of sovereign defaults or restructurings after the pandemic is a worrying development.

(15) Fiscal space is set to shrink, eventually in an abrupt manner. The priority is to preserve it

Low interest rates and favourable financing conditions opened up fiscal space in AEs. But this space is contingent on the economic environment and should not be taken for granted. Higher financing costs and debt service imply less fiscal space. EMDEs know well how it can shrink in times of financial volatility. In those cases, preserving financial stability can require the commitment of large fiscal resources that may not be available. Also in the turbulent era, the shocks have been bigger and the degree of volatility and uncertainty is higher than in the past.

These elements underscore the importance of preserving the fiscal space. Fiscal effectiveness and the convenient financing in the past years have been favoured by the extraordinary environment of the turbulent era and should not be taken for granted. Against this backdrop, prudence advises rebuilding ample fiscal buffers in case risks materialize.

1.3.3   How to Keep Fiscal Policy Effective and Debt Sustainable

(16) A genuine commitment to medium-term fiscal consolidation...

Favourable debt dynamics driven by low interest rates cannot be the recipe to reduce debt. Inflation, neither. Higher financial costs can quickly deteriorate debt dynamics at high debt levels. Inflation only provides a transitory respite and, if entrenched, would translate into persistent higher interest rates. The focus must be on the budget balance.

Protracted fiscal imbalances usually lead to problems. They are difficult to reverse because the political process generates a deficit bias. Even more when fiscal demands are rising, as nowadays. A sustained commitment and effort to reduce deficits with a medium-term perspective is necessary. The current environment is not favourable. Complacency and an 'expansive' fiscal mood have taken hold in recent years. The benign view on fiscal policy can be salutary but it can also be an obstacle to instil the necessary discipline. A medium-term perspective would also allow us to factor in and accommodate – where possible – the expanding fiscal demands.

(17) ...combined with a thorough reflection on the optimal size of the government

Increasing fiscal demands conflict with the already large size of the budget and with the limits to increase fiscal revenues. New expenditures are accommodated generally in an ad hoc manner. Not much thought or resources are devoted to assessing whether the increased expenditures can be sustained through time, also considering the committed future expenses related to ageing. Kicking the can down the road is not a permanent option. At some point choices will have to be made.

(18) Improving the quality of fiscal policy, leveraging on technology

Improving fiscal management and the quality of fiscal policy would help to mitigate the fiscal constraints and risks. The more prominent role of discretionary policy calls for making the process more efficient. Admittedly, the policy reaction to the pandemic was swift and quick. Lessons can be drawn from this positive experience, also for non-emergency situations.

In EMDEs, the gaps to fill are much bigger. There, the fiscal reforms have to be aimed at broadening the fiscal base, as well as improving efficiency. More fiscal resources would facilitate the funding of better public services, fundamental for a more inclusive and sustainable growth.

The challenge in advanced economies is to anchor the fiscal base, avoiding domestic and international leakages. The move towards taxing (global) property and wealth is gaining traction. With the international agreement on taxation it could overcome some of the current constraints for effective and fairer taxation.

Fiscal policy can also exploit the opportunities of digitalization. For instance, digital transfers helped to provide fiscal support in EMDEs to those who needed it during the pandemic and to reveal informal activities. Proper use of digital finance could help in this way to target policies better, contributing to a better approach to mitigate inequality and saving resources. Digital tracking, combined with the international information exchange initiatives developed after the GFC can also help to reduce tax avoidance.

(19) Fiscal rules with the adequate design, complemented in Europe with a central fiscal capacity

Fiscal rules can be useful to discipline fiscal policy, if properly designed. The design, management and implementation of fiscal rules is a learning process. The experience of first-generation rules was generally disappointing but lessons are being incorporated in reshuffled designs. New rules often include provisions for unexpected shocks, are framed in a medium-term perspective, are contingent on debt thresholds and convey enforcement mechanisms. The reformed rules have more chances to serve their original purpose, but the strength of the underlying institutions continues to be key.

The reform of the fiscal rules in the EU follows some of these guidelines, but it says nothing on the establishment of a permanent central fiscal capacity. The case for a central fiscal capacity in the EU was originally related to the stabilizing role of fiscal policy at the regional level. It gathered wide support among analysts and academics before the pandemic, but clashed with political resistance. The rise of economic challenges that can only be properly tackled at the regional or global level (climate change, infrastructure for strategic autonomy and digitalization, etc.) has reinforced the need and urgency of a centralized fiscal mechanism with sufficient muscle.

(20) The overall challenge is to reconcile the central role of fiscal policy with sustainable debt

All in all, the turbulent era has been a good time for fiscal policy. In spite of higher debt, financial conditions widened the fiscal space and it was duly used. Stakeholders favoured a proactive fiscal policy. The demands and expectations on fiscal policy have increased and probably will not recede. But the economic backdrop is changing.

Going forward, an active and effective fiscal policy requires maintaining the fiscal space amid growing pressures. The biggest risk is that markets doubt at some point that debt is sustainable. That would squash the fiscal space when it is most necessary. A fiscal policy that promotes medium-term consolidation is central to reducing debt and safeguarding the fiscal space. The consolidation should be framed in a deep and thorough reflection on the size and limits of public policies.

Will policymakers deliver? The mood for activism remains and fiscal discipline is elusive when there are no strong market or institutional pressures. A disorderly adjustment amid financial stress would be dangerous and that prospect should be enough to force policymakers to act responsibly. Time will tell.

ACKNOWLEDGEMENT

The comments of Javier Andrés and participants in the seminar at Banco de España are acknowledged.

NOTE

1.   The only exception is our most veteran author, Niels Thygesen, who was educated and started his professional career when the Keynesian paradigm was still dominant.

REFERENCES

Furman, J. (2016). The new view on fiscal policy and its application. *VoxEU*, November.

Jacobs, M. and Laybourn-Langton, L. (2018). Paradigm shifts in economic theory and policy. *Intereconomics*, 53(3), 113–118.

Musgrave, R. (1959) *The Theory of Public Finance: A Study in Public Economy.* McGraw-Hill.

Stock, J. and Watson, M. (2002). Has the cycle changed and why? *NBER Macroeconomics Annual*, Working Paper 9127.

PART I

Fiscal resources and the fiscal space

2. Debt explosions and reductions in emerging and developing countries: drivers and implications

Ugo Panizza and Andrew Powell

2.1 INTRODUCTION

Debt has risen fast across the globe during the turbulent era. In 2007 just before the Global Financial Crisis (GFC), public debt was 71 percent of GDP for advanced economies and just 36 percent for emerging and developing economies. In 2019, as the Covid-19 crisis erupted, those figures had risen to 104 percent and 54 percent, and in 2020 they soared to 123 percent and 64 percent, respectively. Total public debt of these nations amounted to a staggering $85 trillion.[1]

Debt can be both good and bad with much depending on what the financing is used for. Public debt harnessed to pursue high-quality investment to improve services should be welcomed. It should also be perfectly sustainable assuming the investment is wealth creating and populations are able and willing to repay borrowed funds through service charges or more general taxation. But debt used to simply live better today, without the expectation of sufficient resources to pay obligations tomorrow, may lead to economic crisis and much future hardship.

The risks tend to be greater, and the tradeoffs involved much harsher, for emerging and developing economies (EMDEs) compared with advanced ones. Arguably, advanced economies (AEs) have become advanced precisely because they have built a set of institutions that contain these types of risks. That is then reflected in lower interest rates and the willingness of investors to hold larger quantities of debt at those rates. The fact that debt levels are higher in AEs may then reflect their higher safe debt-carrying capacity rather than a signal of alarm. Still, the crisis in the eurozone last decade and the recent mini crisis in the UK following an ill-timed tax cutting budget, highlight that advanced economies are certainly not immune.

While public debt levels have increased of late, dependent on the country and the period, debt ratios have both risen and fallen. Debt in the United States reached a peak of about 65 percent of GDP in 1995 and then fell to 54 percent just before the GFC. It rose strongly thereafter and during the pandemic to reach 135 percent of GDP in 2020 and then fell back somewhat given the economic recovery to 120 percent of GDP in 2022. Today's relatively high levels of debt in EMDEs are actually lower than the level in 1990. Still, those levels were built up during the "lost" decade of the 1980s, and, in 1990, several countries were still in default and lacked access to international capital markets (see Chapter 3).

The objective of this chapter is to provide an analysis of the increases and the decreases in public debt with a focus on emerging and developing countries. We provide both a descriptive account and analyses based on econometric techniques. Arguably, debt composition is just as important as the level of debt, and we also discuss the changes in debt composition again concentrating more on the case of EMDEs. Understanding the changes in debt, both increases and reductions, and the role of debt composition leads to a set of conclusions and policy suggestions. Still, we are the first to suggest that further work is required in several areas to pin down more precise recommendations.

The chapter is organized as follows. The next section provides a brief overview of the main trends in public debt levels and in debt composition, comparing advanced economies with emerging and developing ones. Section 2.3 then presents an analysis disaggregating the changes in public debt and then focusing on periods of debt explosions and substantial debt reductions, focusing on emerging and developing economies. Section 2.4 provides a discussion of the main results, draws the conclusions and offers ideas for future research.

2.2   PUBLIC DEBT IN THE NEW MILLENNIUM

This section describes the evolution of the level and composition of debt in relation to GDP with a focus on EMDEs, highlighting the challenges related to measuring sovereign debt and its composition.

2.2.1   Debt Levels

Figure 2.1 plots the evolution of the public debt-to-GDP ratios in advanced economies (top) and emerging and developing economies (bottom) over the last 30 years. Three trends are evident.

First, while in the early 1990s debt ratios were higher in EMDEs (the median value was 75 percent vis-à-vis a median value of 40 percent in AEs), public debt started increasing rapidly in advanced economies in the aftermath of the Global Financial Crisis (GFC), reaching a median value of 66 percent of

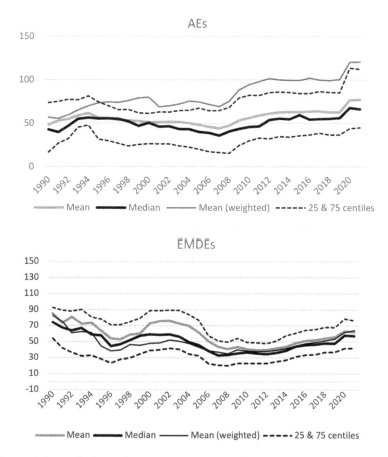

Figure 2.1   *Debt-to-GDP ratio in advanced economies (top) and emerging and developing economies (bottom)*

GDP in 2020. In EMDEs, the average and median debt-to-GDP was higher in 1990, it then fell in the 1990s bottoming out just before the GFC in 2007–2012 (at around 33 percent for the median and 39 percent for the average) and then increased to 2019 and then jumped during the Covid-19 crisis. At the end of the 1980s, several EMDEs faced unsustainable debt levels. While in this group of countries debt-to-GDP ratio remained 20 percentage points below the 1990 level after the pandemic, given rising global interest rates and a strong dollar, there is some resemblance to the late 1970s that heralded the *lost decade* of the 1980s.

Second, debt ratios are more dispersed in AEs than in EMDEs. For instance, in 2020, the advanced economies interquartile range was 55 (from 45 percent to 100 percent), while the interquartile range in emerging and developing economies was 32 (from 39 percent to 72 percent).

Third, large AEs tend to have much higher debt ratios than smaller advanced economies. Over the last 25 years, the GDP-weighted average for the sample of AEs was about 1.5 times the simple average and was always above the debt-to-GDP ratio of the country at the 75th percentile of the distribution. Arguably this might reflect the higher debt-carrying capacity of the larger and more diversified economies. In EMDEs, instead, large countries on average have lower debt ratios than smaller economies.[2] Still, there are some larger emerging economies that have relatively high debt levels.[3]

2.2.2 Debt Composition

Figure 2.2 plots the composition of public debt in EMDEs (top) and low-income economies (bottom) by focusing on the share of external public debt (defined as debt owed to non-residents). Also in this case, three trends are evident.

First, over the last 30 years there has been a marked decrease in the share of external debt. The median share of external debt for EMDEs fell from 70 percent in 1990 to 52 percent in 2019. Second, large economies tend to rely less on external debt. The (debt) weighted average share of external debt for EMDEs decreased rapidly from 2000 to 2010 and it is now below 25 percent.[4] While in middle-income economies there are large differences in external debt shares between larger and smaller economies (with largest economies being characterized by lower external debt shares), in low-income economies the average and weighted average values are almost identical and the dispersion in external debt shares is much smaller than in middle-income economies (results are similar if we drop China from the sample).[5]

Arslanalp and Tsuda (2014) collect detailed data on the holders of government securities issued by 15 emerging markets over 2004–2019. Panizza and Taddei (2020) compare their data with those of Arslanalp and Tsuda (2014) and show that the correlation between the two datasets is high but not perfect; the Arslanalp and Tsuda dataset reports much higher values for holdings of government bonds by non-residents.[6]

The type of external creditor also matters. Lending by private creditors tends to be more expensive, less stable and more procyclical than multilateral lending (Galindo and Panizza, 2018). Moreover, in case of default, there are different seniority structures with a pecking order that places international financial institutions with preferred creditor status such as the IMF and the main multilateral development banks at the top and bilateral debt at the base,

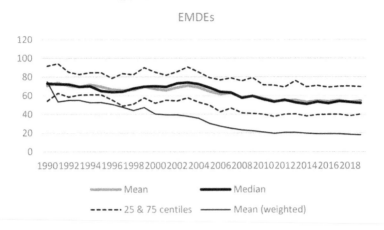

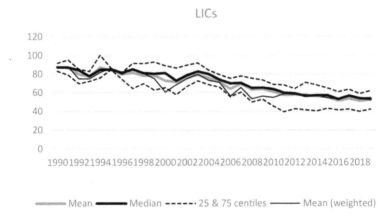

Figure 2.2   Share of external debt over total public debt

with private debt (both bank loans and bonds) being somewhere between the
two (Schlegl et al., 2019; Cordella and Powell, 2021).[7] The dominant type of
lender may also determine the type of process and the challenges in restructuring debt if needed (Powell and Valencia, 2023). Data on the composition
of external debt show that private sector lenders have become relatively more
important, increasing from about 10 percent of the total in 1970 to 60 percent
in 2019. There have been two waves of private sector lending to EMDEs:
a wave of bank loans in the early 1970s and a wave of bond issuances that
started in the early 1990s after the Brady Plan operations. Within the group

of official loans, bilateral lending dominated in the 1970s, but multilateral lending has become relatively more important in the last 20 years.[8]

Two other important elements of debt composition are currency and maturity.[9] Until recently, there was a close match between residency of the lender and currency, with most debt owed to non-residents being denominated in dollar or other hard currencies. This is the original sin problem described by Eichengreen and Hausmann (2005a, 2005b, 2007). In recent years, a limited number of countries started selling local currency domestically issued debt to non-residents (Arslanalp and Tsuda, 2014; Shin and von Peter, 2022; Du and Schreger, 2021). These countries tend to be the same countries for which there is a mismatch between the official debt statistics reported by the IDS and the "true" share of external debt. Data for the 18 emerging economies covered in Arslanalp and Tsuda (2014) show that the share of external public debt denominated in local currency has increased from approximately 11 percent in 2004 to 35 percent in 2020 (peaking at 40 percent in 2017), data for a larger sample of 24 emerging market countries indicate that the share of domestic currency external debt went from less than 10 percent in 1990 to about 20 percent in 2019 (Shin and von Peter, 2022). However, IDS data for the same countries covered in Arslanalp and Tsuda (2014) indicate domestic currency shares which are well below 5 percent.

With respect to maturity, EMDEs tend to borrow at shorter tenors and are characterized by a dynamic in which the share of short-term debt tends to increase during crisis periods (Broner et al., 2013). There is evidence that maturities in both local and foreign currency increased until around 2015, but those advances stalled and maturities decreased during the pandemic (Powell and Valencia, 2023).

As there are issues with standard measures of debt levels and composition, there are also issues with conventional measures of maturity. Most empirical work focuses on contractual maturity (usually the date of last principal repayment). However, debt contracts with similar contractual maturity can have different cash flow profiles. Tomz and Wright (2013) suggest using the zero-coupon equivalent weighted average life of the debt stock. This indicator generates maturities that tend to be significantly lower than contractual maturity.

2.3   THE DRIVERS OF DEBT GROWTH

In this section we describe the drivers of debt growth in a sample of up to 156 developing and emerging economies over 1980–2020. The top panel of Figure 2.3 illustrates the growth in debt in percentage points of GDP over 5-year periods and the bottom panel decomposes the changes.

Debt ratios have grown by 0.5 percent of GDP per annum (2.3 percent for each 5-year period) on average across all emerging and developing countries – and 0.7 percent for the median country (3.4 percent for each 5-year period). Still, there is considerable regional variation. Average debt growth in East Asia is negative (and the median barely positive) and in East Europe and Central Asia it is barely above 0.2 percent per annum. Average and median debt growth is almost 1 percent per annum in Latin America and the Caribbean. Regression analysis indicates that the change in debt is negatively correlated with the initial debt level (the higher is initial debt then, on average, the growth in debt is lower and the results indicate that on average debt follows a stable rather than an explosive path) and is negatively correlated with inflation. The presence of a floating exchange rate is instead positively correlated with the growth in debt.

It is useful to decompose the evolution of the debt-to-GDP ratio into five elements highlighted by the standard debt dynamic equation

$$\Delta d_t = -pb_t + \frac{i_{t-1} - g_t - \pi_t}{1 + g_t + \pi_t} d_{t-1} + SF_t \tag{2.1}$$

where d_t is the debt-to-GDP ratio in year t, pb_t is the primary balance over GDP in year t, i_{t-1} is the average nominal interest rate on public debt, g_t is real GDP growth, π_t is inflation, and SF_t is a residual term capturing what is usually called the stock flow reconciliation. This cumbersome name comes from the fact that this residual entity reconciles the deficit, which is a variable measured over a period of time (i.e., a 'flow' variable), with debt, which is a variable measured at a given moment (i.e., a 'stock' variable). Interest expenditure as share of GDP is equal to the interest rate, denoted i, multiplied by the debt-to-GDP ratio d.

Equation (2.1) shows that the evolution of public debt is driven by fiscal policy decisions as measured by the primary balance, the evolution of the nominal interest rate, real GDP growth, and inflation. Policy discussion tends to focus on these variables.

Applying the decomposition as described to a sample of 5-year debt changes, we find that interest payments and the stock flow reconciliation term are the main contributors to increases in debt ratios (these are the bars above the zero line in the bottom panel of Figure 2.3), with interest payments being especially important in Latin America and the Caribbean.[10] In contrast, the main contributors to falls in the debt ratio are inflation (especially important in Latin America and the Caribbean) and real GDP growth (especially for East Asia). Interestingly, the primary balance plays a relatively small role in the changes in debt ratios on average in most EMDE regions, which, on average,

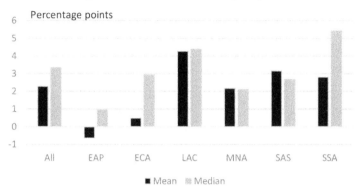

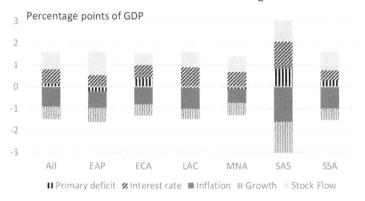

Note: EAP: East Asia & Pacific; ECA: Europe & Central Asia; LAC: Latin America & Caribbean; MNA: Middle East & North Africa; SAS: South Asia; SSA: Sub-Saharan Africa.

Figure 2.3   Changes in debt ratios and their main drivers

have been running close to a zero fiscal balance or even a small surplus. The main exception is South Asia (SAS).

These results corroborate the results of Campos et al. (2006) who found that the stock flow reconciliation is a key driver of the evolution of public debt in EMDEs. For instance, they show that in emerging and developing economies, the overall deficit (primary deficits plus interest payments) explains less than 10 percent of the variance of public debt. The remaining 90 percent is driven by the stock flow reconciliation.

The stock flow reconciliation can be driven by measurement error but also by events that affect the ratios without going through the budget. For example, a banking crisis may force the government to use off-budget resources to inject funds into the banking system; or the recapitalization of a large state-owned corporation, or the bailouts of a pension scheme, or payouts on public guarantees (for example on public–private partnership agreements) may all result in non-budgeted changes in debt. However, more often than not, sudden increases in debt happen when public debt is denominated in foreign currency and the exchange rate depreciates, causing the value of the debt to shoot up relative to GDP (which is denominated in domestic currency). The stock flow reconciliation can also take negative values, for instance in the case of a debt restructuring that leads to a decrease in the face value of debt.

2.4   EPISODES OF DEBT REDUCTIONS AND EXPLOSIONS

The distribution of the change in debt ratios has fat tails (i.e., the distribution has excess kurtosis) suggesting that debt explosions and substantial debt reductions are more common and explain more of the variance than would be expected relative to a normal distribution. To study these relatively frequent debt reduction and debt explosion episodes, we consider the 10th, 20th, 80th, and 90th percentiles of the distribution (–29.5 percent, –14 percent, 19 and 32 percent, respectively) of the 5-year changes in debt ratios. We use these four thresholds to define debt reduction and debt explosion episodes and label them as 10P, 20P (debt reduction episodes), 80P, and 90P (debt explosions).

2.4.1   Debt Reductions

Sub-Saharan Africa (SSA) is the region with more 10P and 20P episodes. The debt reductions in sub-Saharan Africa were largely driven by debt relief associated with the Heavily Indebted Poor Countries (HIPC) and Multilateral Debt Relief (MDRI) initiatives. Latin America and the Caribbean (LAC) has a relatively small share of debt reduction episodes while also having relatively high debt levels. A region that has more debt accelerations than debt reductions will of course tend to have higher debt levels over time. East Asia (EAP), East Europe and Central Asia (ECA) also have a low share of debt reduction episodes, but these regions also have relatively low debt levels. In this case, debt reduction episodes may be less frequent because they are less needed.

Econometric estimates show that, on average, higher levels of debt are associated with a higher probability of observing a debt reduction episode (Powell and Valencia, 2023). The point estimate suggests that when public debt increases from 20 to 80 percent of GDP the probability of observing a P10 episode doubles and goes from 4 percent to 8 percent. Similarly, the probability of observing a P20 episode goes from 11 percent to 19 percent.

Two possible factors could drive the positive correlation between the initial level of debt and the probability of a debt reduction episode. On the one hand, high levels of debt could lead to prudent fiscal policy. This interpretation is consistent with the definition of debt sustainability pioneered by Bohn (1998). An alternative view would be that countries with high debt levels might resort to debt restructuring or high inflation to bring debt down.

To explore these alternative explanations, we use the decomposition of equation (2.1) to classify P10 and P20 episodes into events driven by primary surpluses, real growth, inflation, the real interest rate, and the stock flow reconciliation. Specifically, we define an episode as being driven by a given factor (say primary surplus) if this factor accounts for at least 40 percent of the debt variation in that specific episode. This allocation rule can yield episodes that are not driven by any specific factor (this would be the case if no component of the debt dynamic equation accounts for at least 40 percent of the change in debt) and episodes that are driven by multiple factors.

We find that about 60 percent of episodes are driven by inflation (two-thirds of these are also associated with negative real interest rates), 45 percent of P20 episodes (30 percent of P10 episodes) are driven by real GDP growth, between one-quarter and one-third of episodes are associated with large primary surpluses and about one-quarter of P20 episodes are associated with the presence of a large negative stock flow reconciliation (Figure 2.4, top). Growth-driven debt reduction episodes tend to be more frequent in East Asia and relatively less frequent in the ECA and LAC regions. LAC and the Middle East–North African (MNA) region have instead a relatively high share of primary balance-driven debt reduction episodes. Thanks to debt relief initiatives, sub-Saharan Africa has the largest share of episodes driven by the stock flow reconciliation.

It is perhaps surprising that debt restructurings are not a main driver of debt reductions elsewhere, and especially for LAC, the region that normally scores as having had the most restructurings. But the majority of debt restructurings are actually reprofilings (pushing out maturities with no reduction in nominal debt), and the frequency of multiple restructurings (a restructuring followed by further restructurings) is relatively high, which also suggests that it may take several such restructurings to resolve the underlying problem (see Mariscal et al., 2015; Powell and Valencia, 2023).

Econometric estimates aimed at assessing which economic, political and institutional variables are correlated with different types of debt reduction episodes indicate that primary balance-driven debt reductions are less likely when initial debt is high, while high debt levels increase the likelihood of inflation-driven debt reductions. The likelihood of observing a growth or

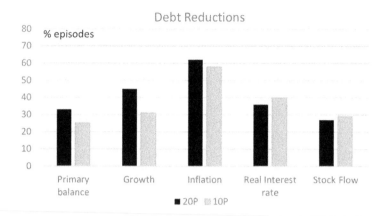

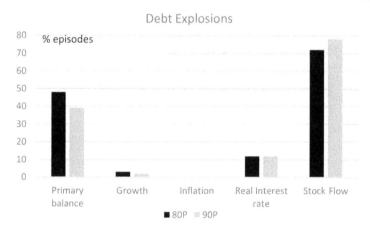

*Figure 2.4   Main contributors to debt reduction and debt explosion
              episodes*

a stock flow reconciliation-driven debt reduction is not associated with initial
debt levels. However, high levels of debt are negatively associated with the
likelihood of observing a growth-driven change in the debt trajectory.

Summing up, inflation appears to be the most common way of addressing
high levels of debt. While there are examples of growth and fiscal adjustment
bringing debt down, these are not the most common approaches. If we think
that debt reduction driven by high growth and primary surpluses is preferable
to debt reduction driven by high inflation, this is not a comforting result. Still,
there is some evidence that a proportion of these inflation episodes is with

moderate inflation and with independent central banks, which may keep inflation expectations anchored (Powell and Valencia, 2023).

2.4.2   Debt Explosions

SSA, MNA and LAC are over-represented in the sample of debt explosions. EAP, SAS and ECA are instead under-represented in the sample. The share of periods characterized by a debt explosion is particularly low in East Asia. The most common driver for debt explosions is the exchange rate, with exchange rate depreciations being significantly associated with the likelihood of observing a debt explosion. We also find that the likelihood of observing a debt explosion is negatively correlated with the initial level of debt, but this correlation is not always statistically significant. Among institutional variables, we find that debt explosions are less frequent in countries with a proportional electoral system and that having high-quality fiscal rules is also associated with a lower likelihood of observing a debt explosion.

When we use the decomposition of equation (2.1) to classify debt explosions into events driven by the various components that drive the debt dynamic, we find that the stock flow reconciliation is the main driver of debt explosions and that large primary deficits are the second most important driver of debt explosions. High real interest rates come a distant third. As one may expect, there is no debt explosion episode driven by inflation (this would require a very significant deflation) and the share of episodes driven by negative GDP growth is negligible (Figure 2.4, bottom). The important role of the stock flow reconciliation is consistent with the finding that movements in the exchange rate are the main drivers of debt explosions, as the joint presence of foreign currency debt and currency depreciations is a key driver of the stock flow reconciliation (Campos et al., 2006).

Debt explosions driven by primary deficits are less likely in countries with high debt levels. This result is consistent with the idea that high levels of debt act as a restraint on discretionary fiscal policy. As expected, debt explosions driven by the stock reconciliation are more likely when the local currency depreciates, and debt explosions driven by high interest payments are more likely in the presence of high debt levels. Debt explosions driven by high interest payments are also positively correlated with GDP per capita. This is expected because, in our sample of emerging and developing countries, low-income economies tend to borrow from official lenders, often at a concessional rate. There is some evidence of a correlation between growth, fiscal deficits, currency depreciation and the stock flow reconciliation leading to a "when it rains it pours" hypothesis (Powell and Valencia, 2023).

2.5   CONCLUSIONS

Global public debt ratios across the world decreased in the late 1990s and in the first 7 years of the new millennium. However, public debt started to grow rapidly in the aftermath of the Global Financial Crises and then ballooned when the Covid-19 pandemic hit.

This chapter focuses on developing countries and emerging economies, where public debt grew by half a percentage point of GDP per annum over the sample period for the average country, with variation across regions. Interestingly, primary fiscal balances do not explain the changes in debt. On average, emerging and developing countries do not run substantial deficits that would lead to ever-increasing debt ratios, nor high primary surpluses that would result in a steady process of debt reduction. If primary balances were the only explanation for the changes in debt ratios, then this might be interpreted as consistent with the Bohn (1998) idea of a fiscal reaction function that delivers sustainability and stationary debt ratios.

But this is far from the whole story. First, as noted, debt ratios on average have risen. The main drivers for these increases in debt are interest payments and the stock flow reconciliation term. The stock flow reconciliation is mostly driven by balance sheet effects associated with the presence of foreign currency debt. However, bailouts of banking systems and loss-making state-owned enterprises, and other payments that are considered "below the line" are also important. Governments may also be tempted to use creative accounting to exaggerate below-the-line items to limit headline fiscal deficit figures. These results then temper the interpretation that there is a fiscal reaction function that overall may keep debt sustainable.

While averages across time are of interest, they cannot explain the variability of debt, we focus on debt explosion and substantial debt reduction episodes. Debt reduction episodes are more likely to happen in the presence of high debt levels, which might be thought of at first sight as consistent with a positive fiscal reaction function. The problem with this interpretation is that most debt reduction episodes are driven by inflation (and associated low real interest rates) rather than improvements in primary fiscal balances. In sub-Saharan Africa and low-income countries, debt reductions are often linked to debt relief which again does not suggest a strong fiscal reaction function. On a more positive note, growth is a main driver of debt reductions in East Asia.

In contrast, debt explosions are driven by balance sheet effects associated with currency depreciations in the presence of foreign currency debt; primary fiscal deficits are the second most important driver of debt explosions. However, fiscal surpluses do not drive debt reductions. The asymmetry suggests a type of ratchet effect. For example, in bad times spending might rise to provide support to families and firms but that may not be matched by lower spending to produce fiscal surpluses and debt reduction episodes. Our results are then consistent with the ratchet mechanism as in Hercowitz and Strawczynski (2004). Currency mismatches then add fuel to the fire.

The differences and asymmetries in the drivers of debt explosions and rapid debt reductions suggest a much more nuanced view regarding sustainability and the idea that debt ratios might be stationary. Debt explosions in bad times may reflect *intended* countercyclical fiscal policy, although with the impact on debt being exaggerated due to currency mismatches, but in order to reduce debt, countries have primarily resorted to inflation rather than a countercyclical response in fiscal balances.

This paper has provided a descriptive analysis and so any policy implications should be considered as tentative. Still, the role of currency depreciation in fueling debt explosions suggests that the continued dependence on debt issuance in dollars and other hard currencies remains a high-level concern. Second, the pattern of the asymmetric drivers of explosions and debt reduction episodes indicates that a continued focus on improving fiscal institutions to promote true fiscal countercyclicality remains relevant; Chapter 7 in this book focuses on fiscal rules. Third, the importance of the stock flow reconciliation term in debt explosions suggests that better monitoring of the determinants of below-the-line items is required. Finally, the absence of debt restructuring as a main driver of debt reduction episodes (with the exception of the case of low-income countries), combined with other evidence in the literature, suggests that further work to ensure debt restructuring processes deliver lasting solutions to the problem of high indebtedness in emerging and developing countries may be in order. The next chapter looks into this issue.

Deeper research would be helpful to yield more specific conclusions. For example, while the finding that inflation is the main driver of debt reduction episodes is concerning (as reducing debt through higher inflation is often considered as more costly than debt reductions driven by higher growth or fiscal consolidation), further research on inflation episodes could be helpful. Intriguing initial evidence indicates that some of these episodes are with moderate inflation, with independent central banks that may keep inflation expectations anchored rather than very high, and variable inflation. Given the current context where inflation is above inflation targets in many countries, further analysis in this area could be very useful.[11]

The current high level of debt among many advanced economies and EMDEs has sparked considerable interest in the historical behavior of debt ratios, how debt rises and how countries have reduced debt in the past. This chapter confirms some results in the pre-pandemic literature with a dataset that encompasses the recent crisis and adds additional results and nuances that we hope will provoke new analysis in this important topic.

ACKNOWLEDGMENTS

Portions of this chapter draw on Gelpern and Panizza (2022), Campos et al. (2006) and on background research conducted for Powell and Valencia (2023). The findings, interpretations, and conclusions expressed in this paper are entirely those of the authors; they do not necessarily represent the views of the Inter-American Development Bank and its affiliated organizations, or those of the Executive Directors of the Inter-American Development Bank or the governments they represent.

NOTES

1. Figures are taken from the IMF's World Economic Outlook, October 2022 database.
2. There is, however, substantial within-group variance. For instance, Brazil is a large country with relatively high debt levels.
3. Figure 2.1 reports data on the face value of sovereign debt (expressed as a share of GDP). However, face value data can be misleading given they measure the undiscounted value of future principal repayments. On the one hand, two instruments with identical cash flows may have different face values if they give different weights to principal and interest payments. On the other hand, two instruments can have the same face value but different cash flow profiles. Unfortunately, the reporting of face values may provide incentives for countries to choose particular structures to attempt to minimize debt ratios – see Dias et al. (2014) for a discussion.
4. Note that the figure includes China. We obtain similar results if we drop China and if we use a GDP-weighted average instead of a debt-weighted average.
5. As in the case of debt levels, standard measures of debt decomposition are not problem-free. We build external debt shares using information on total public debt from the IMF World Economic Outlook (WEO) database and information on public and publicly guaranteed (PPG) long-term external debt sourced from the World Bank's International Debt Statistics (IDS). While, to the best of our knowledge, this is the only way to obtain historical data on debt composition for a large sample of developing economies, there are caveats with this approach (for a discussion of these caveats see Panizza and Taddei, 2020; Panizza, 2008).
6. The difference is particularly large for Brazil, where Arslanalp and Tsuda (2014) report that, in 2018, holdings by non-residents were 3.5 times that reported by IDS, but there are also large differences (of at least 40 percent) for Colombia, Egypt, Peru and the Philippines.
7. Debt composition may also matter as official interventions at the time of crisis may benefit private creditors as much or even more than the "bailed-out" country depending on the composition of debt (Gourinchas and Jeanne, 2013; Jeanne and Zettelmeyer, 2001).
8. Actual bilateral loans could be higher because statistics on official lending by China tend to be incomplete (Gelpern et al., 2021; Horn et al., 2021). For an analysis of the implications of these new bilateral creditors for debt sustainability analysis, see Alfaro and Kanczuk (2019).

9. Another important distinction has to do with the law that regulates the debt contract (Chamon et al., 2018, see also Chapter 3 in this book, on restructuring). In most cases, domestically issued bonds are regulated by domestic law while bonds issued abroad are regulated by foreign law.
10. Subtracting the bars below the zero line from those above, we obtain the annual change in the debt-to-GDP ratio. Note that the values of the bottom panel do not necessarily add up to those of the top panel because the country-year coverage is not the same.
11. See further discussion on emerging economies in Powell and Valencia (2023) and see Andreolli and Rey (2023) on the fiscal consequences of missing inflation targets with a focus on Europe.

REFERENCES

Alfaro, L. and F. Kanczuk (2019), "Undisclosed debt sustainability", *NBER* Working Paper 26347.

Andreolli, M. and H. Rey (2023), "The fiscal consequences of missing an inflation target", *NBER* Working Paper, 30819, January.

Arslanalp, S. and T. Tsuda (2014), "Tracking global demand for advanced economy sovereign debt", *IMF Economic Review*, 62(3), 430–464.

Bohn, H. (1998), "The behavior of U.S. public debt and deficits", *The Quarterly Journal of Economics*, 113(3), 949–963.

Broner, F., G. Lorenzoni and S. Schmukler (2013), "Why do emerging economies borrow short term?", *Journal of the European Economic Association*, 11, 67–100.

Campos, C. F. S., D. Jaimovich and U. Panizza (2006), "The unexplained part of public debt", *Emerging Markets Review*, 7(3), 228–243.

Chamon, M., J. Schumacher and C. Trebesch (2018), "Foreign-law bonds: Can they reduce sovereign borrowing costs?", *Journal of International Economics*, 114(C), 164–179.

Cordella, T. and A. Powell (2021), "Preferred and non-preferred creditors", *Journal of International Economics*, 132(C), 103491.

Dias, D., C. Richmond and M. Wright (2014), "The stock of external sovereign debt: Can we take the data at 'face value'?", *Journal of International Economics*, 94(1), 1–17.

Du, W. and J. Schreger (2021), "Sovereign risk, currency risk, and corporate balance sheets", Columbia Business School Research Paper.

Eichengreen, B. and R. Hausmann (2005a), "The pain of original sin", in B. Eichengreen et al. (eds), *Other People's Money – Debt Denomination and Financial Instability in Emerging Market Economies*. Chicago and London: University of Chicago Press.

Eichengreen, B. and R. Hausmann (2005b), "The mystery of original sin", in B. Eichengreen et al. (eds), *Other People's Money – Debt Denomination and Financial Instability in Emerging Market Economies*. Chicago and London: University of Chicago Press.

Eichengreen, B., and R. Hausmann (2007), "Currency mismatches, debt intolerance, and the original sin: Why they are not the same and why it matters", NBER Chapters, in: *Capital Controls and Capital Flows in Emerging Economies: Policies, Practices, and Consequences*, National Bureau of Economic Research, Inc.

Galindo, A. J. and U. Panizza (2018), "The cyclicality of international public sector borrowing in developing countries: Does the lender matter?", *World Development*, 112(C), 119–135.

Gelpern, A., S. Horn, S. Morris, B. Parks and C. Trebesch (2021), "How China lends: A rare look into 100 debt contracts with foreign governments", Peterson Institute for International Economics, Kiel Institute for the World Economy, Center for Global Development, and AidData at William & Mary.

Gelpern, A. and U. Panizza (2022), "Enough potential repudiation: Economic and legal aspects of sovereign debt in the pandemic era", *Annual Review of Economics*, 14, 545–570.

Gourinchas, P. O. and O. Jeanne (2013), "Capital flows to developing countries: The allocation puzzle", *Review of Economic Studies*, 80(4), 1484–1515.

Hercowitz, Z. and M. Strawczynski (2004), "Cyclical ratcheting in government spending: Evidence from the OECD", *The Review of Economics and Statistics*, 86(1), 353–361.

Horn, S., C. M. Reinhart and C. Trebesch (2021), "China's overseas lending", *Journal of International Economics*, 133, 1–32.

Jeanne, O. and J. Zettelmeyer (2001), "International bailouts, moral hazard and conditionality", *Economic Policy*, 16(33), 407–432.

Mariscal, R., A. Powell, G. Sandleris and P. Tavella (2015), "Sovereign defaults: Has the current system resulted in lasting (re)solutions?", Universidad Torcuato di Tella Business School, *Working Paper* 2015-3.

Panizza, U. (2008), "Domestic and external public debt in developing countries," UNCTAD United Nations Conference on Trade and Development, *Discussion Papers* 188.

Panizza, U. and F. Taddei (2020), "Local currency denominated sovereign loans – a portfolio approach to tackle moral hazard and provide insurance", *IHEID Working Papers* 09-2020.

Powell, A. and O. M. Valencia (2023), "Dealing with debt: Less risk for more growth in Latin America and the Caribbean", *Inter American Development Bank Development in the Americas Flagship Report*.

Schlegl, M., C. Trebesch and M. L. J. Wright (2019), "The seniority structure of sovereign debt", *NBER* Working Paper 25793.

Shin, H. and G. von Peter (2022), "Overcoming original sin", *Journal of Globalization and Development*, 13, December.

Tomz, M. and M. Wright (2013), "Empirical research on sovereign debt and default", *Annual Review of Economics*, 5(1), 247–272.

3. Sovereign debt restructuring and the missing international coordination

Aitor Erce and Mattia Picarelli

3.1 SOVEREIGN DEBT DEFAULT AND RESTRUCTURINGS: A RECURRENT PRACTICE

The global economy appears to be inching towards a wave of sovereign debt crisis. At the end of 2022, eight countries were in default on their international bonds: Venezuela (since 2017), Lebanon, Suriname and Zambia (2020), and Belarus, Russia, Sri Lanka, and Ghana (2022). Going into 2023, multiple countries, mostly low-income countries but also emerging economies such as Tunisia, appear at risk of sovereign debt distress.

This is, unfortunately, nothing new. The historical record shows events of sovereign debt default and restructuring to be recurrent, and to affect all types of creditors, private and official, external and domestic. While there is no unified database recording all episodes, only the subset of official creditors arranged around the Paris Club reports that, since 1956, it has signed 473 agreements (involving over $600 billion in debt) with 100 different countries. Horn et al. (2020) identify 164 restructuring events with Chinese state-owned creditors since 1950. Turning to liabilities held by private external creditors, Meyer et al. (2022), which builds on the work of rating agencies and historical archives, report over 300 episodes since 1815.

The more detailed database by Tamon Asonuma and Christoph Trebesch (2016) reports 197 episodes of debt restructuring, involving both bonds and loans, between 1970 and 2020.[1] Sovereign defaults also affect official multilateral creditors, such IMF, World Bank or multilateral development banks, although this happens way less often, given that the liabilities of these creditors are senior. Schlegl et al. (2019) study the pecking order of external creditors and show that bilateral official creditors are the least senior ones.

Sovereigns have also defaulted domestically. According to the database in Erce et al. (2022), there were 134 events of sovereign debt restructuring of liabilities governed domestically between 1980 and 2018.[2] In fact, over the last couple of decades, defaults on debt issued in domestic markets have become as prevalent as defaults on instrument issued on international markets. Figure 3.1 summarizes these trends.

The historical records also show that debt restructurings are often carried out too late and deliver an amount of relief insufficient to provide a lasting solution to the crisis. As much as two-thirds of debt restructurings led to repeat restructurings (IMF, 2014).

An extensive literature discusses the drivers and consequences of sovereign defaults. The literature shows that delays in acknowledging a debt problem and in completing a debt restructuring operation exacerbate financial instability and hamper growth. These effects need to be weighed against a range of default-related costs, including loss of access to international capital markets and to international trade, spillovers to the domestic economy through the impact of default on residents' balance sheets, and litigation-related costs.

Defaulting countries tend to suffer drops in output.[3] The effect on output of a default on private external creditors can range from zero (Lory Yoyati and Panizza, 2011) to 20 percent of GDP (Furceri and Zdzienicka, 2012). Kuvshinov and Zimmermann (2019) find that the effect on output peaks at 4 percent of GDP after 5 years. The effect is larger in fixed-exchange rate countries, in those with higher external imbalances, and where financial markets are developed.

Debt operations can precipitate capital flight (Gelos et al., 2011), especially at times of global distress. Richmond and Dias (2007) show that regaining partial market access depends on domestic and global conditions. The IMF (2014) argues that the characteristics of the restructuring process affect the shape of market re-access. Cruces and Trebesch (2013) show that restructurings imposing larger losses on creditors (larger haircuts), trigger longer periods of market exclusion and lead to market re-access at higher rates. Kuvshinov and Zimmermann (2019) show that sovereign defaults also affect private agents' ability to borrow internationally.

Borensztein and Panizza (2009) document a negative impact of default on exports. Kuvshinov and Zimmermann (2019) show that following default imports fall sharply. Borensztein and Panizza (2009), Reinhart and Rogoff (2011b) and Asonuma et al. (2018) show that banking crises are likely after a sovereign default. Balteanu and Erce (2018) show that financial spillovers play a key role by triggering credit and investment crunches.

Debt operations are at times considerably delayed by prolonged litigation. Prolonged litigation makes the output costs of default felt for a longer period. Panizza et al. (2009) argue that, over time, as sovereign immunity has been eroded, the legal cost of default has increased, along with creditors' ability to dismiss restructuring negotiations and achieve full repayment. Schumacher et al. (2018) show that creditor lawsuits are becoming increasingly common.

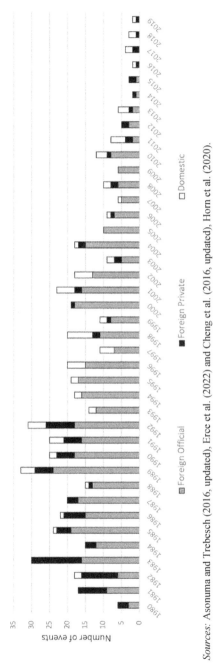

Sources: Asonuma and Trebesch (2016, updated), Erce et al. (2022) and Cheng et al. (2016, updated), Horn et al. (2020).

Figure 3.1 Sovereign defaults at home and abroad

Trebesch (2019) suggests that political instability and strategic government behavior lead to longer restructuring delays.[4]

3.2   THE PROCESS OF DEBT RESTRUCTURING

When a sovereign debtor determines that it needs to restructure its debt, there are a number of decisions that (ideally with the help of legal and financial advisors) it needs to take. First, the authorities need to decide how to announce their intentions, how to treat upcoming payments, and whether to involve the International Monetary Fund. They also need to determine what liabilities will be included in the debt negotiations and the extent of relief needed. Finally, the authorities must negotiate with their creditors how debt relief will be delivered.

Countries have dealt with these steps following different strategies. This has resulted in a wide heterogeneity in restructuring processes, which has translated into markedly different outcomes. Existing evidence shows that the benefits and costs of debt restructuring depend on the characteristics of the negotiation process (coercive or market-friendly, pre-default or post-default) and the restructuring strategy (nominal vs. re-profiling, currency, governing law, with/without official creditors).

3.2.1   Announcing the Process and Managing Upcoming Payments

When a government finds itself in trouble meeting its upcoming debt payments, it can opt to explain that this is the case ahead of the event, and try to stay current on its debt payments while negotiating a debt treatment. Under this pre-emptive approach, governments tend to engage closely with creditors. Asonuma and Trebesch (2016) show that such restructurings are less damaging for growth. Asonuma et al. (2019) argue this improved growth performance is due to the fact that pre-emptive debt restructurings have less effect on credit and investment.

Alternatively, sovereigns can let debt payments go undone and enter into default. Accumulating arrears may allow debtors to signal their intention to achieve significant relief. Countries following this route tend to act unilaterally against their creditors. An advantage for the debtors of this approach is that relief is felt immediately, as upcoming payments are not met, and arrears build up. Still, a sovereign debt restructuring can fail because it may result in a debt relief that most creditors see as excessive and confiscatory or unnecessarily coercive (Buchheit et al., 2020). Moreover, debtors who act in a less collaborative manner tend to suffer higher borrowing costs for longer (Cruces and Trebesch, 2013). Trebesch and Zabel (2017) study external defaults on privately held debt and show that post-default strategies and those that treat creditors in a harsher manner result in a worse growth performance following debt restructuring.

3.2.2   Involving the IMF

While it is not compulsory to speak to the IMF in order to carry out a debt restructuring, in most cases, countries decide to engage with the IMF to get it to support them in their effort. In cases where countries search for IMF support, its debt sustainability analysis (DSA), as prescribed by the IMF's requirement that debt is sustainable with high probability, acts as the gatekeeper of debt restructuring (Gelpern, 2016). The DSA framework guides the IMF in determining when a debt restructuring is needed and how much debt relief is required to bring back debt sustainability. The importance of the IMF remains very large even if countries choose to go it alone. Its DSAs and underlying macroeconomic frameworks almost always form the basis of restructuring negotiations. The IMF has two distinct DSA tools, one for middle- and high-income countries, the Market Access Country DSA (MAC DSA), and another for low-income countries, the Debt Sustainability Framework (LIC-DSF).[5]

Other IMF rules affect countries' incentives to default and creditors' willingness to restructure. First, IMF loans are senior and are not to be restructured. Second, the IMF has arrears policies, which determine the few instances in which a country can borrow if in default with external creditors. This is an important policy, as it provides countries with incentives to remain current on their debt obligations. Last, but far from least, the IMF has a financing assurances policy that requires the existence of credible guarantees, coming from a country's creditors, that the country's financing gap during the program period is fully covered. Promises by creditors, official and private, to restructure debt along the parameters defined by the IMF's DSA are often needed to fulfill this policy. IMF arrears and financing assurances policies distinguish private and official creditors.[6]

3.2.3   Setting the Debt Perimeter: Which Borrowings are Included and Which Not?

Often trade credits, senior or collateralized debt obligations and treasury bills (because of the need for continued short-term financing of the government) are left out of the restructuring perimeter. Still, recent episodes of debt restructuring have seen these unwritten rules repeatedly broken. Both collateralized (including resource-backed loans) and very short-term public debt has been included recently in debt restructuring operations (Independent Evaluation Office, IEO, 2021). This underlines that a main driver of the determination of the debt perimeter is the need to tackle the source of the liquidity pressures threatening debt sustainability.

A key consideration is whether to involve official creditors. Under the umbrella of the Common Framework, determination of the debt to be included lies also with official creditors. As noted above, involving official creditors has additional implications regarding the role to be played by the IMF. Also, key is how to treat claims held by other public bodies (such as social security systems), and whether to include debt from state-owned enterprises. As discussed in Erce (2021), involving debt held by social security systems in a debt restructuring risks leading to increased poverty and inequality, with its negative impact in long-run growth prospects.

Other important decisions are the extent to which relief should be granted by holders of debts governed domestically relative to holders of foreign-law governed debt, and how much to rely on domestic creditors to obtain debt relief. Erce and Mallucci (2018) show that sovereign debtors often differentiate between foreign and domestic creditors, favoring one or the other. They argue that considerations that lead to this type of residence-based discrimination include the origin of liquidity pressures, the soundness of the banking system, and the domestic private sector's reliance on international markets. According to Buchheit et al. (2020), various considerations matter. On the one hand, the restructuring processes differ. Authorities can enact domestic legislation to change the terms of domestic-law governed debt, which gives the sovereign strong tools to prevent disruptive holdouts. On the other hand, because local-law governed debt may be disproportionately held by local residents, including domestic banks, any restructuring could trigger a bank crisis and, through an ensuing credit crunch, worsen the prospects for restoring economic growth.[7] Governments may also have political incentives not to restructure domestic debt, as those claims are often held by voters. Importantly, if debt is in local currency, governments can try to inflate it away, and avoid default in nominal terms. This strategy, however, risks affecting monetary policy credibility.[8]

3.2.4   What to Ask from Creditors: Defining the Extent and Form of Debt Relief

There are three main modifications to the financial terms of sovereign debt that the authorities can propose to creditors. First, the authorities can try to obtain principal debt reductions (so that it is the nominal value of debt that is reduced). Second, they can attempt to extend maturities (this is almost always part of debt restructuring agreements). Third, they can reduce coupons.

The so-called re-profiling of maturities, where bonds maturing in the short term have their maturities extended, is a restructuring technique that has received recent attention. Maturity extensions and interest rate reductions merely smooth out and reduce refinancing needs and only deliver net present value relief; but they do not affect nominal debt stocks and are not generally followed by higher economic growth or improved credit ratings. Reinhart and Trebesch (2016) show that the macroeconomic situation of debtors improves significantly after debt relief operations only if there are principal write-offs. Using Paris Club data, Cheng et al. (2018) find that restructurings involving principal relief not only lead to faster GDP growth. They also lead to a larger reduction in poverty and inequality.

Recent restructurings in Antigua and Barbuda, Ukraine, Congo, and Mozambique have triggered extensive litigation, both with official and private creditors. Sovereign debtors can also use a range of techniques to increase acceptance by creditors, including accepting to issue debt in a more creditor-friendly jurisdiction (as Greece did in 2012), offering collateral or a credit enhancement in the form of seniority. In recent cases, authorities have retrofitted an aggregate collective action clause for restructuring domestic law debt.

They can also value recovery instruments or step-up coupon structures that facilitate that creditors recoup part of their losses if the economic situation of the defaulter improves markedly. Features deployed to foster investor participation can include value recovery instruments, as well as counter-cyclical and state-contingent payouts, or interest rate structures that incentivize prudent fiscal policy.[9] In a few recent cases, partial multilateral guarantees have been successfully deployed to facilitate investors' buy-in.[10]

3.3 THE INTERNATIONAL FINANCIAL ARCHITECTURE FOR SOVEREIGN DEBT RESTRUCTURING

3.3.1 A Historical Overview

Sovereigns cannot be discharged in bankruptcy. That is why, historically, resolution has relied on the willingness of debtors and creditors, both official and private, to negotiate and on their ability to successfully extract concessions from each other. Once the volume of needed debt relief is agreed, the process becomes a zero-sum game among creditors.

During the 1970s and 1980s, most of the financing directed towards developing economies was in the form of multilateral and official bilateral loans, and loans by internationally active banks. When troubles emerged with payments on the latter, issues were resolved within the so-called London Club, an informal forum where international banks coordinated their actions towards countries in default. If, instead, debt troubles linked to official and multilateral creditors, a resolution was negotiated with the Paris Club.

The Paris Club developed over time a number of procedures, in coordination with the IMF and the World Bank, to provide debt relief to less developed and poor countries. The existence of a well-established procedure, with the IMF defining the extent of debt relief required to achieve sustainability, made the process of restructuring official debts relatively easier. Despite this tested process, the fact that the Paris Club debt treatments at that time failed to provide any meaningful relief, implied that debt treatments by the Paris Club simply postponed the resolution of the debt overhang.[11]

By the time of the 1980s debt restructurings, many countries had significant private as well as Paris Club debt. The IMF would guide the debtor countries to settle their rescheduling with the Paris Club and to settle with committees of creditor banks, the London Club. Although there were several rounds of short-term treatment by both Paris and London Clubs in the 1980s crises, it was clear that the banks would bear more of the remaining burden than official creditors. After various attempts, such as the Baker Plan, which merely postponed a resolution of the bank loan defaults, the solution came with the Brady Plan. According to this plan, championed by the IMF, existing loans were exchanged for (partially guaranteed) tradeable bonds (which came to be called Brady bonds). International banks and sovereign debtors spent over a decade without reaching an agreement that could solve the default and unlock the financing from International Financial Institutions.[12] This ineffective framework to resolve sovereign default imposed large domestic costs.

During the 1990s, emerging markets reduced their earlier reliance on official bilateral creditors and internationally active banks, issuing instead bonds in global and domestic markets. This was in part fostered by the success of the Brady Plan, and in part by the fact that during the previous wave of defaults, existing sovereign bonds had continued to be serviced. Unfortunately, the ensuing fragmentation of the creditor base led to the emergence of roll-over risks and (hold-out) creditors that were unwilling to negotiate.[13]

As these problems could not be handled through the London Club, the late 1990s and early 2000s crises reignited the debate on the reforms needed to improve the management of debt crises. For some, crises reflected financial markets' failures. Others blamed inadequate economic policies, and focused on limiting moral hazard. Two main approaches surfaced: one market-based and one statutory-based. Supporters of a statutory approach favored the use of legislation, and defended creating an international institution to guide situations where sovereign debt restructuring is necessary.[14] Supporters of the market-based approach placed good faith negotiations between debtors and creditors at the core. They favored the creation of codes of conduct, and the inclusion of contractual innovations that reduce the likelihood that holdouts block the restructuring process. The main such tool was the inclusion of a voting procedure within sovereign bond contracts in the form of a collective action clause (CAC).

CACs allow a pre-specified majority of bondholders to approve the terms of a restructuring of debt and impose it on dissenting bondholders. This lowers the odds that hold-out creditors derail the restructuring process.[15] Still, CACs do not prevent that a minority of lenders obtain sufficient exposure to a single bond to block its restructuring and prolong resolution.[16]

Despite concerns about the effectiveness of CACs, several restructurings achieved very high participation rates, avoiding successful litigation by hold-out creditors not willing to agree to the operation. In Greece, Barbados, Grenada, Seychelles, Ukraine, and St. Kitts and Nevis, the use of CACs enabled full creditor participation in some instruments, speeding up the restructuring process. However, the use of CACs did not prevent holdouts in some Greek and Ukrainian foreign-law debt where, given the size of the bonds and the thresholds included in the CACs, hold-out creditors built blocking minorities (Fang et al., 2020). In Cyprus and Jamaica, debt was successfully restructured without CACs.

To counteract the ability of holdouts to get around CACs, an improved version of the collective action clauses, which allows bundling different groups of bonds, was published by the International Capital Market Association (ICMA) in October 2014, and was endorsed by the IMF and the Group of 20 (G20) of the largest global economies. The underlying objective of the ICMA CACs reform was to fight hold-out strategies by allowing the debtor and majority holders of one or more instruments to agree on restructuring terms and make them binding on all holders.[17]

In parallel to these legal innovations, after developed countries declined to participate in a comprehensive mechanism with IMF at its center, the Paris Club was given a more central role. In 2003, a new approach for emerging markets was announced, the Evian Approach. This approach allowed the Paris Club to deliver debt relief to emerging markets (Cheng et al., 2018).

3.3.2   The Existing Framework

Zooming into the more recent period, debt instruments and the creditor base have grown even more diverse. They now include collateralized debt and resource-backed loans with commodity traders; non-traditional official creditors, most notably China; a substantial number of Eurobonds held internationally; and (in some countries) borrowing through domestic markets. As a result, coordination has been further challenged, and litigation (also by official lenders) has surged. This negative trend has been exacerbated by a lack of transparency regarding debt structures.

Still, thanks to the use of CACs, various recent debt restructurings involving sovereign bonds have been executed in a pre-emptive fashion, achieving large creditor participation in a relatively short period (IMF, 2020). This recent experience shows that principal-based debt reduction is most effective in bringing debt down to sustainable levels. Re-profiling maturities and lowering coupons also lowers the net present value of debt service, but is less effective against debt overhangs (IEO, 2021). Still, despite improvements in the design of CACs, the rise in the importance of non-Paris Club official creditors and the shift to collateralized instruments substantially complicated debt restructuring negotiations prior to the current wave of distress (IEO, 2021).

Following the pandemic crisis, which raised fears of a wave of sovereign defaults, the G20 announced in April 2020 the Debt Service Suspension Initiative (DSSI), a debt service moratorium by all bilateral official creditors to low-income countries. Coordinated efforts around DSSI enabled the provision of some fiscal space, albeit very limited when compared with upcoming debt payments. In fact, concerned by triggering cross-default clauses and litigation, and by the impact on credit ratings, market access and financing costs, governments participating in DSSI did not manage to convince private creditors to provide debt relief.

Against growing insolvency problems in poor countries, in November 2020, the G20 and Paris Club countries agreed to set up the Common Framework for Debt Treatments (CF), with members of the Paris Club and G20 official bilateral creditors (such as China, India or Saudi Arabia), which will deal with insolvency and protracted liquidity problems in low-income countries that were DSSI-eligible. The objective of the CF is to design and implement a debt restructuring package that can fill a debtor's financing gap in the short term and restore its debt sustainability.

Debt treatments under the Common Framework are initiated at the request of a debtor country and are negotiated by an Official Creditors' Committee, representing all the relevant official creditors. The CF can be used to address different debt challenges. Where public debt is not sustainable, the CF can provide a deep debt restructuring, with a net present value reduction sufficient to restore sustainability. Relief will, in principle, not be conducted using debt write-offs. For countries with sustainable debt but liquidity issues (high debt service payments are a source of vulnerability), it can defer debt service payments.

To benefit from a CF treatment, a country must have (or sign) an IMF program that supports the implementation of suitable policies and reforms. Following a request to enter the CF, the IMF debt sustainability analysis will estimate the scale of debt relief needed.

The CF requires the country to obtain comparable debt relief from external private and other official creditors. Fearing to taint their reputation, countries have been reluctant to enter into the Common Framework. At the time of writing, only Chad, Ethiopia, Ghana and Zambia have asked to be treated under it. Yet, almost three years after its inception, only Chad has reached a restructuring agreement. The process for Chad was long stalled due to problems in involving Glencore's collateralized debt in the restructuring.[18] Zambia, who backed by Chinese lending and Eurobonds issuance saw its public debt jump from 20 in 2010 to 120 percent by the end of 2021, has reached an agreement with the IMF where the loan is conditional on a debt restructuring within the Common Framework. The debt perimeter has been set considering concerns that including domestic debt and domestic creditors could trigger a financial crisis, and excludes foreign holdings of domestic debt. The deal in Zambia is being delayed by the Chinese reluctance to provide debt relief (despite having provided the IMF with assurances that it would) if the World Bank and other multilaterals accept to forego their seniority and also provide debt relief to the country. The process in Ethiopia stalled due to a war outbreak. Ghana was the last country to enter into the framework and, after restructuring its domestic debt, is now facing the restructuring of its external liabilities.

3.3.3   A Critical Overview of the Existing Framework

While international coordination has reached a milestone with the Common Framework for Debt Treatments, which sits together traditional official creditors and the G20, the international architecture remains plagued with issues that make it less effective than it seems. This section describes them and discusses existing ideas to tackle them.

3.3.3.1   The G20 Common Framework lacks teeth

The international architecture in general, and the Common Framework in particular, need to incorporate adequate mechanisms to ensure that private creditors bear a fair share of the burden. While it remains the most promising instrument for achieving comprehensive debt restructuring, for it to achieve such a goal, private and official sector participation needs to be made more binding.

Key is the lack of clarity regarding how comparable treatment will be evaluated and enforced.[19] Western governments are concerned that the multiplicity of Chinese lenders is reluctant to provide debt relief, while simultaneously the Chinese authorities show concerns regarding the lack of contribution by both private sector and multilateral lenders. To complicate matters further, the comparability of treatment places the burden to accomplish comparable participation of other creditors entirely on the debtor and provides no effective means of enforcing it. Private creditors may comply for their own reasons, but any commitment that they may make to participate is not legally binding.

Official creditors may also fudge IMF requirements to provide credible guarantees they will offer the country debt relief.[20] Promises by creditors, official and private, to restructure debt along the parameters defined by the IMF's DSA are needed to fulfill this policy. Within the IMF policy framework, compared with its current role as a financier, the Paris Club has a disproportionate role, as it is the only forum of official lenders that IMF policies recognize.[21] This key role of a Western-countries club is, according to some commentators, one of the reasons China is not as cooperative as debtor countries would like it to be.

Thus, even if a large number of creditors agree to participate in a debt restructuring, the potential for other creditors, private and official, to hold-out and claim full repayment remains. This leaves debtors forced to face lawsuits by creditors. This reluctance to provide relief also helps explain many countries' fears that requesting relief from private creditors will trigger litigation and credit rating downgrades.

Recognizing that creditors' concerns about other creditors receiving better terms is a key driver of delays in conducting debt restructuring, Buchheit and Gulati (2022) propose that most favored creditor clauses are introduced in debt treatments under the auspices of the Common Framework.[22]

Others have proposed that Comparability of treatment be broadened to also imply that creditor governments are required to take steps to facilitate the operation with their private residents. Under this more statutory approach, the creditor governments granting relief would also undertake to seek private creditors under their jurisdiction provide such relief. This could be achieved through the enactment of legislation preventing lawsuits against debtors that are under the umbrella of the Common Framework.

There are other global alternatives that could foster international coordination and lead to faster resolution of debt defaults on private sector creditors. As it was done for Iraq, a UN Council Resolution could shield debtors from creditors (Buchheit and Gulati, 2019; Bolton et al., 2020). Countries could also coordinate to adopt the UN principles on sovereign debt restructuring, which have a strong principle on sovereign immunity. Recently, Belgium and the United Kingdom introduced anti-vulture legislation, intended to shield sovereign debtors from rogue creditors. A similar approach could be followed in other jurisdictions. Still, as tensions during the recent IMF annual meetings show, there seems to be a lack of appetite by official actors for more statutory solutions.[23]

3.3.3.2   No framework to coordinate debt relief for emerging economies

A key gap in the architecture is that despite emerging countries having a much higher exposure to financial markets and roll-over risks than poor countries, there is no Common Framework available for them. This is a remarkable gap that Suriname and Sri Lanka, who have spent months attempting to restructure their public debts, while private and official creditors played hard-ball by not providing the IMF with the necessary text-book financing assurances, know just too well. In fact, five of six countries that defaulted in 2021 were middle-income countries without access to the Common Framework.

One alternative to enhance international coordination on the provision of relief to emerging economies could be for the G20 to replicate within the Common Framework the Evian Approach used by the Paris Club. This is the only treatment accepted by the Club that enables the provision of substantial debt relief to emerging economies.[24]

Additionally, various legal changes to existing debt instruments could enhance the ability of developing-country governments to engage with creditors and limit litigation. Countries could include ICMA CACs on bonds issued by state-owned companies and sub-sovereign bodies. They could also consider the inclusion of aggregation clauses on bank loans. Using such clauses, bank loans could be bundled with bonded debt during debt restructuring exercises.

3.3.3.3   Lack of transparency hinders creditor participation

The reluctance of creditors to provide debt relief is partly based on their fear that, because of uncertainty regarding the stock of public liabilities, they will be forced to provide unfairly large debt relief. The lack of clarity affects especially Chinese loans and collateralized loans with commodity traders, as in Chad (IEO, 2021). Also, the growing presence of collateralized debt can pose problems to setting the debt perimeter, as it can lead to larger losses being imposed on creditors without collaterals (IMF, 2020). This also reduces incentives to participate in de-restructuring.

To tackle this concern, debt transparency must be enhanced across the board, including through the establishment of a detailed public registry for sovereign liabilities, and stricter regulations for the disclosure of debt holdings of private investors (Gelpern, 2016).[25] An area where further transparency could also help is regarding details about financing assurances provided by creditors to the IMF. Their form, size and origin should be systematically monitored by IMF staff and reported to the public (see also Neiman, 2022).

3.3.3.4   Contested determination of debt relief

Another important aspect complicating debt restructuring negotiations is the calculation of the amount of debt relief that is required. This is generally done using the IMF's debt sustainability analysis (DSA), but its ability to determine when and how much debt relief is needed is too low.

This lack of effective modeling of the impact of debt operations, together with general forecasting uncertainty, effectively allows both debtors and creditors to insist on assuming improbably benign scenarios, thereby delaying and limiting debt relief while inflicting undue damage to the debtor country's domestic economy. Current DSA assessments are too optimistic, which further reduces the perceived need for debt restructuring. Moreover, given concerns about market sensitivity, the IMF's precise DSA methodology is confidential. This worsens the lack of transparency, making private actors reluctant to participate.

Decisions on the size of debt relief should be based on improved and transparent DSA assessments. This would give the exercise greater credibility. The DSA could do more to acknowledge the quality of debt rather than just its quantity and adjust thresholds on this basis. Debt can fund capital expenditure, such as infrastructure projects, which can have growth-inducing spinoff effects. These different multipliers should be accounted for in the DSA (IEO, 2021). Additionally, for countries that source the bulk of their market financing via domestic markets, the relevance of domestic sources of financing and their connection to internal demand and growth should be systematically embedded within the framework.

3.4   CONCLUDING REMARKS: A PARADIGM SHIFT?

Despite the remarkable leap forward that the Common Framework represents, much needs to change for the international financial architecture for crisis resolution to be fitting for the challenges of the future.

As a way to improve coordination beyond what the Common Framework has achieved, in February 2023 the IMF launched the Global Sovereign Debt Roundtable, which will sit together creditors and debtors, and work towards finding more expeditive and effective ways to address sovereign debt default and restructuring.

Beyond this initiative, the Common Framework could be better aligned with globally agreed climate goals, and for comprehensive debt relief oriented towards a green and inclusive recovery, in line with the 2030 Agenda for Sustainable Development.[26] Volz et al. (2021) argue that countries undergoing debt restructuring could use the opportunity to obtain additional debt relief in exchange for policy actions that increase the country's ecologic footprint through the use of debt-for-nature agreements. In such a "debt-for-nature" swap, creditors cancel specific debts in exchange for a commitment of the debtor to undertake specified public investments. According to Zettelmeyer et al. (2022) debt–climate swaps can make sense if a selective debt restructuring is sufficient. In contrast, where a comprehensive restructuring is needed, they argue for using a combination of traditional debt restructuring and a separate climate-conditional grant that is senior to debt service.[27] They propose to enhance the design of debt-for-nature swaps by linking them to budgetary spending categories or climate performance commitments.[28]

In turn, multilateral institutions should revamp their toolkits and promote the use of financing tied to policy- or economic contingencies (United Nations, 2017). This would elicit good policies and render debt ratios less pro-cyclical. Further efforts are needed to develop state-contingent and counter-cyclical instruments that help improve the resilience of public debt to shocks. A few multilaterals already offer natural disaster clauses, oil-price linked loans, and export-linked grace periods. In addition, some loans and bonds issued to the private sector contain counter-cyclical features, which should help make public debt less pro-cyclical. Multilateral institutions should promote and scale up the provision of this type of support.

Last but not least, to support long-term inclusive growth, the welcome increased attention paid to the impact of domestic debt restructuring on financial stability should also reach non-financial domestic creditors. Defaulting domestically has macroeconomic effects that go beyond financial stability and the need to receive heightened attention. Of particular relevance are social security systems, often major holders of sovereign bonds. The design of debt operations should avoid leaving them too weak to fight poverty and inequality (IEO, 2021).

ACKNOWLEDGMENTS

We thank Andrew Powell, Enrique Alberola and Ugo Panizza for comments, and Miguel Angel Blanco Martinez for his research assistance.

NOTES

1. Cheng et al. (2018) present a detailed dataset on Paris Club debt restructuring. Beers and de Leon-Manlagnit (2019) introduce a database of default in local currency debt.
2. Reinhart and Rogoff (2011a) report 68 episodes of domestic default during the period 1914–2010.
3. One caveat of this literature is that it has found no clean way to address causality biases, with the implication that the effects reported here reflect that defaults cause economic damage and vice versa.
4. Thanks to the ability of national parliament to legislate over the terms of sovereign debt issued under local law, domestic debt restructuring often proceeds faster (IMF, 2021).
5. The LIC-DSF, which is prepared with the World Bank, analyzes the present value of public debt. Instead, the MAC DSA focuses on nominal debt values.
6. In reaction to the war in Ukraine, and faced with the willingness of its main stockholders to provide support for Ukraine, the IMF reformed its financing assurances policies and increased its lending limits.

7.   Traditionally, domestic debt was governed domestically, denominated in local currency, and held internal, while "external debt" was foreign-law governed, held abroad, and denominated in foreign currency. These lines are increasingly blurred.
8.   In the late 1990s, Russia defaulted on local currency debt to maintain central bank credibility.
9.   Clauses making debt relief contingent on reform implementation build in incentives to pursue responsible fiscal policies but can also reduce the authorities' ability to conduct counter-cyclical policies.
10.   Discussing the recent crisis in Ghana, Gulati and Panizza note that a potential drawback of multilateral guarantees is that they complicate debt restructuring negotiations (Do Rosario, 2022).
11.   For other official creditors, acting outside the Paris Club, debt restructurings proceeded ad-hoc.
12.   The IMF had a policy of no toleration of external arrears, making loans unavailable for countries in default.
13.   Vulture funds purchased distressed debt at a discount and litigated aggressively.
14.   A major exponent of this approach was the Sovereign Debt Restructuring Mechanism (SDRM), championed by Anne Krueger. The SDRM was rejected both by borrowers and lenders.
15.   Most pre-existing sovereign bonds required unanimity from all holders in order for a debt restructuring to be agreed on. This gave huge leverage to bondholders, no matter how small their debt holdings.
16.   Fang et al. (2020) show that CACs are effective in reducing hold-out rates.
17.   The IMF (2020) discusses the recent failure by Argentina and Ecuador to use the single-limb CAC embedded in their bonds and the potential for a strategic use of such clauses by the authorities.
18.   The agreement with Glencore, a commodity trader, provides Chad with no debt reduction. Yet, official creditors determined it ensures the country will achieve the debt metrics set by the IMF's DSA.
19.   Debt relief by creditors is measured by comparing the present value of new debt and the old debt. There are many possibilities to carry out the comparison, each creating biases that can systematically benefit one type of creditor at the expense of other.
20.   Chinese lenders are using the symbiosis of private and official entities in China and the blurred lines in IMF policies, in particular in between the IMF's arrears and financing assurances policies, to have private creditors agreeing to provide debt relief ahead of Chinese actors (Neiman, 2022).
21.   The disputes between China and the IMF regarding the provision of financing assurance for IMF programs with Suriname, Zambia and Ghana testify to the frictions IMF policies can generate.
22.   If a debtor would grant better terms to creditors restructuring later, these better terms should also be offered to earlier creditors who agreed to larger losses. Governments not abiding would risk legal action.
23.   Alternatively, they could elicit private sector participation using regulatory forbearance (such as rating holidays for assets from countries under the framework) or tax incentives.
24.   Inter-American Development Bank (IDB) (2023) argues along similar lines for the specific case of Latin American and Caribbean countries.

25. The IMF (2020) proposes to use negative pledge clauses against the perverse effects of collateralization. Multilateral Development Banks have similar rules.
26. Cosio-Pascal (2008) notes that most Paris Club treatments in the mid-1990s included provisions for partial debt reduction through swaps of debt for social, environmental or investment activities.
27. This approach would make most sense where debtors' climate actions can have an appreciable impact on their creditworthiness.
28. Zettelmeyer et al. (2022) also propose including climate-conditionality in comprehensive debt restructurings addressing unsustainable debt. They also propose that future debt restructurings should be based on DSA analysis that explicitly accounts for the fiscal costs of climate-related expenditures.

REFERENCES

Asonuma, T. and C. Trebesch (2016), "Sovereign Debt Restructurings: Pre-emptive or Post-Default", *Journal of the European Economic Association* 14(1).

Asonuma, T., M. Chamon and A. Sasahara (2018), "Trade Costs of Sovereign Debt Restructurings: Does a Market-Friendly Approach Improve the Outcome?", *IMF* Working Paper No. 16/222.

Asonuma, T., M. Chamon, A. Erce and A. Sasahara (2019), "Costs of Sovereign Defaults: Restructuring Strategies, Bank Distress and the Capital Inflow-Credit Channel", *IMF* Working Paper No. 19/69.

Balteanu, I. and A. Erce (2018), "Linking Bank Crises and Sovereign Defaults: Evidence from Emerging Markets", *IMF Economic Review* 66.

Beers, D. and P. de Leon-Manlagnit (2019), "The BoC-BoE Sovereign Default Database: What's New in 2019?", *Bank of Canada* Working Paper No. 2019–39.

Bolton, P., G. Mitu and U. Panizza (2020), "Legal Air Cover", *Duke Law School Public Law & Legal Theory Series* No. 2020-63.

Borensztein, E. and U. Panizza (2009), "The Costs of Sovereign Default", *IMF* Working Paper No. 08/238.

Buchheit, L. C. and M. Gulati (2019), "Sovereign Debt Restructuring and US Executive Power", *Capital Markets Law Journal* 14(1).

Buchheit, L. C. and M. Gulati (2022), "Enforcing Comparable Treatment in Sovereign Debt Workouts", *Virginia Public Law and Legal Theory* Research Paper No. 2022-67.

Buchheit, L., G. Chabert, C. DeLong and J. Zettelmeyer (2020), "The Sovereign Debt Restructuring Process in Sovereign Debt: A Guide for Economists and Practitioners", (Eds. A. Abbas, A. Pienkowski, and K. Rogoff). Oxford University Press.

Cheng, G., J. Díaz-Cassou and A. Erce (2018), "Official Debt Restructuring and Development", *World Development* 111.

Cosio-Pascal, E. (2008), "The Emerging of a Multilateral Forum for Debt Restructuring: The Paris Club", *UNCTAD* Discussion Paper 192.

Cruces, J. J. and C. Trebesch (2013), "Sovereign Defaults: The Price of Haircuts", *American Economic Journal: Macroeconomics* 5(3).

Do Rosario, J. (2022), "Analysis: Ghana Overhaul a Test for $1 Billion World Bank-backed Debt", *Reuters* (December 2, 2022).

Erce, A. (2021), "Market Debt Operations and Growth in IMF-Supported Programs", *Independent Evaluation Office,* Background Paper BP/21-01/06.

Erce, A. and E. Mallucci (2018), "Selective Sovereign Defaults", *FRB International Finance* Discussion Paper No. 1239.

Erce, A., E. Mallucci and M. Picarelli (2022), "A Journey in the History of Sovereign Defaults on Domestic-Law Public Debt", Board of Governors of the Federal Reserve System International, *Finance* Discussion Papers No. 1338.

Fang, C., J. Schumacher and C. Trebesch (2020), "Restructuring Sovereign Bonds: Holdouts, Haircuts and the Effectiveness of CACs", *European Central Bank* Working Paper No. 2366.

Furceri, D. and A. Zdzienicka (2012), "How Costly Are Debt Crises?", *Journal of International Money and Finance* 31(4).

Gelos, G., R. Sahay and G. Sandleris (2011), "Sovereign Borrowing by Developing Countries: What Determines Market Access?", *Journal of International Economics* 83(2).

Gelpern, A. (2016), "Sovereign Debt: Now What?", *Yale Journal of International Law* 41(2).

Horn, S., C. M. Reinhart and C. Trebesch (2020), "China's Overseas Lending", *NBER* Working Paper No. 26050.

Independent Evaluation Office (2021), "Growth and Adjustment in International Monetary Fund-supported Programs", *Evaluation Report* (International Monetary Fund. Independent Evaluation Office).

Inter-American Development Bank (2023), "Dealing with Debt: Less Risk for More Growth in Latin America and the Caribbean, Inter-American Development Bank (edited by A. Powell and O. Valencia).

International Monetary Fund (2014), "The Fund's Lending Framework and Sovereign Debt – Annexes", *IMF* May (Washington).

International Monetary Fund (2020), "The International Architecture for Resolving Sovereign Debt Involving Private-Sector Creditors—Recent Developments, Challenges, and Reform Options", *IMF* October (Washington).

International Monetary Fund (2021), "Review of the Debt Sustainability Framework for Market Access Countries", *IMF* January (Washington).

Kuvshinov, D. and K. Zimmermann (2019), "Sovereigns Going Bust: Estimating the Cost of Default", *European Economic Review* 119.

Levy-Yeyati, E. and U. Panizza (2011), "The Elusive Costs of Sovereign Defaults", *Journal of Development Economics* 94(1).

Meyer, J., C. M. Reinhart and C. Trebesch (2022), "Sovereign Bonds since Waterloo", *The Quarterly Journal of Economics* 137, August.

Neiman, B. (2022), "Remarks by Counselor to the Secretary of the Treasury Brent Neiman at the Peterson Institute for International Economics", *US Department of the Treasury,* Press releases. Retrieved at https://home.treasury.gov/news/press -releases/jy0963

Panizza, U., F. Sturzenegger and J. Zettelmeyer (2009), "The Economics and Law of Sovereign Debt and Default", *Journal of Economic Literature* 47(3).

Reinhart, C. M. and K. S. Rogoff (2011a), "The Forgotten History of Domestic Debt", *Economic Journal* 121(551).

Reinhart, C. M. and K. S. Rogoff (2011b), "From Financial Crash to Debt Crisis", *American Economic Review* 101(5).

Reinhart, C. M. and C. Trebesch (2016), "Sovereign Debt Relief and its Aftermath", *Journal of the European Economic Association* 14(1).

Richmond, C. and D. A. Dias (2007), "Regaining Market Access: What Determines the Duration of Exclusion?", *Mimeo*.

Schlegl, M., C. Trebesch and M. L. J. Wright (2019), "The Seniority Structure of Sovereign Debt", *NBER* Working Paper No. 25793.

Schumacher, J., C. Trebesch and H. Enderlein (2018), "Sovereign Defaults in Court", *ECB* Working Paper No. 2135.

Trebesch, C. (2019), "Resolving Sovereign Debt Crises: The Role of Political Risk", *Oxford Economic Papers* 71(2).

Trebesch, C. and M. Zabel (2017), "The Output Costs of Hard and Soft Sovereign Default", *European Economic Review* 92.

United Nations (2017), "Sovereign Debt Restructuring: Further Improvements in the Market Based Approach", Financing for Development Office, Department of Economic and Social Affairs, United Nations.

Volz, U., S. Akhtar, K. P. Gallagher, S. Griffith-Jones, J. Haas and M. Kraemer (2021), "Debt Relief for a Green and Inclusive Recovery: Securing Private-sector Participation and Creating Policy Space for Sustainable Development", Boston University, Global Development Center.

Zettelmeyer, J., B. Weder di Mauro, U. Panizza, M. Gulati, L. Buchheit and P. Bolton (2022), *Geneva 25: Climate and Debt*, CEPR Press.

4. Low interest rates, monetary policy and the close links with fiscal policy

Enrique Alberola

4.1 INTRODUCTION

In this chapter, we analyze the interactions between monetary policy and fiscal policy and how they have evolved in the turbulent era. The link between both policies has tightened since the Great Financial Crisis (GFC). This close nexus will remain a defining element of the macroeconomic landscape going forward.

The key element to analyze is the secular decline in the natural interest rate (r^*), also known as equilibrium or neutral rate. The increase in public debt would have pushed r^* up, but trends in real factors, such as demographics and lower productivity, have more than offset the impact of higher debt. The favorable underlying debt dynamics that a low r^* facilitates explained that the surge in debt has had little or no impact on the long-term interest rates of most sovereigns.

The interest rate is where fiscal and monetary policy meet. The main policy instrument of monetary policy is the short-term nominal rate, that takes r^* as the reference for the neutral policy rate. The natural rate thus anchors and guides monetary policy. Its reduction goes a long way in explaining the deep transformation of monetary policy and of its linkages with fiscal policies that we describe in the chapter.

The GFC transformed the monetary policy frameworks. Policy rates collapsed to zero, requiring the adoption of unconventional policies, of which public debt purchases were a central feature. The fiscal environment also changed: while sweeping fiscal support was necessary, the concomitant surge in debt limited the fiscal space.

Against this backdrop, the interaction between monetary and fiscal policy strengthened. In an environment of low inflation and interest rates, fiscal policy is more powerful – by itself, and relative to monetary policy – and the academic and policy consensus has moved towards higher fiscal activism (see Chapter 6). But a high debt overburdens and constrains fiscal policy. After the GFC, monetary policy took the lead in stabilizing the economy, and it has greatly broadened its role, increasing the focus on financial stability. The deployment of unconventional policies and their intensive use of sovereign debt, aimed to reduce interest rates along the yield curve, tightens the link between monetary and fiscal policies. The broadening of the central banks' mandates reinforced further the links, as public finances and policies are also closely linked to financial stability.

The pandemic recession required another round of emergency policies. With the experience and lessons learnt from the GFC, the reaction was swifter, more decisive and more coordinated. A disinhibited fiscal policy has played a decisive role and unconventional monetary policies have supported the fiscal boost. Covid-19 has thus reinforced the nexus.

The closer links between fiscal and monetary succeeded in mitigating and overcoming both crises. But too tight links come with risks. They may erode central bank independence, fiscal discipline and dilute responsibilities, and are prone to generate frictions among authorities when policy objectives become conflicting.

Before the reawakening of inflation, it was already evident that the separation between monetary and fiscal policy had to be restored. With high inflation and slowing growth, the stakes are higher; the policy objectives become conflicting and the interaction between policies becomes more complex. Central banks must tame inflation to avoid it becoming entrenched. Higher policy rates take a toll on activity and constrain the fiscal space. A fiscal expansion would put upward pressures on prices. And the jump in debt in the last years calls for caution: in countries with weak fiscal fundamentals, higher rates could lead to fiscal stress and financial turbulence.

Looking ahead beyond the current tribulations, the base scenario in the medium term is that the close link between policies is here to stay, as the environment of low interest rates is not expected to change dramatically. Central banks will keep the novel instruments devised as a response to the crisis in their toolbox and fiscal policy will remain more active than before the turbulent era, although perhaps more cautious if long-term rates stay at higher levels. Each authority will focus independently on their mandates – the separation principle – although they eventually could clash.

An alternative, risky scenario is that a high inflation regime materializes over the next years. The probability is currently low, but it entails grave consequences. In that case, a prolonged period of high interest rates would constrain the fiscal space. If this is not accepted by fiscal authorities and central banks give in, fiscal dominance of monetary policy could follow. If the risk materializes, the link between monetary and fiscal policy would become toxic and the progress in policymaking achieved in the last 50 years could be reversed.

4.2   THE SECULAR DECLINE IN INTEREST RATES

Interest rates have trended down across the board in the last decades, both in nominal and real terms. The natural rate, $r*$, is usually assimilated to the long-term real interest rate. $r*$ can be seen as a price determined by the supply (saving) and demand (investment) of financing; it also represents the real rate consistent with output and demand at its equilibrium or potential level (Blanchard, 2023). The top panel of Figure 4.1 shows $r*$ for the three main economies. There are multiple methods to compute $r*$, which is an unobservable variable, but all of them point to the dramatic and global decline in the natural rate since the 1980s, from around 5 percent in the 1990s to close to zero or even negative nowadays. Lower natural interest rates reverberate through the term structure of interest rates in the economy, pushing all of them down, with large implications for fiscal and monetary policy.

Public finances and fiscal policy benefit from the decline. The dynamics of debt are governed by the difference between the real interest rate (r) on public debt and the growth of GDP (g), as follows:[1]

$$\Delta \text{ Debt-to-GDP } = \text{ Primary fiscal balance} + (r - g) \times \text{Debt-to-GDP} \qquad (4.1)$$

with $r*$ around zero, a negative $r–g$ is easy to attain, even with low economic growth. In that case, the debt-to-GDP ratio falls unless the primary deficit is large enough. An alternative way to see a negative $(r–g)$ is that it opens up the fiscal space, as it enables primary deficits without increasing the debt ratio.

Figure 4.1 displays the benign impact of the declining trend in interest rates on public finances. In spite of the large surge in public debt since the GFC, the cost of servicing the debt, represented by the effective interest rate, has greatly decreased, from close to 4 percent to less than 2 percent of GDP.

4.2.1   Determinants of the Falling Natural Interest Rate

The definition of $r*$ suggests that real factors are behind the decline in the natural rate. This leaves monetary factors, including inflation, out of the picture, although it may affect long-term rates for protracted periods, as noted in the next section.

The two main determinants of the reduction in $r*$ are demographics and productivity growth. A third factor is the relative preference of economic agents between safe and risky assets, while the increase in public deficits and debt works in the opposite direction. Let us review them in turn.

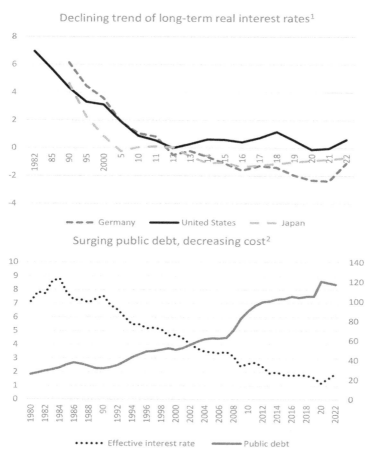

Declining trend of long-term real interest rates[1]

Surging public debt, decreasing cost[2]

Notes: 1. Yield on 10 year bonds minus expected inflation, 10 years ahead. Consensus for Germany and Japan, Cleveland Fed estimates for US. 2. Net government debt; Effective interest rate computed as net interest.
Source: IMF, World Economic Outlook database.

Figure 4.1   The decline in the natural rate reduces financing costs despite the increase in public debt

Ageing and higher inequality lower *r**

The ageing of the population is pervasive in advanced economies (AEs) and, increasingly, at the global level. Economic development usually brings about a demographic transition as a result of lower fertility rates and rising life expectancy. The consequence is an ageing population that spends many more years in retirement. In the 1970s, the expected duration of retirement was 5 years and now is over 20 in AEs (see Chapter 12).

How do ageing and longer retirement play out on the natural rate? There are two main channels, that work in the same direction.

• First, ageing populations depress the demand for capital, while the stock of capital relative to the size of the workforce increases. Also, if the productivity of oldest cohorts is lower, as the evidence tends to suggest (Feyrer, 2007), ageing pushes down growth and investment opportunities.
• Second, rising life expectancy equals longer retirement, increasing the incentives of the state and the individuals, both in the workforce and those retired, to save more. Yet, policies that are becoming widespread under the financial pressure on pension systems due to ageing can mitigate its impact on savings. This is the case of extending the working life or schemes of partial retirement.

The combination of lower desired investment and higher desired saving depresses the natural rate. Estimates calculate the impact in a range of a 1-2 percentage points fall in r^* (Carvalho et al., 2016).

Another factor related to demographics is *inequality*. Poorer households consume a higher share of their income to cover their basic needs and their marginal propensity to consume is higher, too; richer people are more prone to save. So, the increase in within-country inequality feeds into higher saving. Lukasz and Smith (2015) estimate that inequality has contributed to a half percentage point reduction in r^* in the last decades.

Lower productivity growth reduces r^*
The second factor is growth or, more precisely, productivity growth. High economic growth and productivity usually implies a higher return on capital and thus higher real rates. They encourage the saving required for the high investment levels underpinning a fast-growing economy.

The decline in potential growth observed since the 1980s has depressed r^*. World growth has been lower in spite of the incorporation of new emerging countries to the global economy and it is attributable to the overall decline in total factor and labor productivity.

The reasons for lower productivity range from a decline in the rate of technological innovation (Gordon, 2016) to the increase in market concentration and rent-seeking in key industries that has led to higher mark-ups and less business dynamism and investment, as argued by Philippon (2019). Composition effects are also relevant: economic development entails a higher share of services in the economy, and services are usually less productive. Estimates of the impact of the fall in productivity on r^* are around 1 percent (Brand et al., 2018).

Preference for safe assets lowers *r**

One of the first instances where the preference for (foreign) safe assets impacted on *r** was the savings glut of emerging and developing economies (EMDEs). Their savings were invested at the beginning of this century in US dollars, the reserve currency that often acts as the preferred store of value in the international monetary system. Asian economies, with high saving rates and current account surpluses, accumulated massive amounts of US Treasury bonds (the safe asset *par excellence*) in foreign exchange reserves. The policy purpose was precautionary and to keep exchange rates competitive. This demand was seen as a key driver of the reduction of US long-term rates (Bernanke, 2005).

Then came the GFC that increased the preference for safe assets. The large financial shock triggered a run for safety and changed the minds of investors as they have become more sensitive to tail events. The demand of financial assets deemed as risk free – typically public debt of countries with top sovereign ratings – has greatly increased since then. The overall increase in uncertainty has entrenched this behavior. This shift has widened the yield wedge between safe and risky assets – corporate debt, equity – in a persistent way and it has also pushed down *r**, as safe assets of long maturity are used as benchmarks for the measurement of the natural rate.

Other factors have underpinned the relative preference for safe assets. The strengthening of financial regulation in the aftermath of the GFC, requiring thicker capital and liquidity buffers, is one; ageing, again, is another, as older investors become more risk averse.

At the same time, the reassessment of ratings after the GFC and the euro area crisis has shrunk the universe of safe assets, putting additional downward pressures on *r**. Credit risk spreads of economies with high debt and weak fiscal fundamentals have widened, particularly in Europe; EMDEs debt that already had sizable spreads before the GFC were relatively resilient, but the lower growth in the last years has weighed negatively on their credit risk perception, too.

Surging government debt increases *r**

The surge in public debt since the GFC and, more recently, during the pandemic makes compatible the reduction in the universe of safe assets with a much larger supply. A larger supply of debt should imply, *ceteris paribus*, an increase of the required returns, as the sequence of higher deficits that have fueled the higher debt implies a reduction in the national saving. Moreover, the increase of social and health spending underlying higher deficits supports ageing households, implying less need of private savings.

The literature has converged on an estimated impact of higher debt on natural interest rates in the order of 35 basis points per 10 point increase in the debt-to-GDP ratio (Lukasz and Summers, 2019). These authors suggest that the total increase in r^* since the 1980s is 1.5 percent due to higher deficits and debt and from half to a full percentage point due to higher social spending.

The large decline in the natural rate is not expected to reverse
Summing up, the downward forces driving down the equilibrium or natural interest rate have largely dominated. The overall reduction in r^* is around 4.5 percent in the last half century (Brand et al., 2018) and has accelerated in the turbulent era. Without the increase in debt the reduction would have been larger.

Going forward, the trajectory of r^* is not expected to change markedly (Platzer and Peruffo, 2022). The world is still ageing, with the proportion of old people increasing further. The passing of baby boomers (those born in the decades after the Second World War in advanced economies) will stem or even reverse the declining impact on the natural rate in AEs. In EMDEs, the ageing factor still puts strong downward pressure on r^*. Productivity growth is not expected to increase much; if anything, the convergence of EMDEs to AEs in income levels point to an additional global downward pressure in natural rates.

A big question mark lingers on the impact of the ongoing or expected structural transformations of the economy on the saving–investment balances, growth and the natural rate. Under some scenarios (IMF, 2023) r^* could go up. A reduction in the appetite for public debt, given persistently higher levels, or a firming of the recovery in labor shares as a consequence of pandemic-related transformation of the labor market could push natural rates up. On the contrary, other factors could operate in a downward direction: a green transition that entails higher energy prices would bring down the marginal productivity of capital and investment; trade fragmentation would have a negative impact on growth, while the impact of financial fragmentation is uncertain. Current-account deficit countries could face more expensive financing but surplus countries would repatriate savings that would press down r^*.

4.3   INTEREST RATES AND MONETARY POLICY

The natural interest rate anchors monetary policy. Monetary policy aims at keeping inflation at a low level consistent with the paramount objective of price stability. This is achieved by stabilizing the economy around its equilibrium level, where the interest rate equals r^*. There, price pressures wane and inflation stays at the target level. The main conventional instrument of monetary policy is the policy interest rate, which is short term and nominal. Mechanics are simple: policy rates in real terms (r) are raised above r^* to contain demand, and vice versa; when the economy is in equilibrium, monetary policy is neutral and r equals r^*. The neutral policy rate is the monetary incarnation of the natural rate.

But this standard and cyclical behavior of monetary policy intersperses with prolonged periods when it has to deal with too high or low inflation. During the post-war Bretton Woods regime, monetary policy was subordinated to the stability of the exchange rates and, sometimes, to fiscal needs, and there were periods of high inflation. In the 1980s and 1990s, bringing inflation down required a protracted period of monetary tightening. High-for-long policy rates pulled long-term real rates to elevated levels. More recently, too low inflation has required opposite policies, with similar implications as noted below. From this perspective, monetary policy can impact long-term real rates, and thus have an effect on the estimation and assessment of r^*. For this reason, some authors (Borio et al., 2017) consider that monetary policy can have a lasting impact on the natural rate.

The conquest of price stability in the 1990s – first in core AEs and then, progressively, in EMDEs – was achieved through the building up of central banks' credibility within a policy regime of inflation targeting. The achievement generated a sense of mission accomplished at the turn of this century and enabled monetary policy to fulfill its stabilizing role smoothly, while keeping inflation and policy rates low. Terms such as *Great Moderation* or *Goldilocks economy* reflected the triumphalism, but the optimistic mood did not last long.

4.3.1 Monetary Policy Shifts in the Turbulent Era

Low interest rates amid economic exuberance and loose regulation fed the imbalances and financial excesses leading to the GFC in 2008. At that time the decline in the natural rate combined with very low or negative inflation complicated the task of monetary policy that struggled to bring inflation back to target. The need to bring the real policy rate well below the natural rate ($r <$ r^*) to respond to the deep recession, clashed with the zero lower bound (ZLB), as the management of negative policy rates is challenging for central banks.

The ZLB in a context of low natural rates and economic emergency pushed central banks to expand their monetary policy instruments and adopt unconventional policies.

Unconventional monetary policy shifts the focus of central bank's operations from the setting of policy rate to the management of its balance sheet (Borio and Disyatat, 2009). Unconventional policies can take diverse forms, most notably: (i) forward guidance, where the central bank communicates the likely stance of monetary policy going forward; (ii) credit policies aimed at easing the credit constraints of agents at times of financial stress; and (iii) quantitative easing (QE), aimed at reducing the long-term interest rates through the expansion of the central bank balance sheet. The latter two make

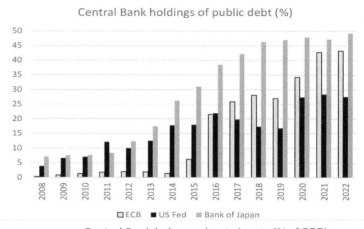

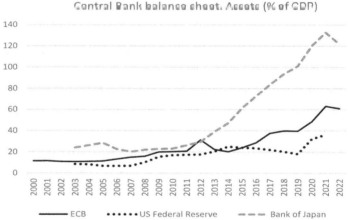

Note: Assets corresponds to eligible bonds for operational or liquidity purposes and asset purchase programs. For the ECB, only bonds of asset purchase programs.
Source: ECB, US Federal Reserve, Bank of Japan, IMF, Reserve Bank of Australia.

Figure 4.2   Balance sheets of central banks have ballooned and now hold a sizable share of the public debt stock

use of public debt securities, either as collateral or as purchases by the central bank. Furthermore, the GFC also induced central banks and regulatory authorities to revamp financial regulation. Now, banks have to hold thicker buffers of capital. This leads to an increase in the demand of safe assets, typically high-rated public debt.

The adoption of unconventional policies in the aftermath of the GFC multiplied the size of central banks' balance sheets in advanced economies (Figure

4.2, bottom). The timing, intensity and typology of QE varied among countries. The Bank of Japan was the pioneer in 2001 to address, unsuccessfully, the deflation malaise. The Federal Reserve implemented several QE programs since 2007. The ECB announced QE and massive purchases later, in 2012, to face the euro fiscal crisis and the fragmentation of the euro debt market, albeit the balance sheet did not surge until 2015. As a result, they have become holders of a substantial share of sovereign debt (Figure 4.2, top).

As the GFC turned the page, unconventional credit policies and some asset purchases programs were discontinued. But, remarkably, the balance sheets hardly shrunk (in Japan, they continued to expand). Inflation remained very low and often below target, so the continuation of very accommodative policies was deemed necessary; furthermore, central banks were very cautious to reverse policies as this could spook markets. This caution was rooted in the experience of 2013 when the Fed announced the reduction or tapering of asset purchases (the taper tantrum), leading to a sudden spike in long-term yields that reverberated across the global economy.

The debate on how to deal with the reduction of the oversized balance sheets in central banks continued until the pandemic hit in 2020. Then, unconventional policies were swiftly reinstated. Central banks implemented new rounds of huge public debt purchases and this time EMDEs also joined in.

The monetary landscape has deeply changed in the last two decades – with hindsight, in unthinkable ways. Central bank balance sheets have multiplied by a factor between four and six relative to 2007 and a substantial part of the public debt (25 percent in the US, 45 percent in the euro area, 50 percent in Japan) is held by the central banks. And unconventional monetary instruments are here to stay.

4.4   THE NEXUS BETWEEN MONETARY AND FISCAL POLICIES

Monetary and fiscal policy have traditionally been intertwined. They are the two main policy instruments for economic stabilization. They complement – and sometimes conflict with – each other. The basic textbook macro model (IS-LM) builds on this interaction, that mainly operates through the interest rate. Fiscal expansions (monetary contractions) increase the interest rate and cool down the economy and inflation, and vice versa. Central bank operations and the institutional set-up also link together both policies. Monetary policy instruments make use of government securities; and central banks' profits are a source of revenue to the national treasuries.

A deeper dimension of the fiscal–monetary interaction is the position of fiscal relative to monetary policies and authorities. Starting with the debasing of currencies in the Roman empire to those in the sixteenth century that triggered infamous price revolutions, the subordination of monetary policy – or the creation of money – to the fiscal needs of the sovereign has a long history. The modern versions of this fiscal dominance are the hyperinflations in the interwar period in Europe and later in emerging economies, when money was created to cover the outsized fiscal needs. A number of countries in Africa and Latin America are still grappling with this malaise. Moderate versions of fiscal dominance underlay the period of high inflation after the demise of Bretton Woods in the 1970s and early 1980s.

Then, the achievement of price stability became a priority as high inflation has deep social implications. An academic and political consensus formed around central bank independence (from fiscal authorities). Independence was seen as a requirement to gain policy credibility and tame inflation. This was the context of the Volcker disinflation in the 1980s in the US and also of the European Monetary System of exchange rates, aimed to benefit from the anti-inflationary reputation of the Bundesbank, EMDEs followed a similar path with fixed exchange rate regimes that evolved to inflation targeting.

Central bank independence and the strong focus on price stability sanctioned the functional separation between monetary and fiscal policy. The relative situation of both policies also changed. As explained in Chapter 1, monetary policy, reinforced by its conquest of price stability took an active, but smooth stabilizing role; fiscal policy, with the hangover of high deficits, took the back seat and became less active.

4.4.1   Strengthened Links in the Turbulent Era

The deep shock of the GFC not only affected the management of monetary policy and the role and space of fiscal policy, but also deepened the links between both.

We have detailed the changes operated on monetary policy: a falling r^*, the success in targeting inflation and the lack of inflationary pressures allowed for very low rates; the challenge became to bring inflation to target from below, when interest rates were close to the ZLB.

Chapter 6 describes how the paradigm of fiscal policy was also shifting from a cautious, contractionary stance in the disinflation period to a more proactive role, and for good reasons. Low interest rates and the lack of inflationary pressures boosted the stabilization role of fiscal policy: (i) fiscal expansions have a larger impact on the economy as they do not push up nominal rates; (ii) fiscal expansions can improve debt sustainability in this set-up, as they increase growth without putting pressure on real rates, pushing down $r–g$; and (iii) the fiscal space expands further as low nominal and real interest rates imply lower financing costs for governments and interest payments. Moreover, under these circumstances, fiscal policy can fill the gap left by monetary policy and even support it to bring inflation back to target if fiscal expansions have an inflationary effect.

The immediate fiscal reaction in AEs to limit the economic damage from the GFC was to launch large fiscal packages, amounting to around 2 percent of GDP in G20 economies (Alberola et al., 2020). Debt shot up and, as the downturn persisted, the fears of a debt crisis compounding with the financial crisis increased. This fear reawakened the ingrained reflex towards fiscal continence, leading to a rethinking of the fiscal stance and a reversal of the fiscal expansion. The point in case was Europe, where austerity was the rule and interest rates were also raised. Indeed, in the euro area, the most vulnerable economies endured a fiscal crisis in 2011. The initial reaction was additional fiscal adjustment that deepened the crisis, with the ECB endorsing the adjustment and providing limited support through liquidity mechanisms. While external bailouts kept the crisis economies (barely) afloat and the euro together, the game changer that overcame the crisis was a monetary policy reaction: the commitment of the ECB's president, to do "whatever it takes" to save the euro in a speech in July 2012.

The contrast between the tribulations of the euro area and the relative success of the US, where fiscal support lasted longer and monetary policy maintained a very accommodative stance, helped to sanction the new state of things: the support of monetary to fiscal policies through unconventional policies and the recognition of the need for an active role of fiscal policy to support activity in emergencies and in close coordination with central banks. The bounds between monetary and fiscal policies had become blurred.

With the economic, inflationless recovery, fiscal policy took a less supportive stance, also to facilitate the reduction of public debt. And central banks kept their activism in their quest to bring inflation back to target and also to entrench financial stability. They were seen in this period as the only game in town as their mandate was overextended (El-Erian, 2016).

But when the pandemic hit, the lessons from the GFC recession were quickly applied and a swift and massive coordinated fiscal and monetary response was implemented. This time not only in advanced but also in emerging and developing economies. The response was quite effective and the massive economic disruptions caused by the pandemic were overcome in spite of new waves of Covid-19. The fiscal support was 4.6 percent of G20 economies' GDP, doubling the response to the GFC. AEs were particularly proactive with a support over 8 percent, while the support of EMDEs was limited to 2 percent of GDP (Alberola et al., 2020).

As the economies recovered from the pandemic shock and the emergency measures lapsed, the dominant view was that fiscal and monetary policy had to disengage from the close cohabitation during the emergency. The joint and coordinated response was facilitated by the consistency of objectives in an environment of deflationary pressures and the size of the recession, but too long and close interaction risked generating problems for both, in particular central banks whose independence could be put at stake.

4.5   WHERE DO WE STAND AND WHAT LIES AHEAD?

The decline in the natural interest rate, the conquest of inflation and the two largest economic crises in generations have reshaped fiscal and monetary policy and their interactions in the last two decades.

Starting with monetary policy, the depth of the GFC required the use of new, unconventional instruments. The success of monetary policy to bring inflation down had a flip side: too low inflation and the challenges to bring it back to target in a world of low r^* and the zero lower bound. This feature has entrenched the unconventional instruments. At the same time, central banks have expanded their scope, first to financial stability and more recently to novel areas, such as green finance and inequality, which are far from their core mandate.

Unconventional policies have a strong fiscal dimension. They aim at reducing long-term rates and imply bringing large amounts of public debt into the central banks. The larger scope of central banks pushes them deeper into the political arena. For institutions that have built their reputation on their independence and close focus on inflation these changes entail risks.

Regarding fiscal policy, there are conflicting views on how to act going forward. On the one hand, the two biggest recessions in generations and a strong policy response have brought debt levels to record levels across the world. The surge in debt would call for fiscal adjustments and a cautious fiscal stance. On the other hand, the reduction of natural rates has boosted fiscal policy as an instrument: it has greatly reduced financing costs for governments, improved debt dynamics and opened up fiscal space; very low rates also make fiscal policy more effective and raise the value of the fiscal multiplier. In this context, fiscal policy can be more active in stabilizing the economy, in particular if demand is structurally weak. It can also be more ambitious, aiming at increasing investment and potential growth, as well as taking a leading role in the green transition (Blanchard, 2023). Overall, the policy consensus has been recently more biased towards the second view, mostly because fiscal concerns have been contained as financing costs continued to be low.

The close interaction and coordination between monetary and fiscal policy has been key to overcome the two crises. As the economies recovered from Covid-19, there was consensus that fiscal and monetary policy should re-establish their separation. The main challenges were how to deal with the related issues of the surge in public debt, withdrawal of the fiscal and monetary stimulus and the salutary reduction of public debt holdings in central banks' balance sheets; the return of public paper to the markets could put pressure on interest rates and worsen debt sustainability (Alberola et al., 2022). There was awareness that this exit process could generate frictions between fiscal and monetary authorities and could make the normalization of monetary policy difficult.

However, the reawakening of inflation that has accompanied the recovery has drastically changed the prospects and is influencing the mainstream view. First, the spike in inflation was related to the sharp recovery in demand (turbo-boosted by large fiscal support packages) and disruptions in supply related to the pandemic. Analysts and central banks first considered this spike as transitory, related to the normalization of activity. However, the energy and food crisis ignited by the Russian invasion of Ukraine has prolonged the inflationary pressures that now look to become persistent and to have second round effects.

The surge in global inflation raises the stakes for policymakers as policy objectives diverge. Central banks must avoid inflation to become entrenched as it did in the 1980s. The hard-won credibility of central banks in their fight with inflation is at stake. Indeed, they have reoriented their efforts to control inflation through an intense monetary policy tightening cycle.

The benign view on fiscal policy and its activism is also under pressure. Fiscal authorities are reluctant to withdraw the fiscal support while the recovery from the deep pandemic recession is not completed. Fiscal policy could offset the effects of tighter monetary policy on activity, but this could fuel demand and prices. Moreover, higher interest rates may constrain again the fiscal space and the jump in debt in the last years calls for caution. True, the surge in inflation provides a temporary relief to public finances as it boosts revenues and the increase in nominal output flattens debt-to-GDP ratios. But in fiscally vulnerable countries, higher rates could lead to fiscal stress that could also stress the interaction between fiscal and monetary authorities.

Even if the inflation is redirected towards the target in the medium run, how fiscal and monetary policies interact in the future is a challenge. The close link between policies is here to stay, as well as the environment of low interest rates, which is not expected to change dramatically. Central banks will keep in their toolbox the unconventional instruments and fiscal policy will remain more active than before. Each authority will focus independently on their mandates, even if they eventually enter into conflict.

The risk scenario is that a high inflation regime consolidates over the next years. If that is the case, a prolonged period of high real interest rates may follow. Fiscal policy would be more constrained. And this might raise the temptation of reducing debt through higher inflation. Fiscal dominance of monetary policy would be a distinct risk. If this risk materializes, the link between monetary and fiscal policy would become pernicious and the conquest of inflation that underpinned economic stability in the last decades and facilitated a greater fiscal activism could be jeopardized.

NOTE

1.   This is a simplified version of the standard debt dynamics equation in Chapter 2.

REFERENCES

Alberola, E., Y. Arslan, G. Cheng and R. Moessner (2020), "The fiscal response to the Covid-19 crisis in advanced and emerging market economies", *BIS Bulletin*, No 23, June.
Alberola, E., G. Cheng, A. Consiglio and S. Zenios (2022), "Debt sustainability and monetary policy: The case of ECB asset purchases", *BIS Working Papers*, No. 1034.
Bernanke, B. S. (2005), "The global savings glut and the US current account deficit", *Sandringe Lecture,* Virginia, 10 March.
Blanchard, O. (2023), *Fiscal Policy Under Low Interest Rates.* MIT Press.
Borio, C. and P. Disyatat (2009), "Unconventional monetary policies: An appraisal", *BIS Working Papers*, 292.
Borio, C., P. Disyatat, M. Juselius and P. Rungcharoenkitul (2017), "Why so low for so long? A long view of real interest rates", *BIS Working Papers*, 685.
Brand, C., M. Bielecki and A. Penalver (2018), "The natural rate of interest: Estimates, drivers, and challenges to monetary policy", *ECB Occasional Paper*, No. 217.
Carvalho, C., A. Ferrero and F. Nechio (2016), "Demographics and real interest rates: Inspecting the mechanism", *European Economic Review*, 88, 208–226.
El-Erian, M. (2016), *The Only Game in Town: Central Banks, Instability and Avoiding the Next Collapse.* Random House.
Feyrer, J. (2007), "Demographics and productivity", *Review of Economic and Statistics*, 89, 100–109.
Gordon, R. J. (2016), *The Rise and Fall of American Growth.* Princeton University Press.
IMF (2023), "The natural rate of interest: Drivers and implications for policy", chapter 2, *World Economic Outlook*, April.
Lukasz, R. and T. Smith (2015), "Secular drivers of the global real interest rate", *Bank of England Working Paper*, 571.
Lukasz, R. and L. H. Summers (2019), "Public boost and private drag: Government policy and the equilibrium real interest rate in advanced economies", *Brookings Papers on Economic Activity*, Spring, 1–76.
Philippon, T. (2019), *The Great Reversal*, Harvard University Press.
Platzer, J. and M. Peruffo (2022), "Secular drivers of the natural rate of interest in the United States. A quantitative evaluation", *IMF Working Paper*, No. 2022/030.

5. A macroeconomic perspective on the challenges of taxing multinationals

Shafik Hebous

5.1 INTRODUCTION

Multinationals are important value-added generators in the economy. In 2022, sales of the *Fortune Global 500* multinational companies reached $37.8 trillion (that is, a multiple of 1.5 of US GDP). Yet, the observation that multinationals tend to face a relatively low effective profit tax rate has sparked a heated debate, eventually placing this topic at the top of the global policy agenda. From a macroeconomic standpoint, three aspects in the debate about the taxation of multinationals are of particular interest: (i) direct implications for tax revenue, (ii) dynamic effects on real investment, and (iii) whether and how tax-motivated activities of multinationals affect aggregate statistics, which could complicate monitoring the economy and interpreting key macroeconomic indicators. The importance of the corporate income tax (CIT) in total tax revenues differs across countries. On average, CIT raises more than 12 percent of total tax revenue in emerging and developing countries (EMDEs), and 8 percent in advanced economies (AEs).

The corporate tax design has not coped with increased digitalization of the economy, increased importance of intangible assets (such as patents, algorithms, and other know-how assets) in generating value added, and the rise of the global firm that produces to the world market with a sophisticated cross-border organization of affiliated companies (rather than 'producing close to consumers'). These developments intensified two fundamental underlying challenges facing the taxation of multinationals. The first is cross-border spillovers on tax rates and bases. One country's tax rules and practices affect other countries (*tax competition* between countries) and multinationals exploit international differences in corporate tax rules to shift profit from high- to low-tax jurisdictions (*profit shifting*). These cross-border spillovers directly affect tax revenue and investment. The second challenge is the allocation of taxing rights between countries – the question is: what country should tax what? Should the country where the affiliate of the multinational company is located tax its profit or should the headquarters country have the right to tax that profit? This question is a century old – existing since the CIT was first introduced – but it has regained importance with increased ability to conduct business without actually having a physical presence in a country (for example through providing cross-border digital services, streaming activities, advertisement on online platforms, and so on). Should the country where consumers are located have the right to tax as well? Currently, countries in principle would not have the right to tax such income under the CIT rules. Therefore, some countries introduced unilateral 'digital services taxes' to capture multinationals that are not present in their countries.

To address those challenges, in 2021, 137 countries agreed on a two-pillar reform of the international corporate tax framework within the OECD-led Inclusive Framework (OECD, 2021):

- Pillar 1 allocates one quarter of profits above 10 percent of revenue to market jurisdictions for multinationals with turnover larger than €20 billion, excluding extractive industries and regulated financial services. While Pillar 1 is mandatory for the agreeing countries, its implementation requires a multilateral treaty and hence needs a critical mass of implementing countries.
- Pillar 2 introduces a minimum effective tax of 15 percent through several rules for multinationals with turnover larger than €750 million (with some exceptions). Pillar 2 is optional – that is, some jurisdictions may opt not to adopt the minimum tax – but jurisdictions must accept adoption by others.

The full details of this OECD-led Inclusive Framework agreement are being finalized for possible implementation in 2024, with a sign of progress particularly regarding the implementation of Pillar 2.

This chapter provides a high-level overview of the challenges that arise from the existing international corporate tax framework and expected impacts of the two-pillar proposal. There is no way to do justice to all the important aspects of this rich topic, but rather the aim here is to give a high-level selective summary through a macroeconomic lens for non-corporate-tax experts.

Section 5.2 looks at pressures to lower domestic taxes (*tax competition*), discusses *profit shifting* and summarizes cross-border spillover effects through real investment. Section 5.3 discusses the impact of a global minimum corporate tax on competition, profit shifting, and investment. Section 5.4 discusses the allocation of taxing rights across countries and the destination-based principle of taxation. Section 5.5 briefly points out potential distortions and measurement errors in relevant macro statistics due to profit shifting. Section 5.6 concludes.

5.2   CORPORATE TAX SPILLOVERS

5.2.1   Tax Rate Spillovers: Tax Competition

Under a strategic interaction of a tax game between countries, the best response to tax changes abroad is likely to change national tax rules too. This tax competition takes various forms, probably the most familiar one is the tax rate setting.[1] The empirical evidence suggests that CIT rates are complement, that is, they tend to move in the same direction (if one country cuts its rate the others would do too). Empirically, the magnitude of the slope of this reaction function has not been tied down with precision due to identification challenges (endogeneity and simultaneity). The IMF (2022) finds that a 1 percentage point cut in the (weighted average) foreign CIT rate leads to a decrease in the home country CIT rate of between 0.25 and 0.6 percentage points. This estimate of the slope is broadly in line with others in the literature based on various methodologies (Leibrecht and Hochgatterer, 2012; OECD, 2021).

Lowering the CIT rate is costly as it lowers revenues from the relatively immobile (domestic) tax base. For example, the average CIT rate in Europe was about 35 percent in 1995 and has declined to 21 percent in 2022. As illustrated in Crivelli et al. (2016), if the EU27 countries plus Norway, Switzerland, and the United Kingdom had applied their 1990 CIT rates to their 2018 CIT bases, they would have collected 1.6 percent of GDP more revenues.[2] The tendency to lower the CIT rate has not been generally accompanied by a parallel broadening of the CIT base. For example, Kawano and Slemrod (2015) report that CIT rate cuts are only 37 percent of the time accompanied by CIT base-broadening measures, while 25 percent are accompanied by CIT base narrowing measures.[3]

Lower CIT rates also put pressure on personal income tax rates and thus could indirectly lead to lower personal income tax revenues and influence the progressivity of the tax system. The CIT plays the role of a withholding tax on income, particularly on retained (undistributed) profits that increase the value of the firm, often without subjecting the owners to capital gains taxes. The CIT is thus linked to the personal income tax (PIT); for example, taxpayers may also avoid income taxes by holding financial assets in the corporate sector (de Mooij and Klemm, 2021; Fuest and Weichenrieder, 2002). If the CIT is lower than the personal income, there would be arbitrage opportunities. Downward pressures on the PIT are costly both in terms of revenues and potentially reducing the average tax rate at the top of income distribution (with equity consequences). The CIT also falls on foreign owners of multinationals, to the extent it falls on economic rent. Therefore, a lower CIT, in principle, implies a lower tax on economic rent in the 'source' country.

5.2.2   Tax Base Spillovers: Profit Shifting

Given international differences in corporate taxation, multinationals use various strategies to minimize their global tax liability. As is well documented in the literature, these strategies shift reported profits from high- to low-tax jurisdictions (thereby eroding the tax base in the high-tax countries). One prominent method, stemming from the hallmark of the current intentional tax framework, is exploiting the vulnerability of the arms' length principle through 'transfer pricing' practices. The arms' length principle states that a related-party transaction should be priced as if it is between unrelated parties – that is, based on the 'world market price'. Often, however, for multinationals it is not straightforward to determine such a price (as if it were an unrelated-party transaction) especially for trade with services, patents, and know-how assets, thereby giving some leeway for the multinationals to determine it. For example, if one affiliate overprices its imports from another affiliate within the multinational group, the cost of the importing affiliate would be inflated, thereby shrinking reported profits, while the other affiliate would see an increase in revenue and hence reported profits.

Cross-border tax planning and avoidance activities of multinationals can be very sophisticated, and are estimated to reduce profits by around about 20 percent in high-tax European Union countries and 10 percent in the United States (Tørsløv et al., 2022). Globally, in 2015, these authors find that one third of multinationals' profits is shifted to low-tax jurisdictions. Other studies focused on specific avoidance strategies – including mispricing international trade with services (Hebous and Johannesen, 2021) and intragroup lending (Feld et al., 2013) – providing a range of estimates. In addition to the direct tax revenue foregone, profit shifting has generated dissatisfaction in the public, raising political pressures to reform international corporate taxation.

5.2.3   Tax Base Spillovers: Real Investment

Beyond the location of 'paper' profit, cross-border CIT base spillovers arise also through real investment decisions. The IMF (2014) finds that a one-point reduction in the statutory CIT rate abroad reduces a country's CIT base by 3.7 percent through lowering real activities. This is a sizable effect considering that CIT rates have fallen, on average, by around 5 points over the last 10 years. Such an estimate includes both channels of tax base spillovers: profit shifting (discussed above) and real investment location decisions.

While profits react to the *statutory* CIT rate, the marginal investor reacts to the *marginal effective* tax rate that takes into account tax deductions, tax depreciations, and other tax base features. A statutory CIT rate cut is more valuable for firms that generate relatively high economic rents (that is those with high mark-ups, for instance from monopolistic power).[4]

As discussed in Hebous et al. (2022), one efficient design of a profit tax is to combine a zero marginal effective tax rate on the 'normal return' (or opportunity cost of the investment) with a tax on the 'excess profit' (or economic rent). There are two broad forms of designing an efficient rent tax: a cash-flow tax (for example with full expensing, while denying interest deductions) or providing an allowance for normal return. Both ways would leave the normal return untaxed. An efficient design makes sure the tax fully falls on economic rent (say that results from monopoly), and the investment decision would be unaffected by the tax because the marginal cost and marginal revenue would remain intact. But the tax would shrink the profit of the monopolist, and thus the tax incidence falls on the monopolist (Mirrlees et al., 2011).[5] In an open economy, the decision to locate investments by multinationals is affected by the international differences in *average* effective tax rates (Devereux et al., 2002), among many non-tax factors.

One costly aspect of tax competition is the spread of ill-designed tax incentives such as tax holidays – especially in EMDEs – that are often motivated by the objective of attracting real foreign direct investment (FDI). The evidence suggests, however, that these preferential tax regimes tend to be ineffective (for example given to investments that would have taken place even without the incentives) and inefficient (implying significant direct and indirect revenue foregone that could have been spent more productively).[6]

5.3 THE EFFECT OF A GLOBAL CORPORATE MINIMUM TAX

Tax competition and profit shifting are costly through directly impacting tax revenues and through affecting investment decisions, as discussed above. Compared with a Nash equilibrium, coordination by agreeing on a common lower bound on the tax rate – set between the highest and lowest Nash tax rates – is welfare-improving for the high-tax country because it reduces its tax base erosion. The amount of profit that is shifted out of the high-tax country becomes lower as the tax rate differential between countries becomes lower under coordination (Keen and Konrad, 2013).[7]

The low-tax country also benefits from such a global minimum tax. This may seem counter-intuitive, but as the low-tax country raises its rate to the minimum, two effects arise: (i) tax revenues from taxing its domestic immobile base go up; and (ii) at the same time, revenues go down from the decline of profit shifted into the low-tax country. As shown in Hebous and Keen (2021), with a modest minimum tax it is possible for the former effect to dominate, leaving the low-tax country better off; while it loses out from having less inward profit shifting, it more than offsets this loss from gains from charging the tax base that remains at a higher tax rate. The calibration in Hebous and Keen (2021) suggests that the most preferred rate for the low-tax country is 15–17 percent.

While Pillar 2 puts a limit on tax competition at an effective rate of 15 percent, it is a limited version of the minimum tax described above due to exceptions and specificities of the rules. For example, some multinationals would not fall in the scope of the agreement if they do not meet the turnover threshold. Also, even for 'in-scope' companies, a portion of profit would not be subjected to a minimum tax under Pillar 2 (called substance-based income exclusion), equal to 8 percent of assets and 10 percent of payroll. Therefore, some forms of tax competition remain intact as discussed in detail in IMF (2023). Estimates of the implication of Pillar 2 on tax revenues suggest that the top-up tax (that is raising the tax on profit that is currently taxed below 15 percent to the minimum), would raise global CIT revenue by 5.7 percent or 0.15 percent of GDP. This estimate considers the main exceptions under Pillar 2 (IMF, 2022, 2023). In addition, if reactions of countries are taken into account, reduced tax competition (by allowing other countries to raise their CIT rates) would raise an extra 8.1 percent of global CIT revenues.

Moreover, EMDE countries have a strong case for revisiting, and potentially abolishing, ineffective and inefficient tax incentives, which would support both revenues and the integrity of the tax system. Multinationals would find a tax holiday, for example, less relevant because they would then be liable for a tax in the headquarters country (if not taxed at the source). Although this effect is somewhat muted under Pillar 2 by the existence of the substance-based income exclusion and out-of-scope companies, the agreement is generally an opportunity to revisit the design of tax incentives as a tool to attract FDI. The case of reconsidering tax incentives is reinforced by the recent trend in capital-exporting countries – such as the United States and EU members – to impose unilateral minimum taxes on their multinationals if they are not sufficiently taxed aboard, which also implies that low taxation in the FDI host country would trigger a tax on the multinational company in the headquarter country. Pillar 2 also reduces incentives to shift profits to low-tax jurisdictions by lowering international tax rate differentials. These are discussed in detail in IMF (2023), which estimates that the introduction of a 15 percent minimum rate increases global CIT revenue by 1 percent. The impact of the agreement on investment by multinationals is rather moderate. Qualitatively, investment would decline as effective tax rates increase due to higher tax rates and less profit shifting. UNCTAD (2022) estimates that the potential decrease in global FDI is around 2 percent (see also IMF, 2023).

5.4   DIGITALIZATION AND DESTINATION-BASED TAXING RIGHTS

Conceptually, if the market countries – i.e., where consumers reside – were to be given the right to tax the profit, then (i) tax competition would be resolved because consumers are generally less mobile; (ii) profit shifting would be addressed because it is harder for the multinational company to 'move consumers'; and (iii) 'selling without physical presence' would imply a tax base for the country where the consumer is, rendering unilateral measures less important. Such destination-based taxation can be achieved for example by consolidating the global profit of a multinational company and next allocating this consolidated profit to countries according to their weights in the sales of this multinational company.[8] Such coordination is superior to unilateral measures (Hebous et al., 2022). Pillar 1 goes in this direction, introducing new taxing rights for market countries. Note also that while Pillar 2 is generally a revenue-raiser, Pillar 1 is a reallocation exercise, shifting a portion of the tax base ultimately from low-tax jurisdictions to market countries. But, by design, it captures only about 100 companies globally, which hardly reallocates 2 percent of global multinationals' profit. Hence, the expected revenue or investment impacts from Pillar 1 are very small (IMF, 2023).

Combining a 'cash-flow' tax with a 'border-adjustment' (i.e., not taxing export while taxing import) has been shown to result in a robust taxation of multinationals.[9] Such an idea, referred to as 'destination-based cash-flow tax (DBCFT)', would resolve known profit shifting practices and eliminate incentives for tax competition (Devereux et al., 2021). It would be, however, a fundamental reform compared with existing rules for profit taxation. One question in this regard is whether a unilateral adoption of a DBCFT would put a country in a more competitive position in international trade. As discussed in Devereux et al. (2021), in principle the exchange rate would adjust (and appreciate in response) to such a fundamental reform, leaving initial trade and investment positions unchanged. Buiter (2017) argues that such an exchange rate adjustment is possible under some conditions, but very different adjustments are also possible.

5.5   TAX PLANNING BY MULTINATIONALS AND MACROECONOMIC STATISTICS

Understanding 'if and how' cross-border profit shifting by multinationals affects macroeconomic aggregates is important for accurate interpretation of statistics, and hence for monitoring the economy and guiding economic policy-making. In this sense, the issue is not a mere statistical concern, but it is rather related to the assessment of a range of macroeconomic elements including GDP, domestic saving, and external balances.

5.5.1   GDP and Productivity

Changes in the books of multinational affiliates can have a significant effect on GDP statistics. For example, in 2015 in Ireland, there was a significant revision to the expected growth of 7.8 percent when the reported GDP growth turned out to be 26.3 percent. This difference was largely driven by a few activities of multinationals, mainly transferring IP assets to Ireland and establishing a new tax domicile of a company. This example – which was studied in detail in Central Bank of Ireland (2016), Avdjiev et al. (2018), and Lane (2017) – raises the general awareness that GDP numbers are influenced by the activities of multinationals. Of course, not all cross-border transactions of IPs and similar arrangements by multinationals are tax motivated, but generally some tax planning and avoidance strategies entail a change in the legal ownership of intellectual properties (IPs), thereby changing the accounts of the resident affiliates of the multinationals without a cross-border physical reallocation of the underlying asset. For example, looking at the United States, Guvenen et al. (2022) report that 38 percent of income generated from US FDI abroad is attributable to US GDP. After adjusting for profit shifting, the authors find that annual aggregate productivity growth rate was 13 basis points higher during 2004–2010 and 12 basis points lower during 2010–2016.

5.5.2   Foreign Direct Investment (FDI)

Conduit entities – in the form of special purpose entities (SPEs), holding companies, among others – are key for understanding the origin and destination of international capital income flows, including dividend, interest, and royalty. A significant share of global FDI is 'pass-through', flowing from country A to country B, through conduit entities in country C without real activities in country C. One motivation behind these flows is exploiting bilateral tax treaties to minimize tax payments ('treaty shopping').[10] Importantly, in some cases, these flows obscure ultimate ownership of capital, thereby jeopardizing transparency with broader consequences than the direct tax revenue impact. It is also difficult to interpret FDI measures in conduit countries in relation to their domestic economies. Damgaard et al. (2019) estimate that investment into corporate shells with no substance and no real links to the local economy may account for almost 40 percent of global FDI. Recently, several countries have imposed substance requirements on resident companies to tackle concerns about shell companies that have little (if any) real activities.[11]

5.5.3   Balance of Payment (BoP)

The BoP records all international transactions of a country with the rest of the world mainly resulting from international trade in goods and services, earnings on investments, and capital transfers. As discussed in detail in Hebous et al. (2021), tax-motivated transfer mispricing does not affect the overall BoP, but it does distort the sub-balances (the trade balance, the income balance, the capital and financial accounts). For example, in high-tax countries the measurement of the trade balance can be biased downward when related-party exports are underpriced (to dwarf firm revenue) and/or imports are overpriced (to inflate costs). This effect is theoretically offset by an upward bias in the income balance (because residents have higher profits abroad). The sub-accounts of the BoP are important indicators of domestic economic activities and net changes in ownership of foreign assets. In addition, BoP statistics are often used in empirical analysis, and thus if numbers are distorted, they can lead to severely biased results and misinterpretation of the findings.

5.6   CONCLUSION

Tax policy and behavioral responses of multinationals are inextricably linked. International tax coordination can be welfare-improving for most countries by reducing the pressures of tax competition and base erosion of the corporate income tax. The two-pillar agreement was envisaged as a package, with Pillar 1 being a reallocation of a portion of the tax base to market countries (thereby creating new taxing rights) while Pillar 2 is a general revenue-raiser. The agreement demonstrates that coordination between countries can work, but the effects are likely to be dampened due to the limited scope.

One issue that has not been discussed in this chapter is how further work can go beyond the two-pillar agreement to consider the circumstances of developing low-income countries (IMF, 2023). With the static revenue impact of the global minimum tax close to 6 percent of the global corporate income tax revenues, reforms of other taxes would remain critical to raise the needed revenues to meet sustainable development goals. Such reforms include the value-added tax, personal income taxes, and property taxes, inter alia (see de Mooij et al., 2020, and Chapter 10, for a specific focus on redistribution). Moreover, from a macroeconomic standpoint, it is important to understand how profit shifting affects aggregate statistics for accurate interpretation of information, and monitoring of the economy to inform policymaking.

Finally, the progress in the area of corporate tax coordination has shown that countries can together deliver tangible results, an inspiration to collectively act on the urgently pressing challenge of global warming and agree on concrete mitigation plans to limit it to below 2°C.

ACKNOWLEDGMENT

The views expressed here are those of the author and do not necessarily represent the views of the IMF, its Executive Board, or IMF management.

NOTES

1. 'Tax rate' here includes not only the statutory CT rate but also policies that affect the base (such as deductions) and hence also the effective tax rate.
2. While this number does not consider tax base changes – whether due to policy changes (such as base-broadening measures) or behavioral responses (such as incorporation decisions and profit shifting), it does indicate a large decline in revenue because of CIT rate cuts.
3. See also Hebous (2021).
4. Some studies, such as Hong and Smart (2010), suggest that ability to shift profit to low-tax jurisdictions raises investment in the headquarters country because it lowers the overall effective tax rate facing the multinational company.
5. This contrasts with the incidence of a tax that includes the normal return (like a common CIT design) that partially falls on wages (see for example Fuest et al., 2018). A significant share of multinationals' profits is, however, economic rent (IMF, 2022).
6. See IMF et al. (2015).
7. There is a counter-effect, though, since residents of the high-tax country benefit less from tax avoidance opportunities.
8. There are other ways. See Devereux et al. (2021), IMF (2019), and Hebous et al. (2021).
9. In 2017, combining a cash-flow tax with a border-adjustment received attention in the policy arena following a proposal by US congressmen Ryan and Brady to introduce a variant of this idea.
10. See for example Lejour et al. (2019).
11. Fischer et al. (2019) show that retained earnings of portfolio investments (which are typically not accounted for in the current account statistics) can be significant, reaching 1.2 to 7.8 percent of GDP. However, these are typically not directly related to tax planning and avoidance that require control over the multinational, as is the case for FDI.

REFERENCES

Avdjiev, Sc., M. Everett, P. R. Lane and H. Song Shin (2018), "Tracking the International Footprints of Global Firms", *BIS Quarterly Review*, March.
Buiter, W. H. (2017), "Exchange Rate Implications of Border Tax Adjustment Neutrality", *Economics*, 11(1), 20170012.
Central Bank of Ireland (2016), "Central Bank Quarterly Bulletin Q3, July".
Crivelli, E., R. A. de Mooij and M. Keen (2016), "Base Erosion, Profit Shifting and Developing Countries", *FinanzArchiv: Public Finance Analysis*, 72(3).
Damgaard, J., T. Elkjaer and N. Johannesen (2019), "What Is Real and What Is Not in the Global FDI Network?", *IMF Working Paper* No. 19/274.

de Mooij, R. and A. Klemm (2021), "Why and How to Tax Corporate Income?". In R. de Mooij, A. Klemm and V. Perry (Eds), *Corporate Income Taxes Under Pressure: Why Reform Is Needed and How It Can Be Designed?* Chapter 2. Washington, DC: IMF.

de Mooij, R., R. Fenochietto, S. Hebous, S. Leduc and C. Osorio-Buitron (2020), "Tax Policy for Inclusive Growth after the Pandemic", *IMF Special Series on COVID-19.*

Devereux, M. P., R. Griffith and A. Klemm (2002), "Corporate Income Tax Reforms and International Tax Competition", *Economic Policy*, 17(35).

Devereux, M. P., A. J. Auerbach, M. Keen, P. Oosterhuis, W. Schön and J. Vella (2021), *Taxing Profit in a Global Economy*. Oxford University Press.

Feld, L. P., J. H. Heckemeyer and M. Overesch (2013), "Capital Structure Choice and Company Taxation: A Meta-Study", *Journal of Banking & Finance*, 37(8).

Fischer, A., H. Groeger, P. Sauré and P. Yeşin (2019), "Current Account Adjustment and Retained Earnings", *Journal of International Money and Finance*, 94.

Fuest, C. and A. Weichenrieder (2002), "Tax Competition and Profit Shifting: On the Relationship between Personal and Corporate Tax Rates", *CESifo Working Paper* No. 781.

Fuest, C., A. Peichl and S. Siegloch (2018), "Do Higher Corporate Taxes Reduce Wages? Micro Evidence from Germany", *American Economic Review*, 108(2).

Guvenen, F., R. J. Mataloni Jr., D. G. Rassier and K. J. Ruhl (2022), "Offshore Profit Shifting and Aggregate Measurement: Balance of Payments, Foreign Investment, Productivity, and the Labor Share", *American Economic Review*, 112(6).

Hebous, S. (2021), "Has Tax Competition Become Less Harmful?". In: R. de Mooij, A. Klemm and V. Perry (Eds.), *Corporate Income Taxes Under Pressure: Why Reform Is Needed and How It Can Be Designed?* Chapter 6. Washington, DC: IMF.

Hebous, S. and N. Johannesen (2021), "At Your Service! The Role of Tax Havens in International Trade with Services", *European Economic Review*, 135.

Hebous, S. and M. Keen (2021), "Pareto-Improving Minimum Corporate Taxation", *IMF Working Paper* October.

Hebous, S., A. Klemm and Y. Wu (2021), "How Does Profit Shifting Affect the Balance of Payments?", *IMF Working Paper* WP/21/41.

Hebous, S., D. Prihardini and N. Vernon (2022), "Excess Profit Taxes: Historical Perspective and Contemporary Relevance", *IMF Working Paper* No. 2022/187.

Hong, Q. and M. Smart (2010), "In Praise of Tax Havens: International Tax Planning and Foreign Direct Investment", *European. Economic Review*, 54.

IMF (2014), "Spillovers in International Corporate Taxation", *IMF Policy Paper* May 9.

IMF (2019), "Corporate Taxation in the Global Economy", *IMF Policy Paper* 19/7.

IMF (2022), "Coordinating Taxation Across Borders", *IMF Fiscal Monitor* April.

IMF (2023), "International Corporate Tax Reform", *IMF Policy Paper* March.

IMF, OECD, UN and World Bank (2015), "Options for Low Income Countries' Effective and Efficient Use of Tax Incentives for Investment", *Report to the G20 Development Working Group.*

Kawano, L. and J. Slemrod (2015), "How Do Corporate Tax Bases Change When Corporate Tax Rates Change? With Implications for the Tax Rate Elasticity of Corporate Tax Revenues", *International Tax and Public Finance*, 23.

Keen, M. and K. Konrad (2013), "The Theory of International Tax Competition and Coordination", *Handbook of Public Economics 5*, Chapter 5. Elsevier.

Lane, P. R. (2017), "The Treatment of Global Firms in National Accounts", *Central Bank of Ireland Economic Letters 2017*, No. 1.

Leibrecht, M. and C. Hochgatterer (2012), "Tax Competition as a Cause of Falling Corporate Income Tax Rates", *Journal of Economic Surveys*, 26(4).

Lejour, A., J. Möhlmann, M. van 't Riet and T. Benschop (2019), "Dutch Shell Companies and International Tax Planning", *CentER Discussion Paper Series* No. 2019-024.

Mirrlees, J., S. Adam, T. Besley, R. Blundell, S. Bond, R. Chote, M. Gammie, P. Johnson, G. Myles and J. Poterba (2011), "Tax by Design", *The Mirrlees Review*. Oxford, UK: Oxford University Press.

OECD (2021), "Statement on a Two-pillar Solution to Address the Tax Challenges Arising from the Digitalisation of the Economy", Paris: Organisation for Economic Co-operation and Development.

Tørsløv, T., L. Wier and G. Zucman (2022), "The Missing Profits of Nations", *Review of Economic Studies.*

UNCTAD (2022), *World Investment Report*. Geneva.

PART II

Uses of fiscal policy: the stabilization role of fiscal policy

6. The effectiveness of fiscal policy

Javier Andrés

6.1 INTRODUCTION

Fiscal policy pursues objectives such as growth, equity, and the provision of basic services to citizens. However, its performance is often judged on the basis of its success in dampening economic fluctuations and preventing recessions. The stabilization capacity of the government budget depends on the strength of automatic stabilizers and on the wise use of discretionary changes in public spending or taxes. When assessing the effectiveness of fiscal policy, we focus mainly on the latter: the fiscal multiplier – the ratio of the change in output as a result of a discretionary change in spending or taxes – summarizes the impact of fiscal changes on economic activity.

The literature on fiscal multipliers is almost boundless, which makes it impossible to come up with a single figure about the response of output to a given change in the fiscal stance. Estimates differ across studies due to the diversity of their geographical and temporal scope, the instrument of interest, the definition and measurement of variables, and the way exogenous fiscal shocks are identified. The identification of shocks uses alternative empirical and theoretical methods whether structural models, Vector Autoregression (VAR) models, studies based on the narrative approach, calibrated or estimated general equilibrium models (DSGE), or even microeconometric studies (Ramey, 2019). This diversity of approaches reflects the different ways in which researchers have tried to identify truly exogenous fiscal shocks in the data and the transmission channels into economic outcomes.

In this chapter we first summarize the evidence on multipliers, discussing their most relevant determinants and the most reliable estimates in diverse circumstances. We separate this evidence into two periods: before and after the Great Financial Crisis (GFC). The enormous research effort devoted to the study of fiscal policy in extraordinary circumstances, such as the ones witnessed in the turbulent era, has addressed issues that were not seen as equally relevant during the previous years, known as the Great Moderation: financial frictions, private debt, debt sustainability, the Zero Lower Bound (ZLB) of interest rates, etc. Much of the evidence is constantly under revision, in particular recently by research based on newly available micro data sets and macroeconomic models with heterogeneous agents. This area constitutes very much work in progress that has already produced some results that confirm previous findings, as well as others that challenge the conventional view about fiscal policy, opening up new avenues for research in the future.

The chapter concludes with a discussion of the main lessons learned from the experience of fiscal policy as a stabilization tool in the last four decades, with special attention to the recent years, when massive fiscal efforts have been applied during the two deep recessions that the world economy has faced. Fiscal policy may be a powerful instrument to stabilize economies, in particular in deep recessions, although its effectiveness is state-dependent and depends on a number of factors, most importantly, the degree of monetary accommodation. The reliance on fiscal stimuli to keep economies afloat during the turbulent era has brought to the fore the importance of debt sustainability to recover and maintain some fiscal space with which to face future recessions and liabilities. Finally, the macroeconomic role of fiscal policy goes beyond short-run stabilization and extends to efforts to get the economies out of the secular stagnation and to successfully cope with longer-term challenges, such as the digital and green transitions, among others.

6.2   FISCAL MULTIPLIERS BEFORE THE TURBULENT ERA

By 2008, after a prolonged period of macroeconomic stability, there was a widespread consensus among academics and policymakers about the use of monetary policy and automatic fiscal stabilizers as the main stabilization tools. There was little confidence in the value of discretionary fiscal changes for stabilization purposes for reasons that had to do with the political processes behind them and with the lack of consensus about the effectiveness of fiscal stimuli. The debate about the effectiveness of fiscal policy focuses mostly on the size of the multiplier, the relative impact of different instruments and how these instruments are affected by the economic environment.

6.2.1   The Government Spending Multiplier is Around 1

A branch of the literature has been skeptical about the output response to changes on government spending. Alesina et al. (2018) studied fiscal consolidations in OECD economies since 1970, concluding that increases in government spending have a small impact on output, whereas some expenditure-based consolidation episodes have been expansionary, implying a negative multiplier. Barro and Redlick (2011) using US annual data (1912–2006) on defense expenditures, obtained public spending multipliers ranging from 0.4 to 0.8, depending on the time horizon. Mountford and Uhlig (2009) found that whereas deficit-financed fiscal stimuli may have a modest positive effect on output in the short run, the need to raise taxes in the future reverses this effect. Similarly, balanced budget fiscal expansions have negative effects on output in the medium term.

On the contrary, some influential papers report a positive and moderate multiplier of public spending. Blanchard and Perotti (2002), using VAR models, estimate multipliers around 1 in the post-war US economy. Government spending crowds-in consumption whereas it reduces private investment. Recently, Caldara and Kamps (2017) have developed a more general VAR method that controls for the restrictions imposed on the fiscal rules that might explain much of the discrepancies in previous papers. They estimate a government spending multiplier of 1–1.3 for the US economy (1950–2006). Also positive, although slightly smaller estimates are obtained by Guajardo et al. (2014). This study applies the narrative approach to a large sample of OECD countries and finds that the two-year fiscal multiplier is close to 1.

Positive output effects are also found in a general equilibrium framework. In a neoclassical general equilibrium model, Baxter and King (1993) calculate the public spending multiplier to be around 1 in the long run. This multiplier is stronger if the fiscal shock is permanent, although it can even be negative if it is financed with distortionary taxes. Galí et al. (2007) confirm the presence of significant government spending multipliers close to 1 in the short run and larger in the medium term. Their model incorporates a significant proportion of liquidity-constrained households, a feature that has proven to be very important to understanding the effects of fiscal policy after the financial crisis. Ramey (2019) finds that the discrepancies among available estimates of the multiplier are mostly due to the time horizon at which they are calculated. Using the present value or cumulative multipliers she narrows her estimate for changes in public spending down to the range 0.6–1.0. Similar results can be found in more general studies (Ramey, 2011).

6.2.2   Alternative Fiscal Instruments

The evidence in favor of higher multipliers for public investment than for public consumption is overwhelming. According to Baxter and King (1993), the effect of public investment on output and private investment is strongly positive if it increases the marginal product of capital and labor. Similar results are found by Auerbach and Gorodnichenko (2012) among others. But public investment projects must be carefully chosen in order to be fully effective. Using a sample of OECD countries, Boehm (2020) finds that when public investment projects are short-lived with no lasting effects on productivity, their impact on output is lower than that of public consumption. In the same vein,

Leeper et al. (2010) show that the timing of public investment and the efficiency of the public investment projects are key conditions to achieve positive long-run output effects from this type of spending.

Gauging the economic impact of changes in taxes is more difficult both theoretically and empirically. According to the basic Keynesian model, the direct demand effect of taxes is weaker than that of public spending, but on top of this effect, taxes have a distortionary impact on households' decisions that may affect the supply side of the economy. The demand and the supply channels have very different timing, and the distortionary effects are more likely to be asymmetrical and very sensitive to the elasticity of labor supply. These considerations explain the variety of outcomes. Blanchard and Perotti (2002) conclude that estimated tax multipliers may be higher or lower than spending multipliers depending on the dynamic specification of the model, and Caldara and Kamps (2017) estimate low multipliers for tax cuts (0.4–0.5). Romer and Romer (2010), applying the narrative approach, find very large tax multipliers in the US; tax hikes reduce investment, which suggests that the distortionary or supply-side effect may be dominant. Alesina et al. (2018) find that tax increases produce a strong multiplier effect at different horizons. Ramey (2019) also obtains cumulative tax multipliers to be between –2 and –3. Mertens and Ravn (2013) find that the responses of output to changes in corporate profit and income taxes in the US are larger than the spending multipliers usually found in the literature. Guajardo et al. (2014) also find that tax increases are more contractionary than spending cuts in their OECD sample.

6.2.3   State-dependence

Other features of the economy are associated with smaller fiscal multipliers. Regarding the effects of the exchange rate regime, Born et al. (2013) find that the government spending multiplier in the OECD is significantly larger under fixed exchange rates than under flexible rates. In addition, the multiplier is significantly higher in larger and less open economies than in more open ones (Ilzetzki et al., 2013).

Fiscal multipliers also differ across phases of the business cycle. In recessions, the usual crowding out channels (interest rates, wages, and prices) are more muted, so multipliers would be larger. Notwithstanding this, in mild recessions or during a boom, when economies are close to full employment, all those prices become more sensitive to movements in the output gap, and the relaxation of financial constraints gives more weight to wealth effects, moderating the impact of fiscal stimuli. The empirical results are nonetheless mixed. Canzoneri et al. (2016) derive substantial differences in the multiplier between booms and recessions in a model with financial intermediation frictions; Cloyne et al. (2021) also obtain higher multipliers in slumps. Auerbach

and Gorodnichenko (2012) find values of the multiplier ranging between 0 and
0.5 in booms and 1 and 1.5 in downturns for the US, and Blanchard and Leigh
(2013) report multipliers close to 2 in the early years of the financial recession. On the other hand, Ramey and Zubairy (2018) attribute these estimated
differences to empirical assumptions inconsistent with critical aspects of the
data generation process. Applying local projection methods, they conclude
that multipliers are very low and non-significantly different across business
cycle states, except for periods when the Zero Lower Bound (ZLB, hereafter)
is binding.

In a study covering 29 OECD economies Riera-Crichton et al. (2015) discuss
one possible cause of the discrepancies in the literature in this respect. Public
spending is often observed to be procyclical, increasing in booms (because
of the favorable fiscal space and interest rates) and falling or increasing more
moderately in recessions, which potentially contaminates the analysis of fiscal
policy during the cycle. The authors control for the sign of the change in public
spending along with the cyclical position of the economy and show that the
multiplier is almost twice as large in recessions than in booms (2.3 vs 1.3).

Many authors have found that multipliers are lower, and even negative, in
countries with high public debt (Ilzetzki et al., 2013). Huidrom et al. (2020)
conclude that multipliers are lower in times of high debt since higher current
interest rates and expected taxes in the future affect private spending decisions.

6.2.4   Monetary Accommodation

Finally, one of the most important determinants of the impact of discretionary
policy changes on employment and output, is the way monetary authorities
respond in the event of a substantial deviation of inflation from target or an
excessive appreciation of the currency. Cloyne et al. (2021) estimate the effect
of the monetary response to government spending shocks and isolate the direct
fiscal multiplier that they estimate to be close to 1. This value is consistent
with very different overall responses that go from zero under standard (non-
accommodative) monetary conditions up to 2 when monetary policy reacts to
mitigate the change in interest rates induced by the fiscal shock.

But the impact of monetary policy on the fiscal multiplier goes beyond the
immediate response of the interest rate. To gather the complexity of channels
at work in the monetary policy mix, Leeper et al. (2017) estimate (1955–2007
US data) the present value multipliers of a shock to government spending in
a full-blown DSGE model with a rich specification of the fiscal structure that
allows for the possibility of a fiscal regime in which monetary policy is subordinated to fiscal policy. The estimated 10-year multiplier is within the range
1.5–1.9 if in the regime of monetary subordination, while it is almost zero in
the standard regime.

6.3   FISCAL POLICY IN THE AFTERMATH OF THE GFC

The global financial meltdown in 2008 dramatically changed the economic landscape of the early 2000s. With the financial system in many countries immersed in a painful restructuring process and with the quick exhaustion of the space for conventional monetary policies, fiscal policy acquired a central role. The G20 summit held in Washington in 2008 called for the "use [of] fiscal measures to stimulate domestic demand to rapid effect … while maintaining a policy framework conducive to fiscal sustainability". These efforts had to be carried out against the backdrop of a world sharply divided between lenders and heavily leveraged borrowers. Once the crisis broke up, the perception of risk overshot and many countries and corporations had to deal with high risk premia. Two additional, deeper, trends predating the financial crisis, the secular stagnation, and the diminished response of the inflation rate to the economic slack, undermined the effect of the conventional monetary policy based on movements of the nominal interest rate.

In this scenario, the discussions about fiscal multipliers took a different tone and focused on the response of the economy to fiscal stimuli in the new reality: high spreads, public and private debt interactions, the ZLB, the persistent risk of deflation, the fiscal limit, financial frictions, inequality, non-linearity in severe recessions, among others.

6.3.1   The Zero Lower Bound (ZLB)

The secular stagnation is characterized by being an extended period of unusually low interest rates. Blanchard (2022) and Chapter 4 in this book argue that the fiscal policy space is, in these conditions, ample, since current deficits may not pose a real threat to debt sustainability. The fact that reasonable fiscal stimuli can be deficit-financed without an expected immediate policy reversal to guarantee sustainability implies that multipliers are bound to be large.

This is confirmed by the empirical evidence. Di Serio et al. (2021) find that the multipliers in the Euro Area are significantly larger in periods in which growth-adjusted real rates are negative than otherwise, both in the short and in the long run. Other authors have found similar results for different countries. Christiano et al. (2011) study the mechanisms that explain the differential impact of government spending when the lower limit of the interest rate is binding in an otherwise standard DSGE model. In their model, government spending multipliers get close to 2 when the policy rate hits its lower limit, clearly above the value obtained when monetary policy operates in normal conditions.

The broad consensus, consistent with the previous discussion on monetary accommodation, is that fiscal policy is particularly effective in times in which the standard monetary policy is at the ZLB, when it is not operative, and that fiscal consolidations at those times may be particularly damaging. Nevertheless, some authors have argued for some caution in the interpretation of these results to justify large and persistent increases in public spending in troubling times. For one thing, a large multiplier can potentially trigger a normalization of monetary policy that will in turn set in motion the conventional crowding out of private spending (Erceg and Lindé, 2014). Also, Christiano et al. (2011) warn that the effectiveness of fiscal stimuli at the ZLB might be diminished due to implementation lags. Finally, in a model with an endogenous fiscal limit and interest rate spreads, Andrés, Burriel et al. (2020) show that increases in public spending at the ZLB may dampen the multiplier even if they do not affect the policy rate to the extent that they increase the borrowing cost in countries with weak finances.

6.3.2 The Importance of Private Debt

The level of private debt may also affect the effectiveness of fiscal policy as a stabilization tool. Jordà et al. (2013) studied a long historical sample (1870–2008) of several advanced economies and found that the level of private credit relative to GDP was a leading indicator of the severity of recessions. High private debt was indeed a salient feature of many economies at the onset of the GFC. For the Euro Area countries, Batini et al. (2019) show that whereas current private debt is a harbinger of future recessions, the level of public debt is not, unless interacted with high private debt. In related work Andrés, Arce et al. (2020) show how high levels of private debt can make front-loaded consolidations particularly costly since the fall of nominal output aggravates the burden of private debt and hence the ability to sustain spending by heavily indebted agents.

Since most household debt is mortgaged, the effect of fiscal shocks on the value of collateralizable assets is another channel through which fiscal policy affects consumption, investment, and output. Mian et al. (2013) show that the consumption response to changes in housing wealth is very significant in the US and heterogeneous across households. Berger et al. (2018) derive theoretically the channels through which the aggregate consumption responds to housing prices; the response depends on the distribution of wealth, age, indebtedness and homeownership across households, as well as on features such as the expected duration of price changes.

According to Eggertsson and Krugman (2012), fiscal policy may help to prevent the consequences of forced and quick deleveraging by indebted households in a recession. In Andrés et al. (2015) the multiplier is higher in a calibrated model with lenders and borrowers than in a model with uncon-strained consumers only. Constrained consumers might be not only poor but also those wealthy households who decide to hold a large amount of illiquid assets (Kaplan and Violante, 2014) and constitute a significant share of population in advanced economies. Andrés et al. (2022) show that a larger share of liquidity-constrained households without access to mortgaged debt may have given rise to a substantial increase in fiscal multipliers. In the same vein, Brinca et al. (2016) find that multipliers increase with the fraction of credit-constrained agents. Several empirical studies have confirmed that government spending and tax multipliers are significantly higher when private debt is high, partly due to the positive response of collateral values to fiscal stimuli (Bernardini and Peersman, 2018; Cloyne and Surico, 2017).

But the interaction between financial constraints and fiscal multipliers is a complex one. Andrés et al. (2016) find that the enhancing effect of collateral constraints on the fiscal multiplier critically depends on the specific (primary) instrument used to apply a discretionary measure as well as on the (secondary) instrument in which the fiscal rule is based to stabilize debt. In addition, Sahm et al. (2015) report a type of "balance-sheet households" who respond asym-metrically to fiscal changes: tax increases are met with reductions in spending, but tax cuts are mostly used to increase savings and to repair their financial bal-ances after a period of debt increase. These features may reduce the multipliers of fiscal expansions even in periods of high private debt and financial distress.

6.3.3   Deep Recessions

Unlike transitory mild fluctuations, severe recessions are singular episodes characterized by the presence of most of the features that tend to increase the size of the fiscal multiplier, such as the ZLB and financial constraints. Riera-Crichton et al. (2015) find that the multiplier is significantly higher in severe, as compared with normal, recessions. Caggiano et al. (2015) show that multipliers differ substantially between moderate and extreme events, being higher in deep recessions than in booms. Klein and Linnemann (2019) estimate a VAR for US data allowing for time-varying parameters and obtain much larger multipliers after the Great Financial Crisis than in previous downturns.

6.3.4   Fiscal Policy During the Pandemic

The Covid crisis and the restrictions it imposed on economic activities have brought the use of fiscal policy as a stabilizing device to a new dimension. The response to the crisis generated an almost unanimous consensus among policymakers in all jurisdictions, giving a prominent role to fiscal impulses, an effort supported by monetary policy in the form of cheap financing for the public and private sectors.

Severe supply shocks such as the result of the pandemic disruptions may induce negative effects on aggregate demand larger than the original shocks themselves, as discussed by Guerrieri et al. (2022). In the presence of what the authors call "Keynesian supply shocks" the multiplier effect of untargeted fiscal expansions might be diminished by shutdowns and firm exit and the optimal response is approximated by the use of targeted fiscal measures to provide insurance to firms and workers affected by the lockdowns. When public spending and transfers have to bear the burden of the recovery in economies in which the circular flow of income is so severely disrupted, the assessment of the effectiveness of fiscal policies goes beyond the size of the multiplier. Its role is to bridge the gap between pieces of the exchange and production system torn apart from each other by the impossibility to trade. When the monetary transmission mechanism is severely impaired and there is just not much monetary policy can do, targeted government spending and transfers can help to maintain whatever trade is feasible, preventing further declines in economic activity (Woodford, 2022).

Bayer et al. (2020) carry out an analysis of the impact of the US main fiscal package (CARES Act) within the framework of a heterogeneous agent New Keynesian model, in which idiosyncratic income risk cannot be fully insured across households. CARES might have helped to reduce the output effect of the quarantine shock in the US to 15 percent, instead of the 20 percent fall that would have happened in its absence. The overall multiplier effect (without taking into account the large direct transfers to firms) is estimated to be around 0.75. Targeted transfers to households with a higher propensity to spend and at the lowest quantiles of the income distribution were particularly effective in reducing income risk. Also, in a calibrated DSGE model for the US, Faria-e-Castro (2021) simulates the effect of the CARES Act during the pandemic and finds that the multiplier is 1.2, whereas it would have been almost zero in the absence of the quarantine shock.

6.4   THE CHALLENGES AHEAD

Discretionary fiscal policy seems efficient when it is most needed, but the limits to its use have grown tighter. The challenge is to maintain sufficient fiscal space and to use it, when needed, in a more efficient way to promote growth, employment, and stability, and in a way that makes debt sustainable (Blanchard, 2022). The fiscal space depends on the distance between the level of debt and the maximum level that the government can service or Fiscal Limit (Corsetti et al., 2013; Andrés, Burriel et al., 2020). Bi (2012) quantifies this limit as the discounted sum of maximum primary surpluses that can be generated in the future, which in turn depends on expected shocks, the cost of servicing the debt net of growth, expected budget surpluses, and the budgetary framework. When the economy approaches this limit, the cost of servicing the debt may increase non-linearly, rendering debt unsustainable.

The efficient use of the space available requires a clear countercyclical stance of discretionary fiscal policy changes, with neutral structural deficits. After two severe global recessions, many economies find themselves with historical record levels of debt-to-GDP ratios, minimal room for maneuvering for monetary policy and old and new structural fault lines needing repair. This legacy calls for a wise choice of fiscal interventions, accompanied by carefully designed consolidations in good times supported by sustained nominal growth. Furthermore, the use of fiscal policy has another dimension, over and above its countercyclical role, that has been to some extent overlooked in the past. The global economy is still on the verge of a chronic deficit of demand (secular stagnation) and faces challenges such as ageing, climate change (analyzed in Chapters 12 and 13 of this book), the digital revolution, and other externalities and social and geopolitical risks that will require substantial increases in public spending, as well as new taxes and regulations. A prudent fiscal framework will have to contemplate some systematic activism beyond the cyclical time frame.

The analysis of the measures undertaken worldwide in the immediate aftermath of the Great Financial Crisis led Romer (2012) to draw two lessons for the conduct of fiscal policy: (i) fiscal policy can have large effects in the short run and (ii) unsustainable budget deficits eventually lead to ruin. A decade later, these two lessons are still valid, but with the benefit of hindsight and the abundant evidence gathered, we can qualify and extend them in the form of conclusions.

6.4.1 Effectiveness of Fiscal Policy as a Stabilization Tool

First, *fiscal policy is a powerful instrument to stabilize economies*. Tackling recessions and unemployment, and doing it quickly, with the most adequate fiscal instruments and with the appropriate size, can help to avoid the worst consequences of negative shocks and their longer-term (hysteresis-driven) effects. Importantly, there are critical times in which fiscal policy is not just effective, but it might be the only policy intervention that can prevent a major crackdown in an economy. In these extreme circumstances, public spending must act to prevent bigger drops in GDP, and monetary policy must concentrate its efforts on maintaining the solvency of the financial sector and facilitating cheap borrowing for governments.

The second conclusion is that *the effectiveness of fiscal policy is state-dependent*, so any attempt to summarize the intensity of the effect of fiscal policy in a single value of the multiplier would be really daring. Before the financial crisis, we knew that many features of the economy condition the size of fiscal multipliers, although the evidence was sometimes weak, mixed, and inconclusive as to which ones were more important. The concurrence of many of the main factors that made fiscal stimuli more effective in the aftermath of the Great Financial Crisis and during the Covid recession has convinced many of the effectiveness of fiscal policy as a stabilization tool, in particular to prevent severe deflationary risks. This notwithstanding, the use of fiscal stimuli must be more appropriate in some types of recessions than in others.

Third, among the many factors that condition the effectiveness of fiscal policies, *the one that appears more determinant is the degree of monetary accommodation.* The widespread consensus about this would be the third lesson to draw from the available evidence. Multipliers are larger the weaker the immediate response of interest rates to the expansionary effects of changes in government spending and taxes, but beyond that what matters is the way the monetary strategy interacts with fiscal policy, i.e. the policy mix.

There has been an intense debate about the fiscal choices in Europe during and in the aftermath of the GFC, more timid and at some points even contractionary, compared with the protracted expansionary stance in the United States. The reaction to the Covid crisis has been swifter and brisker worldwide. Central Banks intensified the purchase of sovereign bonds to finance the massive transfers to households and firms needed to compensate for the collapse of private spending in the worst of the lockdowns. This response has been successful in preventing a bigger fall and has shown the enhanced power of the two instruments working in unison, in the same direction, and complementing each other as described in Chapter 4. A similar strategy of soft policy coordination may be required to navigate the aftermath of the crisis, rebuild the fiscal and monetary space and ensure a more efficient policy mix in the future.

Reis (2022) warns against the subordination of monetary policy to cheapening the service of public debt, with the risk of destroying the framework that has created a friendly environment for the conduct of fiscal policy in the last 30 years. Thus, while more flexibility may be required, in particular in troubled times, monetary policy should preserve full independence to design its strategy to keep medium-term inflation expectations firmly anchored.

6.4.2   Public Debt must be Sustainable: The Speed of Consolidation

The fourth conclusion is that the *effectiveness of fiscal policy must be balanced against the need to maintain debt levels within safe limits.* Public debt facilitates tax smoothing and provides the economy with a safe asset. But, beyond some threshold, public debt may harm growth (Cecchetti et al., 2011). Public debt-to-GDP ratios achieved in many countries by 2021 levels are only compa-rable with wartime years, as shown in Chapter 2. The corridor for a successful consolidation is this time narrower than ever if by success we understand the return to safer public debt levels without endangering the still unequal and uncertain recovery.

When the economy faces very low interest rates, in particular below GDP growth, moderate sustained deficits may be compatible with non-exploding debt. But even in these circumstances, the normalization of public finances to bringing debt-to-GDP ratios to safer levels is of paramount importance since the fiscal space is not unlimited (Mian et al., 2021). First and foremost, to strengthen the stabilization capacity of fiscal policy, severely impaired after the recent recessions (Alloza et al., 2021). In addition, the health of public finances depends on their capacity to face future liabilities associated with ageing, the extension of the welfare state, environmental emergencies, and natural disasters, among others. However, the effort needed to reduce debt-to-GDP to the pre-pandemic levels might be very high, even if spread over the next two decades. The IMF (2021) calculates that in a reasonable sce-nario of interest rates and nominal growth, advanced economies would require an additional 0.5 percent of GDP over the average primary balance observed from 2010–2019 (0.9 percent if the reduction is to be achieved by 2035).

There is a broad consensus about the long-run positive effects on economic growth, investment, and stability of keeping the debt-to-GDP ratio around a reasonable target. After any episode of a sizeable increase in government debt, there is a debate on how to approach the ensuing consolidation. Among the proponents of a front-loaded approach, there are some who believe in the positive effects of consolidations even in the very short run, and others who, despite admitting the cost associated with a quick debt reduction, consider that this strategy is more efficient in present value terms than postponing the bulk of the fiscal adjustment (back-loaded consolidation). The arguments in favor of either alternative rely on the relative importance of long-run and short-run multipliers, credibility, discount factors and hysteresis effects (Fatás and Summers, 2018). The presence of high private leverage ratios, as in the aftermath of the financial recession, adds another important reason to proceed more cautiously (Andrés, Arce et al., 2020).

In 2021 most analysts envisaged an exit from the Covid recession amid low interest rates and low inflation. In these circumstances, the convenience of an exit strategy based on the implementation of expansionary fiscal measures in the recovery phase, without committing to a full consolidation in the future, gathered significant support. The role model for this approach was the extraor-dinary budget of President Roosevelt in the 1930s that combined two different spending programs: one, financed by present or future taxes (normal budget), and another one not explicitly backed by future surpluses (emergency budget).

Bianchi and Melosi (2019) argue that this strategy was the basis of the success in getting the US economy out of the Great Depression. For this kind of policy to be effective, the monetary authority must also renounce pursuing an active inflation stabilization policy, even if the inflation rate goes temporarily and moderately above its target. This combination of passive monetary policy and no commitment to fiscal consolidation characterizes a "temporary fiscal dominance".

Views are changing with the surge of inflation. The success of this strategy critically hinges upon the nature of the shock that caused the recession in the first place. It seems worth considering in deep, demand-driven and deflation-prone, recessions. Since the start of the war in Ukraine and the ensuing energy crisis, many analysts are finding structural factors and increases in medium-term inflation expectations to be the harbingers of a longer period of high inflation. In these circumstances and against a backdrop of higher interest rates the difficulties for a smooth process of consolidation mount. On the one hand, subsidies and transfers to households and firms most negatively affected by the increase in the price of energy will be needed. On the other hand, cautious but determined steps will have to be taken to start reducing deficits to ease the pressure on the financial cost of debt.

6.4.3   Beyond Stabilization: Fiscal Policy to Promote Growth and Structural Change

In the early years of industrialization and later in times of building modern infrastructures and the welfare state, public investment was a key component of total public spending. The succession of deep recessions, followed by more or less intense and ill-designed consolidation processes, has taken its toll on public investment. Many proposals to reform the existing fiscal frameworks advocate for some sort of "golden rule" so that public investment is excluded from the efforts to reduce public debt. Thus, beyond stabilization and sustainability issues, repairing the fault lines in our economies (whether social, technological, or productive) is now an uppermost objective in the management of fiscal policy. This is the fifth conclusion to be drawn from recent fiscal developments.

Rebuilding worn-out infrastructures in the United States, speeding up the digital transition in Europe, and preventing the consequences of climate change and of geopolitical risks everywhere, are now objectives high on the agenda of policymakers in advanced and emerging economies. These challenges generate externalities, but the intervention of public investment in these areas has other justifications besides those of improving the efficiency of the economy and making it more inclusive. In the short run, these projects constitute a stimulus that may help the economies to recover the pre-pandemic levels of output and employment. In the medium term, they should contribute to getting the global economy out of the secular stagnation and increasing the natural rate of interest.

A sustained program of growth-friendly public investment can contribute to this in different ways. First, the increase in public investment may create new opportunities for private investment, thus reducing the excess of corporate savings. In addition, if public investment is financed by fiscal bodies with no significant problems of debt sustainability (like, for instance, the European Commission), the additional debt would contribute to alleviate the global shortage of safe assets and to rebalance the valuation of risk in the market. Finally, to the extent that interest rates remain at low or moderate levels, financing these projects may be done without further endangering the sustainability of public finances in many jurisdictions.

Should the current episode of high inflation persist, consolidation plans will have to be activated earlier than what was considered adequate in the middle of the Covid recession. But fiscal authorities should refrain from the temptation of dismantling large growth-oriented public projects, as was done in the past. Structural reforms and supply-side investments have the potential of generating quick positive effects in economies in all circumstances (Andrés et al., 2017), but it is precisely at times of high inflation, with an important cost-push component, that these measures have the potential to be most beneficial (De Grauwe, 2021).

ACKNOWLEDGMENTS

Financial support from the Spanish Ministry of Economy and Competitiveness (grant PID2020-116242RB-I00), and Generalitat Valenciana (grant PROMETEO/2020/083) is gratefully acknowledged.

REFERENCES

Alesina, A., C. Favero and F. Giavazzi (2018), "What do we know about the effects of austerity?", *AEA Papers and Proceedings*, 108.

Alloza, M., J. Andrés, P. Burriel, I. Kataryniuk, J. Pérez and J. L. Vega (2021), "La reforma del marco de gobernanza de la política fiscal de la Unión Europea en un nuevo entorno macroeconómico", *Banco de España*, DO 2121.

Andrés, J., J. Boscá and J. Ferri (2015), "Household debt and fiscal multipliers", *Economica*, 82.

Andrés, J., J. Boscá and J. Ferri (2016), "Instruments, rules and household debt: The effects of fiscal policy", *Oxford Economic Papers*, 68.

Andrés, J., O. Arce and C. Thomas (2017), "Structural reforms in a debt overhang", *Journal of Monetary Economics*, 88.

Andrés, J., O. Arce, D. Thaler and C. Thomas (2020), "When fiscal consolidation meets private deleveraging", *Review of Economic Dynamics*, 37.

Andrés, J., P. Burriel and W. Shen (2020), "Debt sustainability and fiscal space in a heterogeneous monetary union: Normal times vs the zero lower bound", *Banco de España*, DT 2001, 2020.

Andrés, J., J. Boscá, J. Ferri and C. Fuentes-Albero (2022), "Household's balance sheets and the effect of fiscal policy", *Journal of Money, Credit and Banking*, 54(4).

Auerbach, A. and Y. Gorodnichenko (2012), "Measuring the output responses to fiscal policy", *American Economic Journal: Economic Policy*, 4(2).

Barro, R. and C. Redlick (2011), "Macroeconomic effects from government purchases and taxes", *The Quarterly Journal of Economics*, 126(1).

Batini, N., G. Melina and S. Villa (2019), "Fiscal buffers, private debt, and recession: The good, the bad and the ugly", *Journal of Macroeconomics*, 62, 103044.

Baxter, M. and R. King (1993), "Fiscal policy in general equilibrium", *The American Economic Review*, 83(3).

Bayer, C., B. Born, R. Luetticke and G. Muller (2020), "The coronavirus stimulus package: How large is the transfer multiplier?", *CEPR* Discussion Paper 14600.

Berger, D., V. Guerrieri, G. Lorenzoni and J. Vavra (2018), "House prices and consumer spending", *The Review of Economic Studies*, 85(3).

Bernardini, M. and G. Peersman (2018), "Private debt overhang and the government spending multiplier: Evidence for the United States", *Journal of Applied Econometrics*, 33(4).

Bi, H. (2012), "Sovereign default risk premia, fiscal limits, and fiscal policy", *European Economic Review*, 56(3).

Bianchi, F. and L. Melosi (2019), "The dire effects of the lack of monetary and fiscal coordination", *Journal of Monetary Economics*, 104.

Blanchard, O. (2022), *Fiscal Policy under Low Rates*. The MIT Press.

Blanchard, O. and D. Leigh (2013), "Growth forecast errors and fiscal multipliers", *American Economic Review*, 103(3).

Blanchard, O. and R. Perotti (2002), "An empirical characterization of the dynamic effects of changes in government spending and taxes on output", *The Quarterly Journal of Economics*, 117(4).

Boehm, C. (2020), "Government consumption and investment: Does the composition of purchases affect the multiplier?", *Journal of Monetary Economics*, 115.

Born, B., F. Juessen and G. Müller (2013), "Exchange rate regimes and fiscal multipliers", *Journal of Economic Dynamics and Control*, 37(2).

Brinca, P., H. Holter, P. Krusell and L. Malafry (2016), "Fiscal multipliers in the 21st century", *Journal of Monetary Economics*, 77.

Caggiano, G., E. Castelnuovo, V. Colombo and G. Nodari (2015), "Estimating fiscal multipliers: News from a non-linear world", *The Economic Journal*, 125(584).

Caldara, D. and C. Kamps (2017), "The analytics of SVARs: A unified framework to measure fiscal multipliers", *The Review of Economic Studies*, 84.

Canzoneri, M., F. Collard, H. Dellas and D. Diba (2016), "Fiscal multipliers in recessions", *The Economic Journal*, 126(590).

Cecchetti, S., M. Mohanty and F. Zampolli (2011), "The real effects of debt", *BIS* Working Paper No. 352.

Christiano, L., M. Eichenbaum and S. Rebelo (2011), "When is the government spending multiplier large?", *Journal of Political Economy*, 119(1).

Cloyne, J., O. Jordà and A. Taylor (2021), "Decomposing the fiscal multiplier", *NBER* Working Paper No. 26939.

Cloyne, J. and P. Surico (2017), "Household debt and the dynamic effects of income tax changes", *Review of Economic Studies*, 84(1).

Corsetti, G., K. Kuester, A. Meier and G. Müller (2013), "Sovereign risk, fiscal policy, and macroeconomic stability", *The Economic Journal*, 123(566).

De Grauwe, P. (2021), "Euro Area fiscal policies and capacity in post-pandemic times", IN DEPTH ANALYSIS Requested by the ECON committee.

Di Serio, M., M. Fragetta and G. Melina (2021), "The impact of r–g on the euro-area government spending multiplier", IMF Working Papers *2021/039*, International Monetary Fund.

Eggertsson, G. and P. Krugman (2012), "Debt, deleveraging, and the liquidity trap: A Fisher–Minsky–Koo approach", *Quarterly Journal of Economics*, 127.

Erceg, C. and J. Lindé (2014), "Is there a fiscal free lunch in a liquidity trap?", *Journal of the European Economic Association*, 12(1).

Faria-e-Castro, M. (2021), "Fiscal policy during a pandemic", *Journal of Economic Dynamics and Control*, 125, 104088.

Fatás, A. and L. Summers (2018), "The permanent effects of fiscal consolidations", *Journal of International Economics*, 112.

Galí, J., D. López-Salido and J. Vallés (2007), "Understanding the effects of government spending on consumption", *Journal of the European Economic Association*, 5(1).

Guajardo, J., D. Leigh and A. Pescatori (2014), "Expansionary austerity? International evidence", *Journal of the European Economic Association*, 12(4).

Guerrieri, V., G. Lorenzoni, L. Straub and I. Werning (2022), "Macroeconomic implications of COVID-19: Can negative supply shocks cause demand shortages?", *American Economic Review*, 112(5).

Huidrom, R., M. A. Kose, J. J. Lim and F. L. Ohnsorge (2020), "Why do fiscal multipliers depend on fiscal positions?", *Journal of Monetary Economics*, 114.

Ilzetzki, E., E. Mendoza and C. Vegh (2013), "How big (small?) are fiscal multipliers?", *Journal of Monetary Economics*, 60(2).

International Monetary Fund (2021), "Strengthening the credibility of public finances", *World Economic Outlook*, C. 2.

Jordà, O., M. Schularick and A. Taylor (2013), "When credit bites back", *Journal of Money, Credit and Banking*, 45(s2).

Kaplan, G. and G. Violante (2014), "A model of the consumption response to fiscal stimulus payments", *Econometrica*, 82(4).

Klein, M. and L. Linnemann (2019), "Macroeconomic effects of government spending: The great recession was (really) different", *Journal of Money, Credit and Banking*, 51(5).

Leeper, E., N. Traum and T. Walker (2017), "Clearing up the fiscal multiplier morass", *American Economic Review*, 107(8).

Leeper, E., T. Walker and S. Yang (2010), "Government investment and fiscal stimulus", *Journal of Monetary Economics*, 57(8).

Mertens, K. and M. Ravn (2013), "The dynamic effects of personal and corporate income tax changes in the United States", *American Economic Review*, 103(4).

Mian, A., K. Rao and A. Sufi (2013), "Household balance sheets, consumption, and the economic slump", *The Quarterly Journal of Economics*, 128(4).

Mian, A., L. Straub and A. Sufi (2021), "A goldilocks theory of fiscal policy", *NBER* Working Paper No 29351.

Mountford, A. and H. Uhlig (2009), "What are the effects of fiscal policy shocks?", *Journal of Applied Econometrics*, 24(6).

Ramey, V. (2011), "Can government purchases stimulate the economy?", *Journal of Economic Literature*, 49(3).

Ramey, V. (2019), "Ten years after the financial crisis: What have we learned from the renaissance in fiscal research?", *Journal of Economic Perspectives*, 33(2). doi:10.1257/jep.33.2.89

Ramey, V. and S. Zubairy (2018), "Government spending multipliers in good times and in bad: Evidence from US historical data", *Journal of Political Economy*, 126(2).

Reis, R. (2022), "With public debt set to remain high, price stability matters more than ever", *International Monetary Fund, Finance & Development*, March 2022.

Riera-Crichton, D., C. Vegh and G. Vuletin (2015), "Procyclical and countercyclical fiscal multipliers: Evidence from OECD countries", *Journal of International Money and Finance*, 52(C).

Romer, C. (2012), "Fiscal policy in the crisis: Lessons and policy implications", *International Monetary Fund, Fiscal Forum*.

Romer, C. and D. Romer (2010), "The macroeconomic effects of tax changes: Estimates based on a new measure of fiscal shocks", *American Economic Review*, 100(3).

Sahm, C., M. Shapiro and J. Slemrod (2015), "Balance-sheet households and fiscal stimulus: Lessons from the Payroll Tax Cut and its Expiration", *NBER* Working Papers 21220.

Woodford, M. (2022), "Effective demand failures and the limits of monetary stabilization policy", *American Economic Review*, 112(5).

7. Fiscal rules: challenges and reform opportunities for emerging and developing economies

Martín Ardanaz, Eduardo Cavallo and Alejandro Izquierdo

7.1 INTRODUCTION

Fiscal rules have become a widespread policy tool. They began being implemented, mostly in advanced economies (AEs), in the 1990s and have gained traction since, extending to emerging and developing economies (EMDEs). The surge in debt after the Global Financial Crisis in 2008 has accelerated fiscal rule adoption and prompted changes in their design. The global recession associated with policy responses to the COVID-19 pandemic triggered the suspension of rules, but as countries recover from the pandemic governments are taking the opportunity to rethink and reform their rules-based fiscal frameworks once again.

Fiscal rules impose a long-lasting constraint on fiscal policy by introducing numerical limits on budgetary aggregates (Kopits and Symansky, 1998). If governments followed the textbook prescription of running fiscal deficits during bad times and reverting to surpluses during booms, then rules would not be needed. In practice, however, fiscal deficits often increase when the economy is growing, and deficits generated during recessions are not usually compensated by surpluses during booms, a point also emphasized in Chapter 11. A key reason is that policymakers often have incentives to pursue policies that increase budget deficits, leading to debt accumulation over time. For example, when making budget decisions, lawmakers usually draw upon a common pool of resources financed from a general tax fund to generate concentrated, specific, public spending (Hallerberg et al., 2009). During the budget-making process, each legislator may wish to increase expenditures that benefit their constituency without internalizing the costs on others. Consequently, overall spending is higher than under full internalization.[1]

Persistent fiscal deficits accumulate into growing public debt stocks, which can eventually threaten debt sustainability.

The prevalence of the "deficit bias" provides a rationale for introducing institutional mechanisms to contain it. Fiscal rules are one policy tool that was designed with the purpose of constraining policy discretion and, therefore, of strengthening debt sustainability.[2] Adopters expect that by limiting discretion through a rule-based framework, fiscal policy will become more transparent and predictable, and therefore, debt-to-GDP ratios will not grow over time. In addition, fiscal rules can serve other purposes, such as mitigating the pro-cyclical bias in fiscal policy (e.g., tax rate hikes in recessions, or large public spending expansions during periods of high economic growth). There are often tradeoffs between some of these objectives, and fiscal rule design can contribute to striking a balance between them (Eyraud et al., 2018; Ter-Minassian, 2021).

This chapter discusses selected issues related to the working of fiscal rules in EMDEs.[3] It offers stylized facts on the adoption and key design features of numerical fiscal rules. It then compares fiscal performance between rule adopters and non-adopters in terms of public debt accumulation. The chapter ends with a discussion on the key challenges that emerge from the implementation of rules-based fiscal frameworks in emerging markets and on policy options to address them.

The main message of the chapter is that despite the relative popularity of fiscal rules, they are no panacea for improving fiscal performance. Critical areas to improve fiscal rules can be found in the quality of rule design, the mechanisms behind better compliance, forward guidance on return to the rule, and the impacts on different dimensions of public finances (particularly public spending composition). While certain design features of fiscal rules can help in moderating the "deficit bias", their effectiveness is often hindered by a lack of explicit or relevant policy anchors, low compliance, and lax guidance on how compliance or return to the rules will be achieved in the aftermath of negative shocks. These challenges call for reforming rules-based fiscal frameworks.

7.2   STYLIZED FACTS ABOUT FISCAL RULES IN EMERGING MARKETS

Fiscal rules have become an increasingly popular policy tool. While advanced economies pioneered their use in the 1990s, fiscal rules in emerging economies and low-income countries started gaining traction in the 2000s. By 2021, 106 countries had adopted rule-based fiscal frameworks. Of those, 34 AEs, 43 EMDEs and 10 low-income countries (LIC) had at least one *national* fiscal rule in place (Figure 7.1).[4]

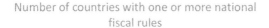

Number of countries with one or more national fiscal rules

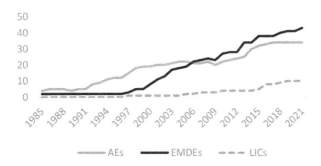

Proportion of countries with each type of fiscal rule, 2021

Source: Own elaboration based on IMF Fiscal Rules Dataset: 1985–2021

Figure 7.1   Evolution and types of fiscal rules

There are different types of fiscal rules, depending on the budgetary aggregate that is subject to control.[5] Budget balance rules (BBR) are the most common (see Figure 7.1). Among emerging economies, debt ceiling or anchor rules (DR) are also common, much more than in developed economies. Expenditure rules (ER), commonly imposed as limits on expenditure growth, are also popular in both emerging and developing economies.[6] Importantly, different rules are often used in combination. While, in advanced economies, BBR are usually combined with ER, the most frequent combination in developing countries is DR with BBR. Expenditure rules are rarely used on their own, but typically combined with BBR or DR across emerging economies.

Some relevant features of rules include the following:

- *Statutory basis*: National fiscal rules can be stated as a government commitment or they can be written into law or even in the Constitution.
- *Institutional coverage*: Some rules cover only the fiscal operations of central governments. Other rules cover other levels of governments and even public sector entities such as nonfinancial enterprises.[7]
- *Monitoring and enforcement mechanisms*: While some rules foresee formal enforcement mechanisms, such as those triggering financial sanctions in case of non-compliance, others do not stipulate formal sanctions, relying only on reputational costs. To raise such reputational costs, fiscal rules are often accompanied by supporting institutions such as autonomous fiscal agencies or councils that verify whether rules are being complied with.
- *Mechanisms to accommodate shocks and investment protection*: Flexibility provisions in fiscal rules allow fiscal policy to accommodate unexpected shocks and involve different features. Clearly defined escape clauses refer to exceptional circumstances that merit the suspension of the fiscal rule, such as natural disasters or severe recessions.[8] Some rules can be defined in cyclically adjusted terms (i.e., that account for the output cycle and other relevant exogenous influences, such as commodity price developments). Public investment-friendly provisions refer to rules that exclude capital expenditures from the numerical targets imposed on fiscal aggregates.

Table 7.1 presents an overview of the main features of fiscal rules in selected EMDEs.

Table 7.1   National fiscal rules in selected EMDEs, 2021

Region	Country	Type of rule[a] ER	BBR	DR	Year[b]	Coverage[c]	Legal basis[d]	Escape clause[e]	Flexibility features Structural target	Investment protection
Latin America and the Caribbean	Brazil	x			2016	GG	C			
	Chile		x		2001/2022	CG	S		x	
	Colombia	x	x	x	2000/2011/2021	CG	S	x	x	
	Jamaica		x	x	2010	GG	S	x		
	Peru	x	x	x	2000/2016	CG	S	x		
Europe	Bulgaria	x	x	x	2006/2003	GG	S	x		x
	Croatia	x	x	x	2012/2009	GG	S	x	x	x
	Poland	x	x	x	2011/2006/1997	GG	S/C	x		
	Romania		x	x	2013	GG	S		x	
Asia and Pacific	India		x	x	2004/2018	CG/GG	S	x		
	Malaysia		x		1985	CG	S			x
	Thailand	x		x	2018	GG	S/PC			x
Middle East	Azerbaijan	x		x	2019	GG	S	x		
	Georgia		x	x	2013	GG	C	x		
Africa	Botswana	x	x	x	2003/2005	CG	PC/S			
	Mauritius			x	2001	GG	CA	x		

Notes: [a]ER – expenditure rule; BBR – budget balance rule; DR – debt rule. [b]Year of implementation. [c]GG – general government; CG – central government. [d]C – constitutional; S – statutory; CA – coalition agreement; PA – political agreement. When rules differ, implementation year, coverage and legal basis are given for ER, BBR and DR, respectively. [e]Checked if at least one rule has an escape clause.
Source: Own elaboration based on IMF Fiscal Rules Dataset (1995–2021) and national sources.

7.3   FISCAL RULES AND PUBLIC DEBT PERFORMANCE

Fiscal rules have been growing in popularity, but how effective have they been in stabilizing debt-to-GDP ratios?[9] We tackle this question by analyzing a large panel dataset covering the period 2000–2019, and comparing the impact of national fiscal rules on debt performance.[10] For each country, we separate periods with no fiscal rule from periods of at least one national fiscal rule in place and analyze three characteristics: average yearly growth rate of debt-to-GDP ratios (in percent), average yearly changes in debt-to-GDP ratios (in points of GDP), as well as the volatility of the debt-to-GDP ratio growth rate throughout each period. Countries with no fiscal rules throughout the whole sample period are also included in the comparison group.

Results are presented in Figure 7.2 with a box plot and reported means for each of the three attributes described above. At first glance, there does not seem to be much difference in average debt growth between periods of no fiscal rule and periods with at least one rule (Figure 7.2, left). As a matter of fact, average debt growth for countries with at least one rule is larger than for countries with no rule. Something similar occurs for the average change in debt expressed in points of GDP (Figure 7.2, center). There is some reduction in debt growth volatility when periods of fiscal rule are in place (Figure 7.2, right). However, mean tests do not account for significant differences in most of these dimensions.

How can this be reconciled with perceptions of better performance with fiscal rule implementation? Figure 7.3 provides an answer: debt performance in all three dimensions improves with better quality of fiscal rules. Considering an index that captures a continuous measure of fiscal rule strength based on *de jure* characteristics, periods of fiscal rule implementation are divided into low, medium, and high quality. The quality index captures relevant design features of fiscal rules: broad institutional coverage, statutory or legal basis, existence of supporting monitoring arrangements, enforcement procedures, and flexibility mechanisms to respond to shocks.[11]

Significant differences are uncovered once design quality is considered, particularly when considering differences between low and high levels of rule quality (see Table 7.2).[12] Average debt-to-GDP growth falls by more than 3 percentage points with high quality fiscal rules, compared with low-quality fiscal rules. Similarly, the average debt change falls by almost 1.4 points of GDP per year with high quality rules relative to low-quality rules. Moreover, volatility in debt-to-GDP growth rates falls to one third under high quality rules.

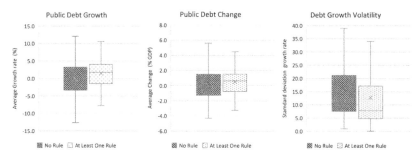

Note: Figure shows the full range of results, the interquartile range (box) with the median line and the mean (cross). Heavily Indebted Poor Countries (HIPCs) are excluded. Only national fiscal rules are analyzed.
Source: Authors' elaboration using IMF WEO data and IMF fiscal rule database.

Figure 7.2   Debt performance with and without fiscal rules

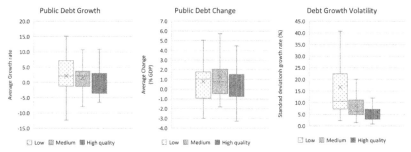

Note: The fiscal rule quality index ranges between 0 and 1, with higher values indicating higher quality rules. Rules with index value lower than 0.33 (greater than 0.66) are considered low (high) quality rules. Values between 0.33 and 0.66 are considered medium quality. The figures show the full range of results, the interquartile range (box) with the median line and the mean (cross). Heavily Indebted Poor Countries (HIPCs) are excluded. Only national fiscal rules are analyzed.
Source: Authors' elaboration using IMF WEO data and IMF fiscal rule database.

Figure 7.3   Fiscal rule quality and debt performance

A conclusion emerging from this analysis is that fiscal rule adoption is not per se a guarantee of success when it comes to stabilizing – or even reducing – debt-to-GDP ratios. In other words, thinking that fiscal sustainability will be dealt with by only imposing any type of fiscal rule is a false premise. Debt sustainability improves when the quality of fiscal rules is considered and enhanced sufficiently. Although this analysis does not provide proof of causation, it suggests that debt sustainability and the quality of fiscal rules go hand

Fiscal policy in a turbulent era

in hand. The next section will cover aspects of fiscal rule design, compliance and guidance that may work in raising the quality of fiscal rules.

Table 7.2   *Fiscal rule quality and debt performance*

	Difference in means test		
	Fiscal Rule Quality[a]		
Variable	Low (A)	High (B)	Difference[b] (A) – (B)
Average growth of debt (%)	2.4673	–0.7654	3.2327*
Observations	20	36	
Average change of debt (% GDP)	0.7002	–0.6727	1.3729**
Observations	20	36	
Average volatility of the growth of debt (%)	13.8337	6.0617	9.9040***
Observations	19	36	

Notes: [a]The fiscal rule quality index varies between 0 and 1, with higher values indicating higher quality rules. Rules with index value lower than 0.33 (greater than 0.66) are considered low (high) quality rules.
[b]Asterisks denote statistically significant differences between the parameters: * $p < 0.10$; ** $p < 0.05$; *** $p < 0.01$.
Source: Authors' elaboration using IMF WEO and IMF fiscal rules data.

7.4   CHALLENGES IN THE IMPLEMENTATION OF FISCAL RULES AND REFORM OPPORTUNITIES

While the specific motivations to adopt fiscal rules vary from country to country, and the timing of adoption is driven by idiosyncratic factors, the overarching objective of adopters is to strengthen governments' commitment to macro-economically sound and fiscally sustainable policies and, thus, to improve creditworthiness. Still, the devil is in the details when it comes to implementing a credible rule-based fiscal framework. Overall, the track record shows a mixed performance in terms of limiting public debt growth.

International experience regarding fiscal rule implementation and empirical evidence on fiscal rule effectiveness suggest that three key elements must be considered for successful performance: rule design, degree of compliance, and attention to spending composition. We cover each of these issues and propose reform opportunities to address them.

7.4.1 Getting Fiscal Rule Design Right

"First-generation" fiscal rules introduced in the 1990s and early 2000s prioritized simplicity. Therefore, they were anchored on nominal budget balances that are easy to verify and understand. However, such rules came under scrutiny for limiting policymakers' ability to respond to unexpected shocks. They also facilitated procyclical policy responses because they did not require saving revenue windfalls during booms and did not allow deficits (even when financeable) during recessions (Ter-Minassian, 2021). In response to these concerns, several countries started introducing rules that consider the output cycle and other relevant exogenous influences, such as commodity prices.[13]

Colombia and Chile provide a case in point on the challenges of implementing more complex fiscal rules in EMDEs. Both countries introduced structural fiscal balance rules in the 2000s considering output and commodity prices. While successful in complying with the rules, they were unable to stabilize debt levels.

In Colombia, a fiscal rule was implemented in 2011 with the objectives of improving the country's credit rating and reducing fiscal policy procyclicality. The rule at inception targeted a declining path for the structural primary fiscal deficit between 2012 and 2022. From then on, the structural primary deficit would not exceed 1 percent of GDP. The estimation of the structural balance hinged on two variables: potential GDP growth, and the long-run price of oil, which is Colombia's main commodity export. Given that the two variables are unobservable, then assumptions about their respective values were used to compute the structural fiscal balance. *Ex post* those assumptions turned out to be exceedingly optimistic and, as a result, fiscal policy was on average significantly more expansionary than what it should have been. Therefore the rule did not prevent debt from growing during the period as originally intended. Moreover, fiscal policy remained procyclical even after the rule was implemented (Arbeláez et al., 2021).

Chile adopted a fiscal rule in 2001 that targeted a structural fiscal balance. While in the case of Chile the estimation of the structural balance itself has been less biased than in Colombia, other features of the rule have proven to be problematic. One feature of the Chilean rule is that every administration can set its own target for the cyclically adjusted balance at the beginning of a four-year term. This has encouraged successive administrations to change the target as needed to pursue more expansionary fiscal policies during crises, without internalizing the behavior of their predecessors. Given that there are no specified mechanisms to offset deviations, or to reverse targets once the crisis ended, the fiscal rule itself became a less binding constraint on fiscal policy over time. As a result, public debt increased from about 10 percent in

2010 to almost 30 percent by end 2019, despite compliance with the fiscal rule (Fuentes et al., 2021).

Both countries have recently enhanced their fiscal frameworks by introducing a debt anchor to their fiscal rules and providing a feedback mechanism from the stock of public debt to the cyclically adjusted fiscal balance to prevent debt from growing to levels that could undermine fiscal sustainability (Betancur et al., 2022; Ministerio de Hacienda, 2022).

The cases of Colombia and Chile illustrate how difficult it is to generate and maintain counter-cyclical buffers and stabilize debt-to-GDP ratios even under sophisticated rules-based fiscal frameworks. In particular, the cases show that implementing a fiscal rule is not sufficient to prevent debt-to-GDP levels from growing, even when the rules target structural fiscal balances, and those targets are met. The consequence of an increasing debt-to-GDP ratio is that, if not eventually stabilized or reversed, it could threaten fiscal sustainability, indeed the main motivation for implementing a fiscal rule in the first place.

Reform options to address this challenge include incorporating a medium-term debt anchor as a key policy objective or target for fiscal rules. Setting the ceiling of the fiscal anchor requires identifying a maximum debt threshold for sustainability and calibrating a "prudent" debt level so that there is a safety margin or buffer ensuring that debt remains below the maximum limit with high probability, even in the presence of adverse shocks (Caselli et al., 2022; IMF, 2018). Once the debt ceiling is obtained, operational fiscal rule targets should be defined to gradually guide public debt to its desired level. For example, the rule should incorporate how structural fiscal balance targets should respond according to the distance between current debt levels and the debt limit, setting more ambitious targets the closer current debt is to the limit. Countries can implement a feedback mechanism based on the outstanding amount of public debt, applying more adjustment pressure as outstanding debt levels exceed prudent ones. That allows them to ensure that debt does not grow to levels that undermine fiscal sustainability with an embedded self-regulating mechanism.

7.4.2   Beyond Design: Compliance Problems and Forward Guidance

Even well-designed fiscal rules will turn out ineffective in improving fiscal outcomes if they are consistently violated. While previous research on fiscal rule effectiveness has traditionally looked at the impact of *de jure* features of fiscal rules, there is emerging evidence emphasizing the relevance of compliance behavior. Overall, the evidence shows that deviations of fiscal outturns from targets are common (Davoodi et al., 2022a; Blanco et al., 2020). For example, during the years preceding the pandemic, more than half of emerging market and low-income countries with budget balance rules (BBRs) saw their deficits exceed the rule limits, with the median deviation exceeding 2 percent of GDP (Davoodi et al., 2022a). More specifically, in a sample of Latin American economies, average compliance with some type of rules was as low as 40 percent, meaning that countries are compliant less than half of the time (Valencia and Ulloa-Suárez, 2022).

While some rules include formal sanctions in cases of non-compliance, these are of limited effectiveness when political incentives are not aligned with fiscal discipline. This creates the need to build complementary institutions oriented at strengthening enforcement. One such institution is fiscal councils, often non-partisan, technical bodies entrusted as a public finance watchdog to strengthen credibility of fiscal policies with a variety of mandates (IMF, 2013). Fiscal councils have mostly materialized in EMDEs in the aftermath of the Global Financial Crisis and they oversee compliance with fiscal rules, providing opinion about a government's fiscal performance and adherence to fiscal rules, among other tasks.[14] Their statements are public and, as such, may inflict some reputational costs for non-compliance. However, and in contrast to central banks – whose compliance with inflation targets has clear implications for the general public – the consequences of government compliance with fiscal rules are less well understood. Thus, there is a limited disciplining effect. Moreover, often resources and technical capacity are not commensurate with the formal tasks assigned to fiscal councils in emerging markets, further limiting their effectiveness.[15] Strengthening the set of tools, resources and staff available to councils in emerging markets for better enforcement would improve their role and the discipline on fiscal policy. Councils could, for example, participate in the preparation of forecasts and perhaps even intervene in recalibrating targets after a prolonged period of non-compliance.

Fiscal authorities could also benefit from another feature that has been adopted by central banks in recent times: "forward guidance" (see Chapter 14). Market expectations are key when assessing the impact of policy, so guiding markets in terms of plans for fiscal policy can be useful for anchoring expectations. Such is the role of medium-term fiscal frameworks (MTFF), which extend the horizon for fiscal policymaking beyond the annual budgetary calendar. This is the tool which should identify and communicate the changes or reforms looking forward that will ensure a path to fiscal sustainability, and fiscal rules should translate such plans into policy actions through the budget process. A key pre-condition for MTFF to work is that they provide credible projections of main macroeconomic and fiscal variables. Independent fiscal councils can play a role in reducing the size of forecast errors typically observed in fiscal policymaking (Caselli et al., 2022). Across emerging markets, while most fiscal councils oversee producing or assessing macroeconomic forecasts, the latter are not actually used during the budget process. Using independent forecasts provided by fiscal councils could help in strengthening the credibility of MTFF and a forward-looking orientation of fiscal policy.

7.4.3   Unintended Consequences for Public Spending Composition and Space to Enhance Flexibility Provisions

Fiscal rule compliance can have unintended and sometimes adverse consequences on public spending composition. For example, fiscal rules have come under scrutiny for unintendedly encouraging large cuts in public investment (Blanchard and Giavazzi, 2004). This is so because pressure to comply with aggregate numerical targets provides incentives for policymakers to cut spending items that may be less salient to voters, but that may have long-term payoffs such as productive public investment, the adjustment variable by default despite its large fiscal multiplier. Moreover, governments in EMDEs often tend to increase current expenditures above trend in the positive phase of the cycle, only to contract spending during the negative phase of the cycle using public investment, introducing a bias against the latter (Ardanaz and Izquierdo, 2022).[16]

In response to these concerns, countries have been incorporating flexible features into their fiscal frameworks. Specifically, those features consist of cyclically adjusted fiscal targets, well-defined escape clauses to address unanticipated shocks, and rules that exclude capital expenditures from numerical targets (Ardanaz et al., 2021a; Guerguil et al., 2017). While, in 1995, there were only seven countries that had adopted at least one such flexible feature (out of a total of 14 countries that had adopted a fiscal rule), by 2021 that figure had increased to 69 countries (i.e., 79 percent of the 87 countries that had adopted a national fiscal rule). Sometimes there is more than one flexible feature operating at the same time, generating overlaps in their use. Recent evidence shows flexible fiscal rules have been instrumental in protecting public investment from budget cuts during fiscal consolidation episodes (Ardanaz et al., 2021a).[17]

How do flexible features help in safeguarding public investment from budget cuts? Investment-friendly provisions do so directly because investment is largely exempted from the rule, thus protecting capital spending from excessive cuts during busts or fiscal adjustment episodes. Fiscal rules in which targets are defined in cyclically adjusted terms also allow policymakers to delink public spending (and thus, investment) from the cycle. The inclusion of well-defined escape clauses in fiscal rules contributes to enhancing the reaction of fiscal policy to unexpected shocks by allowing temporary deviations from the rules' targets. Those clauses give policymakers room to implement discretionary fiscal stimulus in response to shocks. Public investment is the quintessential example of such a counter-cyclical response. Thus, while achieving compliance with a rigid rule may require the compression of public investment during downturns, the activation of an escape clause could stimulate it. This is important, particularly during recessions, as it has been shown that private investment is a complement of public investment – and the reason why public investment multipliers tend to be large (Izquierdo et al., 2019) – meaning that flexible fiscal rules are indeed growth friendly. Another route followed to protect public investment has been the adoption of limits to current expenditure growth. For example, Peru amended its fiscal rule in 2018 to include an additional rule limiting real current expenditure growth – net of maintenance spending – to that of real GDP (Mendoza Bellido et al., 2021). Counterfactual simulations in other Latin American countries suggest that complying with such rules could open up fiscal space for increasing capital expenditures (Artana et al., 2021; Bonomo et al., 2021).

Despite substantial progress in fiscal rule flexibility – and its benefits for public investment protection – little attention has been paid to re-entry to the fiscal rule following departure during shocks. Most escape clauses to date offer little guidance, if any, as to how governments should return to compliance in post-crisis contexts. This is a rule design issue that requires attention, particularly in the aftermath of the COVID-19 crisis, as all emerging markets that had an escape clause made use of it to deal with the pandemic.

The size of adjustment as well as the speed of adjustment to return to compliance with the rule should be set depending on the size of the shock and its impact on both budget deficits and public debt levels. Smaller shocks should call for faster convergence than larger shocks, which may require more time for compliance. Such mechanisms should be part of the rule or should be in the hands of institutions safeguarding compliance with fiscal rules, such as fiscal councils.

7.5 CONCLUSIONS AND POLICY LESSONS

The policy lessons drawn from international experience and empirical evidence on fiscal rule effectiveness discussed in this chapter suggest that fiscal rules on their own are not enough to stabilize debt-to-GDP ratios and ensure fiscal sustainability. However, given ample heterogeneity in design features, improving fiscal rule quality is key for achieving successful debt performance. Evidence suggests that the following features are necessary to improve fiscal rule effectiveness in emerging markets:

- In terms of fiscal rule design:
  - Introducing debt anchors or setting debt limits, that allow the gradual build-up of fiscal buffers as well as feedback mechanisms in operational rule targets that are consistent with those limits.

- Allowing for rule flexibility and/or limitations to current spending that will protect public investment, adding a growth-enhancing dimension to the sustainability concerns that have typically been the focus of fiscal rules.
- Setting clear paths of return to the fiscal rule when escape clauses are invoked.
- In terms of compliance and forward guidance:
  - Establishing fiscal councils with power to increase incentives for fiscal rule enforcement, both by imposing reputational costs on governments that deviate from the rule, and by having a say following periods of non-compliance on how the rule will be enforced.
  - Strengthening medium-term fiscal frameworks that provide "forward guidance" as to how fiscal targets will be achieved in the future, thus contributing to anchoring expectations and providing a path of government reforms for compliance with the rule.

Fiscal rules are one component of a comprehensive fiscal framework, and hence their design cannot be improved in isolation from the quality of the overall policy framework. A well-designed fiscal policy framework should have a clear long-term objective, that is, an explicit anchor that guides fiscal policy, and a rule that orients policy towards that objective. Credible medium-term fiscal frameworks and independent fiscal councils are complementary fiscal institutions that, together with numerical rules, can support the goal of safeguarding fiscal sustainability.

NOTES

1. This is the well-known common pool problem that arises when there are several policymakers (ministers, parties, lobby groups) involved in setting the budget, as formalized by scholars in the political economy tradition, such as Velasco (2000), among others.
2. This chapter focuses on numerical fiscal rules, a key type of budget institution. More broadly, budget institutions affect fiscal policy outcomes by either imposing restrictions on the results of the budget process (fiscal or numerical rules), by distributing agenda power and responsibilities among the various actors that participate in budget negotiations (procedural rules), or by increasing access and quality of information (transparency rules). See Alesina and Perotti (1999).
3. In doing so, we do not offer a comprehensive review of the literature on fiscal rules but rather draw on some of its main insights to shed light on the actual functioning of fiscal rules across emerging economies. For reviews of the vast theoretical and empirical literature on fiscal rules, see for example, Yared (2019), Alesina and Passalacqua (2016) and Wyplosz (2013).
4. The scope of this chapter considers *national* fiscal rules. Supranational rules have been adopted in the European Union (EU) – see chapter 8, Eastern Caribbean Currency Union (ECCU), East African Monetary Union (EAMU), West African

Economic and Monetary Union (WAEMU), and Central African Economic and Monetary Community (CEMAC).

5.   Balanced budget rules (BR) can apply to the observed fiscal balance, the cyclically adjusted, or the structural balance. They impose caps on the size of deficit. Debt rules (DR) set a limit on the stock of public debt. Expenditure rules (ER) can limit the growth of total or certain categories of public spending. Revenue rules (RR) can be set as ceilings to prevent excessive tax burdens or floors to encourage revenue collection (Corbacho and Ter-Minassian, 2013).

6.   Revenue-based rules are barely used in emerging markets.

7.   Fiscal rules that target narrow fiscal indicators run the risk of being made ineffective by moving operations to parts of the public sector not covered by the fiscal rule.

8.   For instance, an escape clause should have (i) a limited and clearly defined set of events triggering the operation of the clause, (ii) time limits on how long fiscal policy can deviate from the targets in the rule, and (iii) a requirement for fiscal policy to return to the targets after the operation of the escape clause is terminated and possibly offset the accumulated deviations.

9.   The effectiveness of fiscal rules in shaping fiscal outcomes has been studied extensively on the national, subnational, and supranational levels (see Heinemann et al., 2018) for a meta-analysis of the empirical literature). Given that the primary focus of fiscal rules is fiscal sustainability, this analysis concentrates on debt performance exclusively. However, as shown later in this and other chapters, fiscal rules can have an impact on other relevant dimensions of fiscal policy, such as cyclicality and on the composition of public expenditures.

10. Highly Indebted Poor Countries (HIPC) are excluded from the sample as they underwent significant debt relief processes which obscure the impact of fiscal rules on debt performance.

11. See Schaechter et al. (2012) for details.

12. These results are consistent with previous studies on the relationship between the quality of rules and fiscal performance in a broader sample of countries (Andrián et al., 2022; Caselli and Reynaud, 2020).

13. Fiscal rule features such as cyclically adjusted targets and well-defined escape clauses have been shown to constrain procyclical behavior (Ardanaz et al., 2021a; Guerguil et al., 2017; Bova et al., 2014

14. As of 2021, fiscal councils are operating in 21 emerging and low-income countries (Davoodi et al., 2022b).

15. Half of the fiscal councils in EMDEs and LICs lack budget safeguards to guarantee their operational independence.

16. In addition to the business cycle, fiscal policy reacts to the electoral cycle, and evidence shows fiscal rules can contribute to tame the political budget cycle across both advanced and developing countries (Bonfatti and Forni, 2019; Eklou and Joanis, 2019).

17. Moreover, Ardanaz et al. (2021b) show that penalizing public investment during fiscal adjustments is costly: a consolidation of 1 percent of GDP reduces output by up to 0.7 percent within three years of the consolidation's onset. By contrast, protecting public investment from budget cuts can mitigate contractions on the short run and can even lead to economic expansion in the medium term.

REFERENCES

Alesina, A. and A. Passalacqua (2016), "The political economy of government debt". In J. Taylor and H. Uhligh (Eds.), *Handbook of Macroeconomics*. Elsevier.

Alesina, A. and R. Perotti (1999), "Budget deficits and budget institutions", *Fiscal Institutions and Fiscal Performance*, NBER Chapters. National Bureau of Economic Research Inc.

Andrián, L., J. Hirs, I. Urrea, and O. Valencia (2022), "Fiscal rules and economic cycles: Quality (always) matters", IDB mimeo.

Arbeláez, M. A., M. Benítez, R. Steiner, and O. Valencia (2021). "A fiscal rule to achieve debt sustainability in Colombia", *IDB* Working Paper Series, Washington, DC: Inter-American Development Bank.

Ardanaz, M. and A. Izquierdo (2022), "Current expenditure upswings in good times and public investment downswings in bad times? New evidence from developing countries", *Journal of Comparative Economics* 50(1).

Ardanaz, M., E. Cavallo, A. Izquierdo, and J. Puig (2021a), "Growth-friendly fiscal rules? Safeguarding public investment from budget cuts through fiscal rule design", *Journal of International Money and Finance* 111, 102319.

Ardanaz, M., E. Cavallo, A. Izquierdo, and J. Puig (2021b), "The output effects of fiscal consolidations: Does spending composition matter?", *IDB* Working Paper Series, Washington, DC: Inter-American Development Bank.

Artana, D., C. Moskovits, J. Puig, and I. Templado (2021), "Fiscal rules and the behavior of public investment in Latin America and the Caribbean: Towards growth-friendly fiscal policy?: The case of Argentina", *IDB* Working Paper Series, Inter-American Development Bank.

Betancur, J.S. et al. (2022), "Cimientos para fortalecer la institucionalidad de la política fiscal en Colombia", *Ministerio de Hacienda y Crédito Público*.

Blanchard, O. and F. Giavazzi (2004), "Improving the SGP through a proper accounting of public investment", *CEPR* Discussion Papers 4220.

Blanco, F., P. Saavedra, F. Koehler-Geib, and E. Skrok (2020), "Fiscal rules and economic size in Latin America and the Caribbean", *World Bank* Publications. Washington, DC: World Bank.

Bonfatti, A. and L. Forni (2019), "Fiscal rules to tame the political budget cycle – evidence from Italian municipalities", *European Journal of Political Economy*.

Bonomo, M. A., C. R. Frischtak, and P. Ribeiro (2021), "Public investment and fiscal crisis in Brazil: Finding culprits and solutions", *IDB* Working Paper Series No 1185.

Bova, E., N. Carcenac, and M. Guerguil (2014), "Fiscal rules and the procyclicality of fiscal policy in the developing world", *International Monetary Fund*, Working Papers No. 14/122.

Caselli, F., H. Davoodi, C. Goncalves, G. Hee Hong, A. Lagerborg, P. Medas, A. Minh Nguyen, and J. Yoo (2022), "The return to fiscal rules", *Staff Discussion Note*, IMF.

Caselli, F., and J. Reynaud (2020), "Do fiscal rules cause better fiscal balances? A new instrumental variable strategy", *European Journal of Political Economy* 63.

Corbacho, A. and T. Ter-Minassian (2013). "Public financial management requirements for effective implementation of fiscal rules". In R. Allen, R. Hemming and B. H. Potter (Eds.), *International Handbook of Public Financial Management* (pp. 38–60). Palgrave Macmillan.

Davoodi, H. R., P. Elger, A. Fotiou, D. Garcia-Macia, X. Han, A. Lagerborg, W. R. Lam, and P. Medas (2022a), "Fiscal rules and fiscal councils: Recent trends and performance during the COVID-19 pandemic", *IMF* Working Papers (11), Washington, DC: International Monetary Fund.

Davoodi, H., P. Elger, A. Fotiou, D. García-Macía, A. Lagerborg, W. R. Lam, and S. Pillai (2022b), *Fiscal Councils Dataset: The 2021 Update*. Washington, DC: International Monetary Fund.

Eklou, K. and M. Joanis (2019), "Do fiscal rules cause fiscal discipline over the electoral cycle?", *IMF* Working Paper No. 2019/291.

Eyraud, L., M. X. Debrun, A. Hodge, V. D. Lledo, and M. C. A. Pattillo (2018), "Second-generation fiscal rules: Balancing simplicity, flexibility, and enforceability", *International Monetary Fund*, Washington, DC.

Fuentes, S. M., J. R. Schmidt-Hebbel, and R. Soto (2021), "Fiscal rule and public investment in Chile", *IDB* Working Paper Series No. IDB-WP-1189, Washington, DC.

Guerguil, M., P. Mandon, and R. Tapsoba (2017), "Flexible fiscal rules and countercyclical fiscal policy", *Journal of Macroeconomics* 52.

Hallerberg, M., C. Scartascini, and E. Stein (Eds.) (2009), *Who Decides the Budget? A Political Economy Analysis of the Budget Process in Latin America*. Harvard University Press.

Heinemann, F., M. Moessinger, and M. Yeter (2018), "Do fiscal rules constrain fiscal policy? A meta-regression-analysis", *European Journal of Political Economy* (51).

International Monetary Fund (IMF) (2013), *The Functions and Impact of Fiscal Councils*. IMF Policy Paper, July.

International Monetary Fund (IMF) (2018), "Fiscal policy: How to calibrate fiscal rules", *IMF* How to Note, Washington, DC.

Izquierdo, A., R. Lama, J. P. Medina, J. Puig, D. Riera-Crichton, C. Vegh, and G. Vuletin (2019), "Is the public investment multiplier higher in developing countries? An empirical investigation", *NBER* Working Papers 26478.

Kopits, G. and S. Symansky (1998), "Fiscal policy rules", *IMF* Occasional Paper 162. International Monetary Fund, Washington, DC.

Mendoza Bellido, W., M. Vega, C. I. Rojas, and Y. Anastacio (2021), "Fiscal rules and public investment: The case of Peru, 2000–2019", *IDB* Working Paper Series. Washington, DC: Inter-American Development Bank.

Ministerio de Hacienda (2022), "Bases de la política fiscal de acuerdo a ley sobre responsabilidad fiscal", *Ministerio de Hacienda*, Decreto No. 755. Santiago, Chile.

Schaechter, M. A., M. T. Kinda, and M. N. Budina (2012), "Fiscal rules in response to the crisis: Toward the 'next-generation' rules: A new dataset", *International Monetary Fund*, Washington, DC.

Ter-Minassian, T. (2021), "Strengthening the Institutional Fiscal Framework in the Caribbean". In M. Schwartz and D. Beuermann (Eds.), Economic Institutions for a Resilient Caribbean", Inter-American Development Bank.

Valencia, O. and C. Ulloa-Suárez (2022), "Numerical compliance with fiscal rules in Latin America and the Caribbean", *IDB* Working Paper Series, Washington, DC: Inter-American Development Bank.

Velasco, A. (2000), "Debts and deficits with fragmented fiscal policymaking", *Journal of Public Economics* 76(1).

Wyplosz, C. (2013), "Fiscal rules: Theoretical issues and historical experiences". In A. Alesina and F. Giavazzi (Eds.), *Fiscal Policy after the Financial Crisis*. University of Chicago Press.

Yared, P. (2019), "Rising government debt: Causes and solutions for a decades-old trend", *Journal of Economic Perspectives* 33(2).

8. Fiscal governance in the European Union

Niels Thygesen

8.1 INTRODUCTION

Designing fiscal policy within national borders is already a complex process with multiple objectives, as described in the previous chapter: counter-cyclical stabilization, improvements in allocative efficiency and hence potential growth, and a distribution of incomes which is regarded as fairer than that produced by market forces – all facing the constraint of preserving the sustainability of public finances in the medium to long term. Adding a European dimension to fiscal policymaking, in the currently 27 Member States of the European Union (EU), implies some EU influence on national budgets which make up 40–50 per cent of GDP in most countries, while the EU budget has been stuck around 1 per cent for decades.

Over the last 60–70 years, the perspective on how best to design fiscal policy to achieve its multiple objectives and accept its constraint has varied remarkably, as explained in Chapter 1. The early post-war decades were marked by a growing emphasis on the Keynesian perspective on fiscal policy as providing essential stabilization of economic activity around high levels of capacity utilization. The supply shocks and inflation of the 1970s and early 1980s undermined that perspective and the emphasis shifted to commitment in both monetary and fiscal policy to medium-term objectives – price and output stability – and hence to sustainable public finances. After nearly two decades this regime was interrupted by the Great Financial Crisis (GFC), and fiscal policy gradually came back to be perceived as the essential source of stimulus and stabilization. Evidence for the view that fiscal policy becomes particularly effective in such circumstances accumulated during the COVID-19 pandemic. And confidence in the ability of fiscal policy to mitigate serious downturns spread to its potential for raising long-term growth in an economy due to more efficient allocation of resources.

These long swings in the perspective on what fiscal policy can deliver could be well illustrated by the experience of several European economies individually over this long time span. However, more interesting in the context of this chapter, there may be no example that better illustrates the evolving views than the swings in the way the EU and its Member States have tried to design the most appropriate way of how EU decisions can best influence national fiscal policy. This tortuous process of half a century of trial and error is helpful in understanding where the EU is today and how its fiscal governance may evolve further.

The first systematic effort goes back to the Werner Report of 1970 (Commission of the European Communities, 1970) on Economic and Monetary Union (EMU). It combined deep attachment to European integration with the then prevailing Keynesian confidence in what fiscal policy can do. The Report proposed a centre for economic policy decisions at the level of the EU Council of Finance Ministers (ECOFIN) with authority to override and coordinate national budgetary decisions. But consensus on such ideas evaporated under a decade-long pressure on the cohesion of the EU from inflation, energy price hikes and supply constraints.

The second effort came around 1990 with the Maastricht Treaty on EMU. It marked a low point of confidence in fiscal policy. The vision that fiscal policy was hard to control and subject to long-term biases in public deficits and debt made it essential to use whatever EU influence obtainable to constrain it: national policies should be subject to upper guidelines for public deficits and debt to prevent undesirable spill-overs to partner countries. The emphasis on medium-term commitments as expressed in these indicators was justified by the need to protect the prospective European Central Bank (ECB) against the risk of "fiscal dominance".

This very different paradigm for EU fiscal governance has proved more durable. Formally, it is still in existence, but its implementation has been increasingly challenged over the past decade since the GFC and, particularly, since March 2020 when the pandemic led to a de facto suspension of the fiscal framework. The ongoing debate on reforming EU economic governance focuses on how to reconcile the many investment needs in the EU economies with attention to the sustainability of public finances. More specifically, how can the EU dimension in fiscal policymaking be taken care of most constructively – by influencing national decisions or by taking more direct responsibilities at the EU level – or by combining the two approaches? The debate has at times returned to the ideas and arguments considered half a century ago when the roles of fiscal policy were last seen in the ambitious perspective of recent years.

This chapter has three main sections. The first traces the long swings in fiscal ambitions at the EU level, linking them both to the evolution of macroeconomics and to the EU experience. The second looks at the proposals for reforming economic governance that have gradually matured since the pre-pandemic period. Their aim is to reconcile protection of growth-friendly national public expenditures with sustainable public finances; the emphasis remains on a decentralized approach. The third section looks further ahead – to an evolution of EU economic governance to meet more jointly some of the major challenges that have faced its economies with increasing frequency and intensity in recent years. A brief final section concludes.

8.2 FISCAL GOVERNANCE: THE LONG SWING IN PERSPECTIVES

The Werner Report (Commission of the European Communities, 1970), prepared by a group of senior EU and national officials, headed by the Prime Minister of Luxembourg, built on the encouraging experience of the post-war period. Since the 1950s rapid progress in goods–market integration among the initial six EU Member States had accelerated economic growth, as had expansionary national fiscal policies. Rapid growth had been reconciled with moderate inflation. Public expenditures were rising fast, but revenues kept pace; the average of national debt ratios was around only 30 per cent by 1970, making later concerns over medium-term sustainability of public finances seem superfluous.

However, the benign experience had begun to look precarious. The inflation–output trade-off was worsening as very low levels of unemployment were reached, while an independent driving role for inflationary expectations emerged – "the inflation-augmented Phillips curve". Policymakers in the EU attributed some of these developments to the global environment, notably overheating in the US threatening the stability of the international monetary system. European integration required a regional replacement, if the favourable external environment provided by the Bretton Woods System of stable exchange rates were to unfold. More joint decision-making in both monetary and fiscal policies, not just informal efforts at coordination, would then be needed.

The Werner Report (Commission of the European Communities, 1970) is mostly remembered for its insistence on the need for "parallelism" between the two policies. It took this vague notion very literally in outlining it as central both in a complete EMU, and over the stages towards it. The Report was ahead of its times in referring to a single currency and a unified central banking system as end-objectives to be reached over a decade. But the proposal to set up "a centre of decision for economic policy" was its most innovative and controversial idea: the ECOFIN Council, would be upgraded to "influence the national budgets on the basis of quantitative objectives for growth, employment, prices and external equilibrium".

Warnings against excessive centralization can be found in the Werner Report, but these ambitions were striking in two dimensions: confidence in the efficiency and predictability of fiscal instruments in achieving desired macroeconomic outcomes, and support for European integration. The combination was to lead to political union via both monetary and fiscal instruments.

But the authors were not only European idealists. They had internalized the perspective of mainstream macroeconomics of the late 1960s – in retrospect, a high point in the confidence in what fiscal policy may achieve as a tool of demand management. That perspective emerges with clarity from an OECD Report (1968) led by Heller, and a companion volume, Hansen and Snyder (1969).[1] The implications of this perspective are that fiscal policy can deliver significant and predictable improvements in economic performance; decisions at the EU level might even improve outcomes by taking account of cross-border effects. And more refined indicators of fiscal policy in the shape of structural (or cyclically adjusted) budget balances were emerging. It did not appear unreasonable on economic grounds to propose tight EU oversight of national fiscal policies.

The very ambitious views of fiscal options were certainly far from shared by several EU governments at the time. But the efforts in the early 1970s to prolong the long post-war boom through tight coordination amid growing economic difficulties illustrate some persistence of aspirations. However, any remaining consensus in the EU on fiscal policy disappeared as inflation picked up, the first energy price hike hit, and the global monetary system broke up – all in the course of 1973, within three years of the launch of the EMU plans. Even before that it had become clear that transfers of budgetary authority to the EU would be blocked by France on political grounds.

Divergence within the EU widened as the impact of the massive supply shock revealed major asymmetries in reactions due to different attitudes to the inflation–output trade-off. Some saw the external shock as temporary and hoped to bridge the gap in demand by fiscal expansion, while Germany wanted to prevent inflation from becoming entrenched. The divergences could not be contained by the residual stability of exchange rates – and floating created wider space for further divergence in inflation and in fiscal actions.

With the disappearance of any common perspective on fiscal policy, a search for alternative approaches to integration flared up briefly. One such approach was crisis management: setting up a regional IMF-like institution to finance temporary external imbalances. Proposals for a joint EU unemployment fund were also elaborated over 1975–1977.[2] The experience with fiscal federalism outside the EU inspired efforts to regenerate integration; the idea was to exploit possible efficiency gains of assigning the provision of public goods with a clear transnational dimension to the EU, rather than to national governments. But the estimates of the required size of even a modest "pre-federal" EU-budget – around 3 per cent of collective GDP – discouraged the Commission and *a fortiori* the national governments from pursuing this approach.

Anyway, the initiatives soon focused on a monetary approach to integration with the Franco–German initiative of the European Monetary System (EMS).[3] That the EMS was of only of indirect relevance for fiscal policies was illustrated by the divergent fiscal policy in France in 1981–1983. But after three sizable devaluations, a reversal of the French very expansionary fiscal stance became essential for stabilization and convergence in the EU – and for any new initiatives in integration to become realistic.

The plan to develop the Single Internal Market for goods to be achieved by 1992 triggered new ambitions to combine this major initiative with moving towards a single currency. The focus was concentrated on monetary unification, but it was well understood that such a process would need an underpinning from national fiscal policies. The context had changed radically since the first EMU project two decades earlier: pro-cyclical policies had often been observed, due to both misjudgements and objectives other than stabilization, while public debt ratios had more than doubled to 60–65 per cent on average for the (now 12) EU countries. This experience undermined the case for short-term fiscal prescriptions from the EU; the main focus in the coming EMU had to be the defensive one of limiting the risk of high and rising debt in one or more countries spilling over into financial instability also in partner countries.

The major change in fiscal approach was also determined by the major shift in mainstream macroeconomics over the previous decades. A preference for rules rather than discretion in the conduct of both monetary and fiscal policy had emerged (see Chapter 1). In the context of EMU, that implied protecting a new common central bank, committed to price stability in the medium term as its primary objective, against the risk of "fiscal dominance", i.e. pressure from the political authorities to accommodate rising public debt through lower interest rates than warranted by the outlook for inflation.[4]

The Werner Report was written near the peak influence of the Keynesian positive view on the scope for fiscal policy. The preparations of the Maastricht Treaty were made, as the neo-classical paradigm became widely accepted: what matters for policy is a firm commitment to medium-term objectives by those responsible for monetary and, indirectly, fiscal policies. It was a vision for monetary dominance which aimed to anchor expectations and help to steer economies through temporary instability. National fiscal policies would be guided by reference values for public deficit and debt; keeping a safe distance below them would allow the automatic stabilizers, powerful in most EU countries, to operate. No need for a central fiscal authority, seen anyway as politically unrealistic, but compliance with a rules-based framework, monitored by the Commission and sanctioned by the Council in case of "gross errors".

The Treaty set the upper guidelines – "reference values" – of 3 per cent of GDP for the deficit and 60 per cent for debt. Both were close to the then average for the EU; they would be mutually consistent on the then commonly accepted assumption that the EU economies would grow in nominal terms by around 5 per cent a year in normal times. The intended message was: do not take on additional debt-financed expenditures. However, that message was not adequate for all EU countries: two (Belgium and Italy) already had public debt ratios of twice the reference value by 1990; they were asked to reduce debt "at a satisfactory pace", a notion left undefined for more than two decades.

Although the prime justification for introducing the rules-based framework was the risk of high debt spilling over into financial instability, in practice the monitoring came to focus on deficits. That was particularly evident in the Stability and Growth Pact (SGP) of 1997, which implemented the fiscal framework at a time when respecting the 3 per cent deficit was seen as the central criterion for admitting a country into the single currency. On four subsequent occasions the fiscal framework has been modified to become more, then less flexible. A very brief overview will have to suffice.

The first rebellion against recommendation of annual deficit adjustment was led by the two largest EU economies – Germany and France – in 2003. It was agreed two years later to take national circumstances more fully into account; but during the good years 2005–2009 imbalances built up, though in some cases not primarily in public finances. The crisis that began in the EU in 2008 exposed the failure to anticipate risks to public budgets from overextended banks; capital flows reversed towards the stronger economies, requiring massive efforts of refinancing of financial institutions, and triggering a sovereign debt crisis that brought the very survival of EMU into question.

The response centred on crisis management, reviving the notion of an EU crisis lender – a role the ECB was not mandated to assume – in the shape of the European Stability Mechanism (ESM) to oversee adjustment in four Member States, and of steps towards strengthening financial institutions and markets, initially through joint EU supervision of major banks – led by the ECB – and a common framework for bank recovery and resolution. But, in recognition that fiscal buffers had not been built prior to crises, the SGP was tightened by efforts to make debt-related enforcement more operational, while opening a large number of Excessive Deficit Procedures (EDP). The so-called six- and two-pack reforms have clearly been the most comprehensive efforts so far at updating the SGP.

However, as the recovery after 2013 proved to be slow, partly because of the simultaneous tightening of fiscal policies in most EU countries in the previous period, additional flexibility was opened up by the Commission in

2015. The main purpose was to better reconcile the sustainability and stabilization objectives, and to increase the scope for public investment which had borne the brunt of expenditure cut-backs during the GFC. This more explicit multi-dimensionality of objectives was, however, not well reflected, neither in economic outcomes, nor in compliance with the framework. Still there was only limited appetite to consider further reforms when the SGP came up for review in 2019.[5] Most were critical of what had been achieved, but there was no sense that reform was urgent; hence agreement seemed a distant prospect.

The outbreak of the COVID-19 pandemic in March 2020, just as the reform debate had been launched, changed the agenda drastically. A severe downturn clause was invoked to de facto suspend the rules-based framework for the entire EU – the popular label of the General Escape Clause (GEC) catches the wide scope. At the time of writing, the GEC is still to be deactivated, although most Member States had returned to their pre-pandemic GDP around the end of 2021; continuing uncertainty and the need to await an updated SGP have motivated the prolongation of the interregnum; an intention to deactivate the clause with effect from 2024 has been indicated.

The environment for a reform was changed by bold joint EU initiatives triggered by the pandemic. The European Council in July 2020 took the unprecedented step to agree to a near-doubling of the EU budget for 2021–2027, mainly to set up the Recovery and Resilience Facility (RRF) enabling national governments to undertake investments and accompanying reforms, monitored by the Commission and signed off by the Council. Nearly half of the funds raised by the EU were to take the form of grants to Member States; there is a substantial element of redistribution of resources, determined by objective criteria. The two transitions – green and digital – are the priorities in the recovery plans, indicated by minimum shares in the allocations.

Will the RRF initiative (and other bold 2020 decisions) fundamentally change EU economic governance? The answer remains unclear. On the one hand, the initiative has a sunset clause: it expires in 2027 with the current EU medium-term budget, and some Member States made their ratification depend on its character as a one-off initiative, making it almost certain that it will not be extended in anything like its present shape. The truly exceptional and exogenous nature of the pandemic may only temporarily have pushed aside traditional concerns about moral hazard. On the other hand, the RRF experience, though not yet evaluated, looks promising in having created new willingness in a number of EU countries to improve priorities in public spending as well as opportunities for the EU institutions to combine fiscal and structural surveillance. Looking in the following two sections, first at the Commission's proposals to improve fiscal governance, then at elements absent from them, may permit a clearer picture of how to assess the options for combining sustainability and growth-friendly public expenditures – the current fiscal ambition of the EU.

8.3 THE EU COMMISSION'S PROPOSALS FOR ECONOMIC GOVERNANCE[6]

On 9 November 2022, the Commission published a Communication on orientations for a reform of EU economic governance. In several respects it marks a new departure in surveillance by updating and simplifying the SGP.

The proposals focus explicitly on debt-reduction strategies over the medium to long term, but they do so in a nationally differentiated and, hopefully, realistic way. The central element is now to be nationally tailored fiscal–structural plans to fit into a debt-reduction path; the plans span over initially a four-year horizon to set debt on a "plausibly declining" path for a decade beyond that. The 60 per cent reference value will stay as a (very) distant marker. Governments with high debt, i.e. more than 90 per cent, and some with debt in the 60–90 per cent range, will produce and commit to plans, to be signed off by the Council on a Commission recommendation.

Focus on fiscal prudence for high-debt countries – six Member States have debt well into excess of their GDP – is seen as warranted: the extended period when sustainability concerns were below the radar with borrowing costs to remain low for long, may be about to end. Renewed attention to sustainability by means of a rules-based fiscal framework will become important in keeping financial conditions moderately favourable.

While sustainability remains the primary objective, the Commission's proposals do not disregard the other two objectives: allowing for counter-cyclical stabilization and improving the quality of public expenditures. Tension between sustainability and stabilization should be reduced in a medium-term rather than an annual perspective on policy intentions and outcomes. As for the quality of public expenditures, the proposals devote much attention to closer interaction with governments, balancing more national ownership with stronger commitments. Some reservations as to how this balance is to be attained are taken up below, but the approach seems superior to the half-hearted experiments with so-called Golden Rules in the pre-pandemic period.

The focus in the proposals facilitates additional simplifications. Emphasis on identifying, preventing and correcting "gross errors" of policy becomes more meaningful in a medium-term perspective, making it possible to roll back much of the structure built up to offer more flexibility in annual implementation, notably in the so-called preventive arm of the SGP. Most of it relied on short-term policy indicators subject to major *ex post* revisions. Indicators derived from estimates of the output gap are analytically valuable, but not readily useful for fiscal policy recommendations in real time.

That the proposals move towards recommendations based on observed outcomes rather than on policy intentions is confirmed by the retention of the 3 per cent reference value for the headline deficit. This policy indicator is easy to monitor and communicate in the national political environment; and it remains the best known in the arsenal. But it too should be seen in a multi-annual perspective: a reminder to governments to maintain fiscal buffers that make transgressions rare and temporary.

Another simplification is the dominant role of the expenditure benchmark in monitoring by the Commission. The relationship between the growth of expenditures and of the economy's potential is not beyond observational ambiguities – expenditures are adjusted for estimated discretionary revenue changes to remove the perception that the benchmark is just a tool to restrain the public sector. But the benchmark remains easier to observe and to communicate than the structural deficit while leaving scope for automatic stabilizers to operate.

Independent national fiscal councils – popularly known as IFIs – were set up a decade ago in nearly all Member States that did not have them already. They have brought more transparency into the domestic debate, by validating the macroeconomic and budgetary forecasts of governments, occasionally marked by excessive optimism. The current proposals build on the promising record of the IFIs by extending it to assessing – though not designing – the national medium-term fiscal–structural plans, the central elements in the future framework. A number of IFIs are already well placed for these tasks; assuring minimum standards is to be explored.

Enforcement has been a particularly weak area for the SGP throughout its existence. The proposals indicate that debt-related EDP will begin to be applied. Financial sanctions, the final step in the EDP, were to be imposed when transgressions become more than modest and temporary and no escape clause can be invoked. But sanctions have never been applied. One reason may be that imposing a significant fine on a government in economic difficulties was regarded as overly idealistic. The proposals now envisage lowering the financial sanctions to make them a more credible deterrent, and to supplement them by reputational sanctions.

All the points in the proposals mentioned so far have to be acknowledged as advances based on past experience; they are both bold and pragmatic. Finding a convergence of views on them among governments may be within reach, but some issues and reservations remain unresolved.

The two initial steps in future surveillance will be: first, the presentation by the Commission of a reference debt adjustment path – relabelled "technical trajectory" during negotiations to soothe national government concerns about its immutable status – for a country with high or medium-high debt; then a fiscal–structural plan prepared by the government, both taking a four-year horizon to represent the medium term; finally, an assessment of whether the plan follows the trajectory.

The proposals envisage that, in cases where congruence is incomplete, the government may ask for a slower pace of debt adjustment over seven rather than four years. The Commission and the Council are presumed not to object, provided a revised government plan includes investment projects and reforms that promote sustainability and keep the debt ratio on a "plausibly declining" path beyond the extended horizon, assuming unchanged policies. The government must also to show that it can observe the 3 per cent reference value throughout the planning horizon.

These steps to introduce additional flexibility raise two questions that should be clarified before the proposals are agreed and implemented. The first relates to the horizon over which a government can commit to a plan and to the nature of its incentives to do so; the second to whether the grounds for extending that horizon can be made operational.

The normal life of a government is 3–5 years; the Commission's proposed four-year horizon is an approximation to the period over which a government can be expected to commit to a medium-term plan. That is already a stretch: many EU governments have struggled to adopt such a plan and even more then to have it respected in annual budgets. Backloading of expenditures has been a regular feature in the past. Extending planned adjustments well beyond the life of a government looks hazardous; it may lead to strategic behaviour rather than to fiscal prudence.

Sustainability is a very long-term notion which cannot be "ensured" by policy recommendations over four, seven or even ten years beyond that. Therefore, the Commission will evaluate whether the declining debt path looks plausible beyond the short horizon over which governments can commit. An extension up to seven years may seem minor, but it could prove risky for the credibility of the new framework; the incentives for governments to design and properly implement investment and reform proposals will weaken when disbursements from the RRF peter out in a few years. Obtaining a prolonged debt adjustment path is anyway not an attraction comparable to EU funding.

On the second question – the grounds for extending adjustment – the Commission has been inspired by what is seen as a promising experience with the Recovery and Resilience Facility (RRF). Integrating fiscal and structural surveillance – the SGP and the Country-Specific Recommendations (CSR) – has long looked unappealing due to the limited impact of the latter, subject until recently only to informal coordination. While the experience with the RRF is yet to be carefully evaluated, the prospects for integrating the two dimensions of surveillance have been enhanced by the intensive dialogue between the Commission and governments on their plans, including monitoring of milestones and targets before disbursements of RRF funds.

A basic difference between the fiscal and structural dimensions of surveillance nevertheless persists. The "virtue" of the SGP is the macroeconomic nature of its aggregate indicators, deficits and debt. That makes the SGP both more quantifiable, but also less central and controversial in a domestic political context than the CSR; national budgetary debates focus more on the composition of expenditures than on deficits and debt. That could make commitments to detailed investments and structural reforms more controversial domestically – despite the good intentions.

Could the impact of individual investment projects and sectoral reforms on the economy, ultimately on sustainability, be reliably assessed? The analytical challenges are major; the more detailed the structural elements, the more surveillance enters into unquantifiable territory. The Commission may choose to perform only a qualitative evaluation, leaving the benefit of doubt to the national government. But that might not be adequate to maintain respect for its recommendations.

Trying to develop a strategy different from that followed after the GFC is understandable. Budgetary consolidation in 2011–2013 may, in retrospect, have been overly rapid, while structural reforms were underemphasized. It would be preferable to grow out of a crisis, rather than risk a prolonged period of low activity while consolidating. Unfortunately, the preferred strategy may not deliver the measurable contributions to the growth of productive potential intended. However necessary the investment and reforms may be in preventing worse future outcomes, their role in replacing existing capital stock warrants caution in presenting them as inevitably raising potential growth and the debt-servicing capacity of an economy; sustainability may be stretched regardless of the purpose for which debt is issued.

The two questions raised do not undermine the conclusion that adoption of the Commission proposals would mark a significant improvement in surveillance. But the efforts to negotiate extra flexibility bring elements of complexity, intransparency and bilateralism. Complexity is inherent in the granularity of the fiscal–structural recommendations. Transparency may suffer for the same reason, despite the intention of the Commission to maintain a high level of openness in procedures. Bilateralism will be hard to avoid; only the Commission has the resources to keep up with the detailed surveillance emerging. The committees of national officials serving the ECOFIN Council can hardly take the time to monitor the surveillance process in the detail they seem to require. The ECOFIN Council will find it difficult to challenge what has been agreed between a government and the Commission, all the more so since a qualified majority against a recommendation is required to overturn it. This procedure may now appear more logical due to the complexity of the policy recommendations; but it remains objectionable by reducing the role of the Council.[7]

A simple way to mitigate the concerns raised by the two questions would be to retain scope for extending – and *a fortiori* for revising – a national debt adjustment path only in two situations: when a severe downturn clause can be activated for a country, or when a new government comes into office after elections asking for a limited revision of an agreed path. These are objective circumstances for moving to more flexible implementation that can be taken into account in a rules-based framework. There are limits to what fine-tuning engineering of national budgets can achieve.

A simplification of this nature may be seen as going too far in reducing national ownership – the counterpart to the firmer commitments undertaken by a government. Such a balance is desirable in the governance framework, particularly if the ambition is to extend its aims to improve the quality of public expenditures by protecting investment better than in the past. However, such aims might also, at least in part, be addressed by joint EU initiatives, omitted from the Commission proposals – with the understandable argument that such an extension would have put a broad agreement on the update and simplification of the SGP out of reach. Nevertheless, such a longer-term agenda has recently advanced in realism.

8.4   A LONGER-TERM AGENDA

The Commission announces its Communication as "addressing the key economic and policy issues that will shape the EU economic policy coordination and surveillance for the next decade". That is a surprisingly strong claim at a time when a major gap in the proposed economic governance has been identified by the ECB, the IMF and the OECD as the absence of a Central Fiscal Capacity (CFC) to provide two main contributions to economic governance: to support the supply of well-defined public goods with an EU dimension; and to strengthen the automatic stabilizers in national budgets.[8]

Providing strategic EU public goods could be taken on through joint decisions and financing within a narrow range of major investment projects of a cross-border nature with a clearer EU dimension than the many smaller-scale national investment projects and reforms funded by the RRF. But that would require a review of the preferences in the EU for decentralization and subsidiarity.

An economically appropriate division of responsibilities between the national and the EU level has come up in the political debate only rarely. As noted above, it became a subject briefly in the mid-1970s, at a time when economic divergence had eroded the political will to take further steps towards EMU. Inspired by analysis of fiscal federalism in large countries, some categories of public expenditures with obvious economies of scale or spill-over effects, implying a case for placing shared responsibility for them at the EU level, were examined. The discussion ended quickly.

It did not resume in detail even at the time of the Maastricht Treaty. The design for a common central bank implied full centralization, but narrowly delimited to monetary policy. Not even regulation and supervision of financial institutions and markets were regarded as a contiguous responsibility; banking supervision was added to the ECB mandate only in 2014.

A general principle of subsidiarity was introduced in the Treaty (TEU Art. 3b): the power of EU institutions should be limited to functions that cannot be adequately performed nationally. The constraints on centralization are tighter in Art. 5: "in areas which do not fall into its exclusive competence, the Union shall act only if and in so far as the objectives of the proposed action cannot be sufficiently achieved by the Member States, and the content and form of Union action shall not exceed what is necessary to achieve the objectives of the Treaty." The burden of proof is meant to be on those who argue in favour of joint action, e.g. to provide better counter-cyclical stabilization or public goods, the two functions for a CFC.[9] The approach in a decentralized rules-based framework – to limit risks of harmful spill-overs – may be difficult, but it is clearly in a different and safer category.

The deterrent impact of the subsidiarity principle has proved highly durable. With respect to several categories of public expenditures it can be argued that greater efficiency from moving decision-making, sometimes implementation, beyond the national level may not be sufficient to justify overcoming national preferences for acting one by one. The efforts of the Commission in stressing the element of "national ownership" of investments and reforms illustrate how this dilemma may be approached. The more detailed the involvement in national expenditure allocation and hence in the domestic political debates, the stronger the need to emphasize national ownership and to downplay EU influence becomes.

However, recent experience with new and comprehensive challenges suggest that the need for public goods with an EU dimension is growing rapidly. Two criteria may underpin greater efficiency of joint action: the scale of an activity transcends the resources of at least smaller Member States; and/ or spill-over effects on partners are important. To take the new challenges in the rough order they appeared – the green transition, the pandemic and the Russian invasion of Ukraine – they have all strengthened the need to supplement national efforts through EU decisions and actions.

For at least a couple of decades the green transition has been on the EU agenda; it was given the highest priority in the RRF. National projects contribute to saving energy and to shifting supply away from fossil fuels. A decentralized approach maintains elements of competition between Member States to offer examples as models and to develop new technologies for the transition.

They may also be the best way of mobilizing private industrial and financial resources. But to become fully effective, the EU will have to take more than a coordinating role. Strategic decisions to assure central facilities for energy linkages, storage and security are becoming key areas for the EU, emerging in the RePower EU initiative. The need to implement as uniform guidelines as possible for how the green transition is to be advanced may be more of a challenge to the state aid regime than to EU budgetary resources or borrowing. More joint economic responsibilities will follow the joint decisions.

Similar remarks can be made on the other, less foreseeable, events facing the EU. The pandemic prompted unprecedented joint action to develop, purchase and distribute vaccines. The war in Ukraine required a joint EU response to mitigate the challenges of constrained energy supplies and a large wave of migration; it also triggered new perspectives on how defence capabilities could be more efficiently raised by joint equipment acquisition. The eventual reconstruction of Ukraine may prove the largest task of all, going well beyond coordination, without undermining the extra sense of commitment that national involvement can bring. The EU faces over the next decade not only the task of helping Ukraine from destruction to near membership, but also of taking in several new West Balkan members in need of support for their transition.

Economic governance over the next decade or so will impose a wider fiscal agenda than the update of the SGP. Making some top-down decisions, followed by a gradual build-up of an EU budget and borrowing that allows strategic, but limited participation in seeing the decisions implemented, will continue to crowd out traditional agenda items in the European Council, and even in the ECOFIN Council.

This is not a criticism of the past economic governance or, even less, of the Commission proposals. Underlining the new challenges and the need for the EU to jointly provide public goods is simply intended as a reminder: a bottom-up approach focusing on national policies within a reformed and simplified SGP framework will have to be complemented before long by the requirements of a new and more demanding agenda.

Compared with assuring the supply of certain strategic public goods, the role of a CFC in enhancing automatic counter-cyclical stabilization in the EU may seem at the same time less significant and more straightforward. It appears, however, to be politically (even) more controversial. A modest version of the idea could be to build up an EU rainy-day fund through national contributions, topped up by the authority to supplement them through joint bond issues at times of major crises. Member States would then draw on the fund for shorter periods on the basis of objective criteria.

During the pandemic the Council agreed to set up a temporary mechanism (SURE) to mitigate unemployment risks during the emergency by compensating Member States for some of their expenses in keeping employees attached to their work while temporarily idle. The experience was seen as successful; no funds had been accumulated; hence EU borrowing had to provide all the financing. The SURE experience could be repeated and help to keep the EU more cohesive in the face of significant but temporary disturbances. The idea was not taken up prior to 2020, due to the perceived risk of moral hazard in any insurance mechanism, but the pandemic was evidently well beyond any national responsibility.

Two other omissions, besides the central one of the CFC, also reflect an optimistic view of the environment in which the reform will operate. The authors of the reform of the rules-based framework a decade ago had to pay attention to crisis management. They did so primarily by setting up the ESM to provide loans with conditionality. Together with the start of a banking union and an ECB announcement that sovereign bonds issued by countries with an ESM adjustment programme could be purchased by the central bank, these initiatives ended the sovereign debt crisis. There is no mention of the need for any crisis mechanisms in the proposals. Yet the ESM has the experience and the unused resources that could prove valuable in a future crisis, even in preventing one.

Finally, the Communication touches only in passing on the appropriate mix of fiscal and monetary policy. It recognizes the responsibility of the political authorities "to help the ECB attain its goals, particularly as it faces the challenge of delivering on its mandate to maintain price stability while avoiding financial fragmentation in the euro area". It may be that is all that can be said on a sensitive subject and in respect of ECB independence, but the contrast to what was said and done in 2012 is striking. Today the ECB is in the front line of protecting the cohesion of the euro area, and it is unprotected by ESM conditionality, while the revised fiscal framework may provide only limited protection. The new anti-fragmentation tool of the ECB – the Transmission Protection Instrument (TPI) – offers a potentially powerful reinforcement of the fiscal framework, but only if governments are seen to put sustainability high on the agenda.

One argument in favour of moving to rules-based governance was to provide both the ECB and financial markets with signals on economic performance in vulnerable Member States and on the likely EU policy reactions to them. However, the purpose of promoting smoother market evaluations based on fundamentals, has not been served well so far. There is a need to become more specific on how the help from fiscal policymakers in containing fragmentation can be reinforced. The ECB cannot be expected to achieve stability on its own.

8.5 CONCLUSIONS

The perspective on the purposes and the realism of fiscal governance in the EU has gone through major changes. Strong confidence in the stabilizing properties of national fiscal policies, combined with apparent political momentum for European integration, led – half a century ago – to proposals for a supranational EU centre for decision-making on budgetary policies. Both elements in the combination disappeared when unfamiliar economic challenges arose from the early 1970s, prompting a resurgence of divergent policies in EU Member States.

By the late 1980s the EU was preparing for a very different approach to integration, not least to fiscal governance. The disappointments with the ability of fiscal policies to contribute to stabilization and the doubling of public debt over two decades prompted an attitude of restraint; public deficits and debt should respect rules to limit the risk of an unsustainable build-up of debt spilling over into financial instability also for the country's partners. The design of the coming central banking system with medium-term price stability as its primary objective was to be underpinned by firm commitments by the political authorities to sustainable public finances.

This model, representing what was seen in 1990 as a politically feasible and economically adequate, governance framework, has basically survived until recently. It was modified in several later reforms to make the framework more flexible by allowing for national circumstances. During the recovery from the GFC, tensions in the policy mix arose. Even massive monetary accommodation did not raise inflation to the target of 2 per cent, while public deficits and debt in the most indebted Member States did not comply with recommendations to build fiscal buffers. And postponement of public investment accounted for an important share of any fiscal consolidation observed during and after the GFC.

The ambition to allow for a greater role of fiscal policy in general, especially to better protect growth-friendly investment, marks a swing back towards the perspectives of half a century ago. A long period of very low interest rates has reinforced this swing, as economists and, even more so, policymakers began to see sustainability of public finances as a less severe constraint, as argued forcefully by Blanchard (2019, 2022). The tensions in the EU fiscal framework were initially addressed by suspending the SGP and by the extraordinary joint efforts of 2020. As the governance debate resumed three years later, the environment may appear to have changed once more: inflation has risen as the combined result of a strong recovery from the pandemic and energy shortages, adding a more cautionary perspective to the design of fiscal policy – at least temporarily. However, this does not hide the basic shift in fiscal ambitions

Fiscal policy in a turbulent era

towards protecting national and joint investment efforts while taking steps to monitor sustainability.

These tensions in the framework were temporarily eased by effectively suspending the SGP and by adding unprecedented joint EU steps when the pandemic hit in 2020. The governance debate has resumed three years later in an environment which, once more, appears to have changed. Energy shortages combined with a strong recovery in output and employment have made inflation a concern in 2022–23. But the EU has also been faced with several challenges in the last few years which call for new ideas, both on how to improve resource allocation within each country, and on how to harness and coordinate efforts at the EU level.

The main theme of this chapter is the long swings in EU efforts to develop an appropriate fiscal framework for a group of closely integrated countries seen from a macroeconomic perspective. Keynes provided a perceptive account of how such swings may be characterized to illustrate the power of ideas".[10] At most a decade after a shift in mainstream macroeconomics, new ideas break through into policy decisions. As noted in Chapter 1, that was observed in 1970, some years after the Keynesian confidence in the stabilizing role of fiscal policy became dominant. It happened around 1990 when medium-term policy commitments were undertaken, about a decade after the new credibility-oriented paradigm had become dominant. And it is now happening a third time, as sustainability may seem less difficult to assure and fiscal ambitions break through the barriers created by concerns over their own past use and misuse. The EU will remain an interesting case study in the current revival of fiscal policy.

ACKNOWLEDGEMENTS

Discussions with EFB colleagues are gratefully acknowledged, but the views expressed should not be attributed to the EFB. Comments from Enrique Alberola and Vítor Gaspar greatly improved the chapter; the author retains sole responsibility for the interpretation of events.

NOTES

1.   Starting from the arrival of the Kennedy Administration in 1961, US fiscal policy became highly ambitious in pushing up economic growth and conducting more active stabilization. This process was driven by a desire for political change, enabled by macroeconomic research and model-building in universities, think tanks, the Fed and the President's Council of Economic Advisers. Hansen and Snyder (1969) give an overview of this effort. Heller chaired the CEA over that period and conveyed a strong message in the OECD report he co-authored with leading European economists.

2. First in the Marjolin Report (Commission of the European Communities, 1975), further elaborated in the MacDougall Report (Commission of the European Communities, 1977).
3. For an account of the EMS and the limited constraints imposed on fiscal policy, see Gros and Thygesen (1998).
4. Such a "game of chicken" was first analysed by Sargent and Wallace (1981). The emphasis on credibility and commitments to reduce the risk of time inconsistency in both monetary and fiscal policy was pioneered by Kydland and Prescott (1977) and taken further by Rogoff (1985) and Giavazzi and Pagano (1989).
5. European Fiscal Board (2019) reviewed the record of the reforms undertaken just after the GFC and made a number of proposals to update and simplify the SGP. Most of them have recently reappeared in the Commission's 2022 orientations for reform, now with better chances of agreement. Gaspar (2020), speaking at a conference just before the outbreak of the pandemic, gives a more wide-ranging perspective on the agenda as it looked at the time.
6. The chapter was completed in March 2023, shortly before the full legislative proposals of the Commission were known in late April. The final shape of the EU governance reform may thus differ to some extent from the account in this section.
7. For a critical review of the Reverse Qualified Majority Vote (RQMV) see EFB (2019). The RQMV was introduced to allow the Commission as the Guardian of the Treaty an easier passage for its recommendations in Council. However, since 2014 the Commission has increasingly emphasized that it is a political, not a technocratic body. That implies that the Council as the other political EU institution should have more influence (though it did not use it well in 2003).
8. For detailed comments on these two separate functions of a central fiscal capacity, see EFB (2022, chapters 5.5–6).
9. An early comprehensive discussion of subsidiarity may be found in Begg (1993). A strong case for EU provision of strategic public goods is made by Furst and Pisani-Ferry (2019) – before the pandemic brought another unforeseen and persuasive example of the usefulness of joint EU action.
10. I am grateful to Vitor Gaspar for suggesting to me to reread the final pages of Keynes (1936) where the maestro brings up the image of powerful men as slaves of a "defunct economist" – until new ideas force their way through. The three examples in this chapter of a breakthrough of a new paradigm in designing fiscal governance in the EU brings forward an alternative image of this process: finance ministers and central bank governors today are well briefed by economic advisers. The latter are very attentive to new paradigms in macroeconomics about to become mainstream, and particularly when the new ideas fit into current political preferences. Ministers then become proponents of these ideas – in powerful versions with fewer qualifications and with the keenness of recent converts to a new orthodoxy.

REFERENCES

Begg, D. (1993), "Making sense of subsidiarity: How much centralization for Europe?", *Center for Economic Policy Research.*
Blanchard, O. (2019), "Public debt and low interest rates", *American Economic Review* 109(4).

Blanchard, O. (2022), *Fiscal Policy under Low Rates.* The MIT Press.

Commission of the European Communities (1970), "Report to the Council and the Commission on the Realisation by Stages of Economic and Monetary Union in the Community". Supplement to Bulletin 11 ("The Werner Report"), Brussels.

Commission of the European Communities (1975), "Report of the Study Group on Economic and Monetary Union 1980". ('The Marjolin Report'). Brussels.

Commission of the European Communities (1977), "Report of the Study Group on the Role of Public Finance in European Integration". The MacDougall Report Vol. III. Brussels.

European Fiscal Board (2019), *Assessment of EU Fiscal Rules.* EFB.

European Fiscal Board (2022), *Annual Report 2022.* EFB.

Furst, C. and J. Pisani-Ferry (2019), "A Primer on Developing European Public Goods", *EconPolicy Report* 16(3).

Gaspar, V. (2020), "Future of Fiscal Rules in the Euro Area", Keynote Address at Workshop of DG ECFIN on *Fiscal Rules in Europe*, 28 January 2020.

Giavazzi, F. and M. Pagano (1989), "Confidence Crises and Public Debt Management", NBER Working Paper No. 2926

Gros, D. and N. Thygesen (1998), *European Monetary Integration*, 2nd Edition. Pearson Education.

Hansen, B. and W. Snyder (1969), *Fiscal Policy in Seven Countries 1955-65.* OECD.

Keynes, J. M. (1936), *The General Theory of Employment, Interest and Money.* Macmillan & Co.

Kydland, F. and E. Prescott (1977), "Rules Rather than Discretion: The Inconsistency of Optimal Plans", *Journal of Political Economy* 85.

OECD (1968), *Fiscal Policy for a Balanced Economy: Experience, Problems and Prospects.* OECD.

Rogoff, K. (1985), "The Optimal Degree of Commitment to an Intermediate Monetary Target", *Quarterly Journal of Economics* 100.

Sargent, T. and N. Wallace (1981), "Some Unpleasant Monetarist Arithmetic", *Quarterly Review of the Federal Reserve Bank of Minneapolis* 531.

9. Fiscal policy and financial stability: revisiting the nexus

Claudio Borio, Marc Farag and Fabrizio Zampolli

9.1 INTRODUCTION

The Great Financial Crisis (GFC) prompted policymakers to tighten prudential regulation and supervision (Borio et al., 2020b). While essential, these efforts are not enough to safeguard lasting macro-financial stability. Much attention has been devoted to how best to combine monetary policy, macroprudential policies, foreign exchange intervention and capital management tools to achieve that objective. By contrast, the role of fiscal policy in such a macro-financial stability framework has not been explored as thoroughly (Borio et al., 2023b; BIS, 2022).

In fact, fiscal policy was at the heart of many past financial crises or episodes of severe financial stress, including in the recent euro area debt crisis. In some cases, it was an unsustainable fiscal situation that precipitated a crisis in the financial sector. In others, it was an unsustainable credit boom that led to strains in financial institutions, bail-outs and the need for large fiscal stimulus to fight the crisis-induced recession. In both types of episode, however, fiscal and financial risks reinforced each other, giving rise to so-called "doom loops".

This chapter begins by describing the channels through which these adverse feedbacks may arise (Section 9.2). In one direction, an increase in fiscal risk reduces the value of the explicit and implicit government guarantees that protect financial institutions and diminishes the value of government bonds held in their balance sheets. This weakens financial institutions. In the other direction, an increase in financial risk makes it more likely that public debt exceeds a sustainable limit, thus raising the risk of a sovereign default or of high inflation wiping out bondholders. If left unchecked, these vicious cycles can increase the probability and the cost of a financial crisis. And even if they do not result in a full-blown crisis, they can severely damage economic activity.

The chapter next deals with how to break or lessen these vicious loops. This requires action in two dimensions.

First, it requires incorporating explicitly financial stability considerations into fiscal policy, so as to prevent financial instability from undermining fiscal sustainability and to protect the room for manoeuvre to address crises (Section 9.3). In practice, this can be done in three ways: by improving the assessment of the potential costs of possible future banking crises; by extending the principle of a countercyclical policy to address the impact of financial expansions and contractions – the financial cycle – on the fiscal accounts; and by reducing the debt bias in tax/subsidy regimes.

Second, it requires addressing effectively sovereign exposures in prudential regulation and supervision, notably for banks (Section 9.4). A better treatment of sovereign risk in prudential policy would help shield banks from sovereign crises and possibly also inhibit the excessive accumulation of public debt in the first place. The implementation of this principle would need to take into account the special role of sovereign bonds in the financial system as well as country-specific characteristics and circumstances. That said, banks would continue to be exposed to sovereign risks indirectly, through the increased macroeconomic instability that unsustainable fiscal positions can generate – hence the need for fiscal sustainability more generally, regardless of the factors that may impair it.

9.2   THE TWO-WAY PROPAGATION CHANNELS OF BANK–SOVEREIGN RISK REDUCTION

The financial and public sectors are closely intertwined. Banks (and other financial institutions) are a key source of funding for governments.[1] Governments, in turn, provide the ultimate backstop for the financial sector and underpin an economy's performance. As a result, risks can propagate both ways through various channels.

9.2.1   Propagation from the Banks to the Sovereign

Banks can affect the sovereign in several ways, all of which raise the risk of a substantial increase in public debt.

First, the sovereign is directly exposed to bank risk. This is so both explicitly – through deposit insurance or other guarantees – and, implicitly – through the expectation that it would bail out institutions in trouble.

Second, the sovereign is indirectly exposed to financial sector risk through the macroeconomic fallout of crises. In the wake of a banking crisis, fiscal balances tend to deteriorate much more and for much longer than following ordinary recessions. One reason is the size and persistence of output and employment losses, which reduce tax revenues and increase spending through automatic stabilizers. Another reason is the compositional change in tax revenues linked to the collapse in asset prices and financial activity. For instance, in a financial bust, housing transactions and the revenue associated with them fall sharply.

Third, sovereigns tend to respond to crises with discretionary fiscal expansions. Provided a country has sufficient fiscal space, such a response can help stabilize output and prevent a financial crisis from deepening. However, unless properly calibrated, it may leave a stubborn legacy of higher debt.

Finally, the currency depreciation that typically goes hand in hand with financial stress or an outright banking crisis can weaken the sovereign further. Whenever a large share of public debt is denominated in foreign currency or indexed to it, the depreciation would significantly raise the domestic currency value of the public debt, as noted in Chapter 2. If the depreciation is large enough, the sovereign may also be forced to support other sectors that run currency mismatches.

One way to capture both the direct and indirect fiscal costs of a banking crisis is to look at the change in public debt in its aftermath (Figure 9.1). The historical record indicates that these costs are very large. For instance, between 1970 and 2017, the median cumulative increase in the government debt-to-GDP ratio in the five post-crisis years for advanced economies (AEs) is about 20 percentage points (pp) and almost 40 pp, depending on whether one considers the pre- or post-GFC sub-sample.[2] For emerging and developing economies (EMDEs), the post-banking crisis median increase is smaller but still sizeable, at 12 pp. In all cases, there is a considerable variation across countries and episodes.

9.2.2   Propagation from the Sovereign to the Banks

An increase in sovereign risk (which reflects the probability of various types of sovereign credit event)[3] may increase financial risks in three ways (e.g. Committee on the Global Financial System, CGFS, 2011).

First, the drop in the price of government securities weakens banks' balance sheets directly. Even short of a government default, an increase in sovereign risk premia will generate losses on direct holdings and depress the value of sovereign bonds as collateral. The size of these effects depends on the amount and duration of the government bonds held and the extent of their recognition varies with accounting treatment (e.g. historical cost versus marked-to-market).

Second, an increase in sovereign risk can tighten banks' funding conditions. Investors are likely to perceive banks with exposures to the sovereign as riskier and therefore charge higher spreads. It also saps the value of explicit and implicit government guarantees, which works in the same direction.

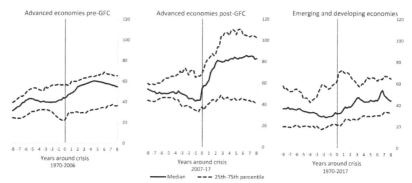

Note: In percentage of GDP. Median value across countries in the region and period. The vertical line indicates the year when the crisis starts.
Source: Bova et al, (2016); Laeven and Valencia (2018); Reinhart, www.carmenreinhart.com/data; IMF, International Financial Statistics and World Economic Outlook; OECD, Economic Outlook; national data; authors' calculations.

Figure 9.1   Government debt level after banking crises

Third, an increase in sovereign risk can weaken banks through its broader impact on the economy. The higher cost of funding and diminished bank credit availability that accompany a marked increase in sovereign risk weaken aggregate demand. In addition, fiscal policy may have less room for a counter-cyclical response and any additional support to the banking system. Economic weakness, in turn, tends to depress credit demand as well as boost debt arrears and defaults among bank customers.

The evidence confirms the quantitative relevance of the transmission from fiscal to financial risk. Research finds that higher sovereign risk tends to depress bank valuations, raise bank risk and curtail bank lending (see Borio et al., 2023a, for a review and references therein). In particular, the relationship tends to be stronger in countries where banks' sovereign exposures are higher. This does not simply reflect country risk: within the same country, banks with larger domestic sovereign exposures cut credit by more than their peers in response to increased sovereign risk.[4] Interestingly, even well-capitalized banks without significant sovereign exposures face higher borrowing costs and cut credit supply, largely reflecting the increase in default rates among borrowers that accompany a weaker aggregate demand.

9.2.3   Risk Amplification and "Doom Loops"

The previous discussion indicates that sovereign and financial risks can be mutually reinforcing and may therefore generate "doom loops". Banking crises are a major source of deterioration in fiscal positions and, in turn, a weaker sovereign can weaken banks. Indeed, banking and sovereign crises have frequently occurred simultaneously or have followed one another in quick succession (e.g. Bordo and Meissner, 2016).

Outside default episodes, bank and sovereign risks tend to move in tandem. This is the case, regardless of how these risks are measured, e.g. by CDS spreads, expected default probabilities or interest rate spreads. Many studies focusing on euro area countries in the aftermath of the GFC generally find evidence of a direct causal interdependence: the correlation between the two risks is stronger than can be explained by common factors, such as the state of the economy, market volatility and aggregate global risk. However, the strength of this correlation varies depending on a host of factors. For instance, it tends to be stronger in countries with less fiscal space – that is, higher government debt to GDP ratios – and where banks are weaker – that is, are more leveraged, more reliant on wholesale funding and holding larger amounts of government securities. Balance sheet variables also explain the strength of the correlation between individual bank risk and sovereign risk within the same country (see Borio et al., 2023a, for a review).

The evidence also suggests that, in general, the correlation between bank and sovereign risks is strong in EMDEs, too, although it varies considerably over time and across countries. It tends to increase with the level of distress in the banking sector and with tighter global financial conditions. Furthermore, the spillovers vary across sectors: they are on average stronger from sovereign to bank than in the opposite direction. And they vary across countries: they are larger in those with higher public debt and larger banks' holdings of public debt (IMF, 2022).

9.3 FISCAL POLICY TO SUPPORT FINANCIAL STABILITY

How can fiscal policy support financial stability? Having sufficient fiscal space is a prerequisite for financial stability. Not only is fiscal sustainability essential to avoid a crisis, but it is also a necessary condition for solving a crisis in an orderly way once it arises, including by backing up any lender-of-last-resort or buyer-of-last-resort central bank operations. As is well known, many factors can undermine fiscal sustainability. But how can one specifically measure those linked to financial stability? That is, how can one assess in real time the potential impact of future financial (banking) crises on fiscal space (stock) or that of a financial boom on cyclically adjusted fiscal positions (flow)? Consider each question in turn.

9.3.1   Fiscal Buffers

There is no hard and fast rule for determining the minimum or optimal size of
a fiscal buffer against banking risk. To get a sense of the potential magnitudes,
one can look at the mean or median fiscal cost experienced in past banking
crises, which are quite large (as shown in Figure 9.1). However, since the
direct and indirect fiscal costs vary greatly across countries and episodes,
to come up with an assessment more suitable for policy, it is important to
understand what explains this variation. And because any such assessment is
shrouded in uncertainty, it is best to base it on a distribution of possible outcomes rather than on point estimates.

Borio et al. (2020a) put forward a method for computing the distribution of
the potential fiscal costs of a banking crisis based on the distribution of past
crises' fiscal costs. This approach is equivalent, in credit risk management
parlance, to estimating losses given default as opposed to estimating default
probabilities. It comprises three steps.

The first step is to approximate the overall *ex post* fiscal cost with the
increase in gross public debt over a five-year window, as is standard in the
literature (e.g. Laeven and Valencia, 2013; Bova et al., 2016). Such a measure
includes both direct and indirect costs; and because it calculates the change
over several years, it is less likely to overstate the true fiscal cost.[5]

The second step consists of finding the risk (and mitigating) factors that
best predict the fiscal cost in past banking crises. Here, the authors find that
a relatively small set of variables appears to provide the best prediction.[6]
One variable pertains to the fiscal position itself: the pre-crisis government
debt-to-GDP ratio tends to raise the fiscal cost – probably acting as a proxy for
policy headroom. The other variables include the pre-crisis level and growth
rate of domestic credit to the private non-financial sector (aggravating factors)
as well as foreign exchange reserves and bank capital (mitigating factors).

The third step consists of computing the mean and various percentiles of
the conditional distribution of the fiscal cost given a crisis. This is done based
on quantile regressions that include the risk factors identified in the previous
step. The projected quantiles are then interpolated to obtain a smooth distribution using a method akin to the one employed by Adrian et al. (2019) in the
"growth-at-risk model".

Based on data available at the end of 2018 the approach finds significant
estimates of the fiscal cost. The expected average fiscal cost is within a range
of 5–30 per cent of GDP for AEs, with a cross-country average of 20 per cent.
The range is similar for EMDEs, although the cross-country average is lower.
At the tail of the distribution, the fiscal losses can be substantial. On average
across advanced economies, the 95th quantile is about 38 per cent of GDP and
the 99th quantile exceeds 40 per cent.

Comparing estimates of these fiscal costs with typical estimates of fiscal space for OECD countries (e.g. Fournier and Fall, 2017; Fournier and Bétin, 2018) suggests that the available space should be sufficient to absorb the cost of the crisis for most, but not all, economies in our sample. However, these measures of fiscal space are likely to overstate the true amount of space available as they do not consider several sources of uncertainty. In the case of EMDEs, considering the calculations of, for instance, Ganiko et al. (2016), which account for various sources of uncertainty, fiscal sustainability in a number of countries looks vulnerable in the case of serious financial stress.

One important caveat to the above estimates of fiscal cost is that they probably do not capture the full benefits of the post-GFC financial reforms. These have not just raised bank capital, but also improved its quality and robustness, introduced liquidity standards, implemented macroprudential frameworks, and put in place specific arrangements to ensure the orderly resolution of systemically important banks (Borio et al., 2020b). Moreover, large estimates of the *ex ante* fiscal cost do not imply that the best solution is necessarily or exclusively of a fiscal nature: prudential regulation is always an essential part of the solution (see also below).

9.3.2   Cyclical Adjustments

Once policymakers have decided on the optimal size of fiscal space to use as a buffer, the key challenge is to prevent that the fiscal space is eroded inadvertently over time. Indeed, fiscal positions fluctuate cyclically with the state of the business cycle, but should remain constant over time to avoid a dangerous drift.

While measuring cyclically adjusted fiscal positions is generally difficult, a major limitation of standard approaches is that they fail to take properly into account the flattering impact of financial booms – a typical source of subsequent recessions and outright banking crises (e.g. Borio and Drehmann, 2009; Schularick and Taylor, 2012). During such booms, estimates of potential output and potential growth will tend to be skewed upwards, raising the share of any increase in the fiscal balance that is deemed permanent. Compositional effects, especially those reflecting unsustainable rises in asset prices, may boost revenues further. Asset price booms, in turn, will affect transaction volumes and similar metrics, raising tax revenues for any given level of asset prices.

The recent experience of Spain and Ireland is quite telling. In both cases, government debt-to-GDP ratios were falling before the crisis and as events unfolded (i.e. in real time) measures of cyclically adjusted fiscal positions pointed to surpluses. However, once the crises erupted, and measures were re-estimated following the standard methods, it turned out that countries had been running cyclically adjusted deficits during the boom. Their (unobservable) potential output had been overestimated. History, as it were, had been rewritten.

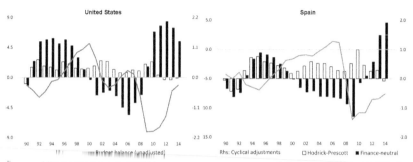

Source: OECD; Borio et al. (2017b).

Figure 9.2   Cyclically adjusted fiscal balances (real time)

Borio et al. (2017a) developed a method designed to capture the flattering impact of financial booms on the output gap in real time – so-called "finance-neutral" measures. The method is an improvement over standard ones, such as production function approaches or those based on filtering methods that use information on inflation rather than the financial cycle. The main reason is that proxies for the financial cycle, including the behaviour of credit and property prices, contain useful information about output fluctuations at typical frequencies. Furthermore, unlike conventional measures, finance-neutral measures of the output gap obtained in real time tend to be quite close to those based on *ex post* data. The output gap measure thus obtained is then used to adjust the fiscal balance (see Borio et al., 2017b).

The comparison between different measures of the cyclically adjusted fiscal balances is striking (Figure 9.2). In the boom that preceded the GFC, the fiscal balances adjusted according to standard measures of the output gap (white bars) indicated a surplus, while the fiscal balances adjusted using the finance-neutral output gap (black bars) indicated a deficit.

Admittedly, such a finance-neutral measure of the fiscal balance does not incorporate all the channels through which fiscal strength may be overestimated. Further research could seek to incorporate factors such as the compositional effects or the build-up of implicit liabilities. But it does represent an improvement, which could be included in a richer and more granular assessment.[7]

9.3.3   Reducing the Debt Bias in the Tax System

In most countries, tax systems favour debt over equity. In the household sector, several countries allow tax relief on mortgage interest payments. Similarly, in the corporate sector, income taxes generally allow interest payments to be deducted when determining taxable profits, whereas the return-on-equity, either through dividends or capital gains, is typically not deductible. Removing, or at least reducing, the debt bias in taxation would lower leverage significantly. This, in turn, would lower the probability and cost of a banking crisis.

The "debt bias" is well documented for the corporate sector. Across countries, financial and non-financial firms tend to have higher leverage where effective tax rates on corporate income are higher. And meta-analysis of studies that control for confounding factors finds consistent results (e.g. Feld et al., 2013). Country-specific studies of changes in the tax code have also reached similar conclusions. A case in point is Belgium in 2006, when the tax law was changed to enable firms to deduct a notional interest expense from their return-on-equity. Following the change, banks reduced leverage and increased the share of lower risk private-sector loans at the expense of government securities. They also managed their risks more conservatively, as weakly capitalized banks directed new lending to firms with lower default probabilities (Schepens, 2016). Likewise, similar effects are visible in countries that introduced so-called "thin capitalization rules", which allow deductibility only up to a certain threshold of debt or interest (De Mooij and Hebous, 2018).

9.4   FINANCIAL REGULATION OF SOVEREIGN EXPOSURES

The financial sector is highly exposed to sovereign risk, both directly and indirectly. While not a substitute for fiscal prudence, prudential regulation and supervision can help protect both the financial system and the sovereign. The treatment of bank exposures is critical in this context: it needs to adequately safeguard banks' resilience for sovereign stress while also reflecting the pervasive role played by government bonds across financial markets.[8]

In the Basel prudential framework, sovereign exposures are treated more favourably than other asset classes (BCBS, 2017). For example, national supervisors have the discretion to apply a preferential risk weight to domestic sovereign debt. In practice, all Basel Committee member jurisdictions exercise this discretion and apply a zero per cent risk weight. Domestic sovereign debt also enjoys a preferential treatment in other parts of the risk-weighted capital and liquidity standards, while all sovereign exposures are exempted from the large exposures framework.

Conceptually, the case for such a favourable treatment of sovereign exposures is debatable. First, sovereign claims do carry credit risk: sovereigns
default, even on their domestic currency debt. This is recognized in credit
ratings (e.g. Amstad et al., 2020). The fact that defaults have been extremely
rare in advanced economies might not be a good guide for the future. And,
even short of default, changing perceptions of fiscal risks and associated
changes in asset values and funding conditions can hurt banks. Second, sovereign exposures are subject to market risk. In fact, the perceived market risk of
sovereign bonds is in part shaped by market participants' view on the ability
of the sovereign to issue more of its own currency in a sustainable manner and
to avoid default.

Eliminating the present favourable treatment of sovereign exposures would
have several benefits. *Ex ante*, it would discourage the build-up of large bank
exposures in domestic sovereign bonds and provide an important signal that no
asset class is risk free. This would limit banks' incentive to undertake regulatory capital arbitrage by shifting their investment towards higher yielding but
zero risk-weighted assets. And it would limit the incentive of troubled banks to
"gamble for resurrection" by loading up on riskier government bonds.

Ex post, it would make banks better capitalized and better able to withstand
sovereign distress. Thus, better risk management would also lead to greater
macroeconomic resilience, not least by attenuating the "doom loop". This
could ultimately translate into lower long-term funding costs for both banks
and governments.

Several arguments have been proposed to support the current treatment.
Upon closer examination, however, none appears to be sufficiently strong to
rule out regulatory changes.

One argument is tighter regulation could reduce the liquidity of the bonds
and the markets that depend on them for collateral. Government bonds are
typically the most liquid asset available; and in economies with less developed
financial systems often the only liquid domestic asset available. By the same
token, it might also complicate monetary policy implementation. These effects
can arise, but it is easy to overstate their impact. Recent studies (BCBS, 2021;
FSB, 2022) have found that prudential regulation is not a primary driver of
bank dealer behaviour and of market dislocations. Moreover, if banks become
more resilient, so that market stress becomes less likely in the first place,
market liquidity should become more robust – reduce the risk that it is just
a fair-weather phenomenon.

A second, closely related, argument is that prudential regulation could
constrain banks' demand for government debt in times of stress, or limit their
role as contrarian buyers when market moves are excessive, such as when
self-fulfilling elements are involved. But this need not be the case. In fact,
having *ex ante* capital requirements for sovereign exposures should make

banks more resilient in stress and more capable to act as a stabilizing force if needed. And in cases where banks comprise the dominant investor base for sovereign exposures, more structural measures should be the first line of defence. This means, in particular, establishing deeper and broader capital markets with a diverse set of investors (BIS, 2019).[9]

While these arguments point to a clear direction of travel, the devil is in the detail, as is often the case. Any change to the current treatment of sovereign exposures would have to address a number of difficult issues. It is worth at least listing them to provide a sense of the technical challenges involved.

The first issue is how exactly to define sovereign exposures. For example, to what extent do central government and central bank exposures differ in their risk profile? How should subnational government entities and public-sector entities be treated? And how should the regulatory perimeter for the universe of sovereign exposures be defined to avoid any leaks? Balancing risk sensitivity with simplicity is an important consideration when it comes to definitional issues.

The second issue is how to measure sovereign risk. Internal models may be insufficiently robust owing to the limitations of historical data, especially among advanced economies. Credit ratings summarize a large amount of information and are designed to be forward-looking. Yet they also tend to change infrequently and abruptly, as rating agencies seek to avoid ratings volatility. Alternative measures could be based on market indicators such as CDS spreads, which are readily available and easy to translate into default probabilities. However, these are more procyclical and volatile than credit ratings. This leaves more standard non-market metrics such as debt-to-GDP ratios and other indicators of fiscal sustainability or country risk. Still, the translation of these indicators into risk weights is inevitably sensitive to modelling assumptions.

The third issue is what regulatory instruments to use: risk weights, large exposure limits or a combination of the two? Higher risk weights raise the required capital on each unit of investment in sovereign bonds, aiming to ensure that banks are sufficiently capitalized to withstand eventual losses. Large exposure limits constrain risk concentration more directly. Soft limits – increasing risk weights based on a bank's concentration of sovereign exposures – are also possible. For instance, an increasing capital charge may be imposed for exposures above the limit or for step-wise thresholds.

The fourth issue concerns the consistency of credit risk regulation with the treatment of other risks. For example, government securities eligible to meet liquidity requirements should be held in the trading book, on account of the market-related risks that they present. Similarly, sovereign debt held in the banking book should also be capitalized against interest rate risk.

The final issue is how to handle the transition to any new sovereign risk requirement. Positive risk weights and/or exposure limits may require banks to adjust their balance sheets. The transition to any new treatment would have to be gradual to avoid any adverse impact.

More generally, the calibration of any regulatory requirements for sovereign exposures will need to tread a careful balancing act. The clear benefits from such prudential safeguards should be weighed against the broader role played by sovereign debt, including for monetary policy implementation and the smooth functioning of financial markets.

9.5   CONCLUSION

The GFC triggered major policy efforts to strengthen financial regulation and supervision. However, the link between fiscal policy and financial stability has attracted less attention. Such a link is critical in the design of macro-financial stability frameworks aimed at delivering lasting macroecnomic and financial stability (Borio et al., 2023b; BIS, 2022)

To reduce the amplification of risk, we have highlighted a number of policy directions.

First, policymakers should build adequate fiscal buffers. This means having fiscal space proportionate to the size and features of the financial system. This would instil confidence in the strength of the financial sector and allow the sovereign to act as an effective backstop in case of need. Critically, building adequate buffers also means striving to improve the measurement of fiscal positions over the financial cycle. This would address an important factor behind the (involuntary) erosion of fiscal buffers in good times. We have indicated practical ways to meet these two challenges – measuring fiscal space and financial-cycle adjusted fiscal positions – although clearly more work is needed to make them fully operational.

Second, policymakers should continue to make progress towards reducing the favourable tax treatment of debt over equity. Several countries have introduced such measures, but there is still scope to reduce this debt bias further.

Third, in prudential regulation, a lot has been done to improve bank resilience to episodes of stress (Borio et al., 2020b). But more should be done to assure that regulation better reflects banks' sovereign risk exposures. This greater risk sensitivity would need to be calibrated in light of the special role of sovereign debt in the financial system – as a source of liquidity and a potential buffer for the macroeconomy.

Finally, the evolving landscape of finance implies new challenges. In particular, much more focus should be given to the sovereign linkages with non-bank financial intermediation (NBFI). NBFI now accounts for almost half of total financial assets. As witnessed over the past few years, episodes of NBFI market dislocations could trigger sovereign support, which could exacerbate moral hazard and increase fiscal pressure. Similarly, gyrations in sovereign debt markets have tested the resilience of NBFI entities. While global efforts are underway to address NBFI vulnerabilities, these have so far been insufficient (Carstens, 2021). Looking forward, it will be important to recognize the role of NBFI in the broader nexus between fiscal policy and financial stability.

ACKNOWLEDGEMENTS

This chapter draws partly on Chapter V of the BIS 86th Annual Report entitled "Towards a financial stability-oriented fiscal policy" (BIS, 2016), and Borio et al. (2023a). The views expressed in this paper are those of the authors and not necessarily those of the BIS. The authors thank Dietrich Domanski and Ingo Fender for close co-operation and Enrique Alberola, Fernando Avalos and Aitor Erce for insightful comments. Berenice Martinez provided excellent research assistance.

NOTES

1. Henceforth we use the terms government and sovereign interchangeably. We sometimes use the term "banks" as a shorthand for the financial sector as a whole.
2. Approximating these costs with changes in public debt over a sufficiently long horizon allows us to account for a large share of any recovery rates and any reversal in fiscal stimulus. See also Note 5 below.
3. Sovereign credit events may come in different forms (BCBS, 2017): missed payments, debt restructuring or outright defaults, currency redenomination (or the risk thereof), loss from unanticipated inflation owing to sovereign distress, debt monetization and/or sharp currency devaluations, and fluctuations in the value of sovereign exposures resulting from non-default events such as sovereign downgrades or market stress. Defaults may also involve domestic debt, especially when inflation is high (Reinhart and Rogoff, 2011).
4. Country- and bank-level data show that this effect holds for a large set of countries, including EMDEs (Gennaioli et al., 2014, 2018). There are numerous studies that confirm the relevance of sovereign exposures – see the references cited in Borio et al. (2023a).
5. Estimates of the direct bail-out fiscal costs may not consider recovery rates, but after a few years any recovery would be recorded as a reduction in the debt stock, other things equal. Besides, any initial discretionary fiscal stimulus may be subsequently reversed, at least partly.
6. See also Amaglobeli et al. (2017).
7. As a complement, for countries that rely heavily on commodity exports, it may be useful to make a cyclical correction of fiscal balances using information about commodity prices (e.g. Alberola et al., 2017).
8. A related issue is how to deal with interest rate risk linked to sovereign exposures. See Borio et al. (2023a) for a discussion.

9.   A third argument is of a different nature: the post-GFC reforms aimed at ending too big to fail (TBTF), such as better resolution regimes, mean that banks are less likely to be a source of stress for sovereign finances. This weakens the case for changing the current treatment of exposures. True, great strides have been made by such reforms, but there are still gaps that need to be addressed in order to truly end TBTF (FSB, 2021). More generally, better regulation in some dimensions is not a good argument for refraining from improving it in others, where possible.

REFERENCES

Adrian, T., N. Boyarchenko and D. Giannone (2019), "Vulnerable growth", *American Economic Review*, 109(4).
Alberola, E., R. Gondo, M. J. Lombardi and D. Urbina (2017), "Output gaps and policy stabilisation in Latin America: The effect of commodity and capital flow cycles", *Ensayos sobre Política Económica*, 35.
Amaglobeli, D., N. End, M. Jarmuzek and G. Palomba (2017), "The fiscal costs of systemic banking crises", *International Finance*, 20.
Amstad, M., F. Packer and J. Shek (2020), "Does sovereign risk in local and foreign currency differ?", *Journal of International Money and Finance*, 101.
Bank for International Settlements (2016), "Towards a financial stability-oriented fiscal policy", *Bank for International Settlements 86th Annual Report*, Chapter V.
Bank for International Settlements (2019), "Establishing viable capital markets", *CGFS Papers*, 62, January.
Bank for International Settlements (2022), "Macro-financial stability frameworks and external financial conditions", Report submitted to the G20 Finance Ministers and Central Bank Governors, *BIS Other*, July.
Basel Committee on Banking Supervision (BCBS) (2017), "The regulatory treatment of sovereign exposures", December.
Basel Committee on Banking Supervision (BCBS) (2021), "Early lessons from the Covid-19 pandemic on the Basel reforms", *BIS* Implementation reports July.
Bordo, M. and C. Meissner (2016), "Fiscal and financial crises". In *Handbook of Macroeconomics*, Vol. 2, Ch. 7.
Borio, C. and M. Drehmann (2009), "Assessing the risk of banking crises – revisited", *BIS Quarterly Review*, March.
Borio, C., P. Disyatat and M. Juselius (2017a), "Rethinking potential output: Embedding information about the financial cycle", *Oxford Economic Papers*, 69(3).
Borio, C., M. Lombardi and F. Zampolli (2017b), "Fiscal sustainability and the financial cycle". In L. Odor (ed.), *Rethinking Fiscal Policy After the Crisis*, Cambridge University Press.
Borio, C., J. Contreras and F. Zampolli (2020a), "Assessing the fiscal implications of banking crises", *BIS* Working Papers, 893.
Borio, C., M. Farag and N. Tarashev (2020b), "Post-crisis international financial regulatory reforms: A primer", *BIS* Working Papers, 859.
Borio, C., M. Farag and F. Zampolli (2023a), "Tackling the fiscal policy–financial stability nexus", *BIS* Working Papers, 1090.
Borio, C., I. Shim and H. S. Shin (2023b), "Macro-financial stability frameworks: Experience and challenges". In C. Borio, E. Robinson and H. S. Shin (eds), *Macro-Financial Stability Policy in a Globalised World* (Ch. 1), World Scientific Publishing Company.

Bova, E., M. Ruiz-Arranz, F. Toscani and H. Ture (2016), "The fiscal costs of contingent liabilities: A new dataset", *IMF* Working Papers, 16/14.

Carstens, A. (2021), "Non-bank financial sector: Systemic regulation needed", *BIS Quarterly Review*, December.

Committee on the Global Financial System (2011), "The impact of sovereign credit risk on bank funding conditions", *CGFS* Papers, 43, July.

De Mooij, R. and S. Hebous (2018), "Curbing corporate debt bias: Do limitations to interest deductibility work?", *Journal of Banking and Finance*, 96.

Feld, L., J. Heckemeyer and M. Overesch (2013), "Capital structure choice and company taxation: A meta-study", *Journal of Banking and Finance*, 37.

Financial Stability Board (2021), "Evaluation of the effects of too-big-to-fail reforms: Final report", *Financial Stability Board*, March.

Financial Stability Board (2022), "Liquidity in core government bond markets", *Financial Stability Board*, October.

Fournier, J.-M. and M. Bétin (2018), "Limits to government debt sustainability in middle-income countries", *OEDC Economics Department* Working Papers, 1493.

Fournier, J.-M. and F. Fall (2017), "Limits to government debt sustainability in OECD economies", *Economic Modelling*, 66.

Ganiko, G., K. Melgarejo and C. Montoro (2016), "How much is too much? The fiscal space in emerging market economies", *Banco Central de Reserva del Perú*, Working Paper 002-2016, November.

Gennaioli, N., A. Martin and S. Rossi (2014), "Sovereign default, domestic banks and financial institutions", *Journal of Finance*, 69.

Gennaioli, N., A. Martin and S. Rossi (2018), "Banks, government bonds and default: What do the data say?", *Journal of Monetary Economics*, 98.

International Monetary Fund (2022), "The sovereign–bank nexus in emerging markets: A risky embrace", *Global Financial Stability Report*, Ch. 2, April. IMF.

Laeven, L. and F. Valencia (2013), "Systemic banking crises database", *IMF Economic Review*, 61.

Laeven, L. and F. Valencia (2018), "Systemic banking crises revisited", *IMF* Working Papers, 18/206.

Reinhart, C. and K. Rogoff (2011), "The forgotten history of domestic debt", *Economic Journal*, 121.

Schepens, G. (2016), "Taxes and bank capital structure", *Journal of Financial Economics*, 120.

Schularick, M. and A. M. Taylor (2012), "Credit booms gone bust: Monetary policy, leverage cycles, and financial crises, 1870–2008", *American Economic Review*, 102.

PART III

Uses of fiscal policy: redistribution, allocation
and emerging demands

10. Fiscal policy and income redistribution in the turbulent era

Benedict Clements, Sanjeev Gupta and João Tovar Jalles

10.1 INTRODUCTION

A substantial body of research in recent years has underscored the adverse effects of inequality on the economy and society, which has sharpened interest in how fiscal policy can be used to dampen (at least partially) these effects. This is because fiscal policy is the government's most powerful tool to achieve distributional objectives in both the short and the long term. This expanding literature shows that income inequality has negative consequences for economic growth and its longer-term sustainability (Ostry et al., 2014; Berg and Ostry, 2017). A rising income share of the top income group lowers GDP growth in the following five years (Dabla-Norris et al., 2015), which has implications for the pace at which growth reduces poverty.

These concerns are of even greater importance going forward as high income inequality affects social cohesion and makes it difficult to gain broad political support for growth-enhancing structural reforms (Duval et al., 2021). This may even prompt governments to adopt populist policies, threatening economic and political stability.

This chapter is organized as follows. In Section 10.2, we discuss trends in income distribution in recent years, both globally and within countries. The section highlights the inequality in wealth, which tends to be larger than income inequality. It also presents evidence on the impact of COVID-19 on income inequality. In the subsequent section, we discuss the channels through which fiscal policy affects income inequality and the relative effectiveness of fiscal instruments in addressing distributive concerns in advanced (AEs) and emerging and developing economies (EMDEs). Section 10.4 highlights the consequences of fiscal tightening on income distribution. In the concluding section, an agenda for reforming taxation and spending to achieve better redistribution in turbulent times is presented.

10.2   TRENDS IN INEQUALITY

On a global level, inequality has been declining, given the faster economic growth of EMDEs, especially in developing Asia. Figure 10.1 displays the Gini index, the main gauge to measure inequality. A Gini index of zero would imply that income would be evenly spread among the population. Within countries, median market income inequality (reflecting household income from wage and non-wage sources before taxes) has been rising in AEs, on average. In contrast, it has fallen somewhat in EMDEs, although the trend has changed in recent years.

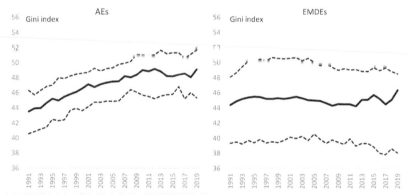

Note: The market Gini index is before government tax and transfers. Interquartile range of Gini coefficients; median (solid line), top and bottom quartiles (dashed lines) or respective distributions. Data cover 32 advanced (AEs) and 66 emerging and developing economies (EMDEs).
Source: Authors' computations based on Solt's (2009) Standardized World Income Inequality Database (SWIID).

Figure 10.1   Income inequality: market Gini in AEs and EMDEs

Household wealth is much more unequally distributed than income (Clements et al., 2015). The main reason is that high-income individuals have higher saving rates and thus they accumulate wealth faster than do poorer households. Differences in risk tolerance – which is higher among rich individuals – prevailing tax systems, and the share of private pensions also explain differences in wealth accumulation across countries. What is worrisome is that wealth inequality has risen since 2000 in most advanced and developing countries, reversing a declining trend from the end of the Second World War until the 1970s (Piketty, 2014). Figure 10.2 shows trends in wealth Gini between 2000 and 2020 in selected countries. Germany is the only country in this sample where wealth inequality has declined somewhat since 2000.

Preliminary evidence indicates a worsening of inequality since the COVID pandemic, due to sharp declines in output and increased poverty, especially in the developing world (Blofield et al., 2021). The design and coverage of social assistance programs in certain countries in Latin America was targeted to protect low-income groups, leaving middle-income ones out of the safety net. In other parts of the developing world – such as sub-Saharan Africa – all income classes were equally impacted by the pandemic. The pandemic has had significant adverse effects on school attendance of low-income students (IMF, 2021), which portends further increases in inequality (of income and opportunities) in the future.

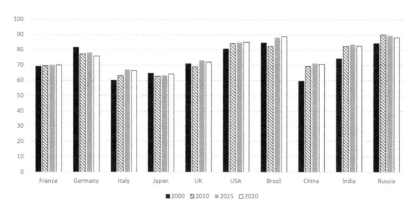

Source: Credit Suisse Global Wealth Databook (2021).

Figure 10.2   Wealth Gini in selected countries, 2000–2020

10.3   THE REDISTRIBUTIVE ROLE OF FISCAL POLICY

Fiscal policy affects inequality through its effects on direct taxes and income transfers, as well as in-kind benefits such as education and health care. These in-kind benefits strengthen an individual's ability to earn higher market income, including through social mobility, thereby also impacting economic growth.

One way to measure the redistributive effect of fiscal policy is by examining the difference between the household market income before taxes, as defined above, and the income they have left after paying income and property taxes and receiving government transfer payments ("disposable" income). From this

Table 10.1   *Redistributive effects of fiscal policy in AEs and EMDEs, 1990 vs 2019*

	Gini disposable		Gini market		Absolute redistribution (market – disposable)	
	1990	*2019*	*1990*	*2019*	*1990*	*2019*
AEs (#32)	28.8	29.8	43.1	48.1	14.3	18.3
EMDEs (#66)	41.1	39.9	44.4	43.9	3.3	4.0

Note: Figures refer to mean Gini coefficients.
Source: Authors' computations based on Solt's (2009) SWIID.

perspective, AEs undertake much more fiscal redistribution than in EMDEs (Table 10.1). Fiscal redistribution through this channel reduces inequality by about a third, much more than in EMDEs. Most of this reduction is achieved through transfers, which account for about three quarters of the decrease in the Gini (Gupta, 2018). Within transfers, public pensions and family benefits account for the bulk of the redistribution. Unemployment benefits are included in this category and also play a role in buffering the distributional effects of the business cycle (see Chapter 11). On the tax side, personal income taxes make an important contribution to reducing inequality in AEs; the redistribution achieved through income taxes is higher than that achieved through means-tested transfers, in countries such as Belgium, Finland, Greece, Italy and the Netherlands. As explained in Chapter 11, the redistributive role of fiscal policy in AEs diminished in the pre-pandemic era because of the combination of increasing market income inequality and decreasing progressivity of personal income taxes, reflecting inadequate reforms of the tax system (Granger et al., 2022). In addition, the cash transfer system in the OECD countries had become less progressive over time (Causa and Hermansen, 2017).

The low degree of redistribution outside AEs reflects several factors. First, a small share of revenues in emerging and developing countries comes from personal income and property taxes (Figure 10.3, left panel), which are more progressive than indirect taxes (Abdel-Kader and de Mooij, 2022). Second, lower revenues (as a share of GDP) in EMDEs leave fewer fiscal resources for public spending. As a result, expenditures as a share of GDP in EMDEs countries are lower, most notably on social protection (pensions and social assistance). The present-day AEs also had low tax-to-GDP ratios in the early 1900s. It was only when they instituted taxes (including on income and inheritance) that they were able to engage in redistribution during 1914–1980 – a period that Piketty (2022) labels as the "Great Redistribution". Third, pension systems in EMDEs benefit a small share of the poor population, given the high degree of labor market informality that effectively excludes them from paying contributions and receiving benefits from these systems. Fourth, there is imperfect coverage of social assistance for lower-income households. In developing Asia, for example, less than half of households from the poorest 20 percent of the population receive assistance, while in Latin America, about two-thirds are covered (Clements et al., 2022). Finally, a substantial share of benefits accrues to the non-poor, blunting the potential redistributive effect of social assistance. In developing Asia, for example, the poorest 20 percent of the population receives about 10 percent of social assistance payments, and in Latin America, they receive just 5.5 percent (Clements et al., 2022).

Governments in EMDEs can influence income distribution through indirect taxes (such as the value added tax, VAT) and subsidies (such as those for energy). The net effect of indirect taxes and subsidies on distribution is about zero, reflecting the offsetting effect of policies that increase inequality (such as energy subsidies, that favor upper-income groups) and other subsidies and indirect taxes that reduce inequality (Granger et al., 2022). Indirect taxes have a less progressive incidence than direct taxes, given that low- and middle-income groups consume a higher share of their incomes. The incidence of different indirect taxes, however, varies both between AEs and other countries and by tax. In EMDEs, the incidence of import duties varies, depending on the composition of imports and differences in the consumption basket between low- and high-income groups. Reductions in trade taxes for luxury products, for example, can increase inequality. In OECD countries, excise taxes on alcohol, tobacco, and energy have a regressive incidence (OECD, 2014), while in EMDEs the picture is mixed.

The distributive incidence of the VAT has generated considerable controversy. In AEs, the VAT is a regressive tax as it is applied to a broad base of consumption, including products consumed by the lower- and middle-income classes. In EMDEs, however, the evidence is less conclusive. Because small traders in agriculture and the informal sector are often outside the tax system (because they are too small to file or too difficult to tax), the VAT does not affect the prices they charge for their products. Because the poor purchase a significant share of their total consumption from these sellers, the VAT may not have a regressive incidence (Jenkins et al., 2006; Bachas et al., 2021). The overall progressivity of the fiscal system can be improved if revenues from consumption taxes are used to finance pro-poor spending. Thus, any analysis of the incidence of consumption taxes should be combined with the incidence of the spending that taxes finance.

Many EMDEs have been implementing tax reforms, but their impact on income distribution has not been universally positive across all countries (Gupta and Jalles, 2022). In these countries, the tax reforms that have the most favorable impact on income distribution are those involving the personal income tax and revenue administration. However, the implementation of such reforms did not improve income distribution in sub-Saharan Africa (and

fragile states in particular). In fact, personal income tax reforms worsened the
distribution of income, reflecting their poor design.

Government spending on health and education (Figure 10.3, right panel)
results in significant redistribution in AEs, but less so in other country groups.
In AEs, health and education outlays reduce the Gini by 0.05 (when measured
on a scale from 0 to 1), reflecting the more intensive use of these services by
lower- and middle-income segments of the population than upper-income
groups. In other country groups, the smaller effect reflects lower levels of
spending and the fact that in many countries, a sizeable share of this spending
is for services that benefit higher-income households (for example, outlays for
tertiary education and curative health). For example, such in-kind spending
lowers Gini by an average of 0.03 in EMDEs, with the smallest effect in
low-income countries (Granger et al., 2022).

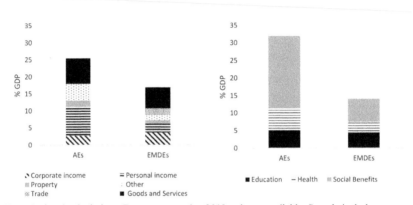

Note: Authors' calculations. Data correspond to 2019 or latest available. Sample includes
a maximum of 35 advanced (AEs) and 68 emerging and developing countries (EMDEs).
Source: World Bank, United Nations WIDER Government Revenue Dataset (November 2022),
IMF World Economic Outlook dataset.

Figure 10.3   Average taxes and spending in AEs and EMDEs

Fiscal policy became more redistributive in AEs during the pandemic,
although in many cases this is the result of temporary measures launched
during this period. Simulations for the European Union suggest that tax and
benefit systems (including new measures) offset 75 percent of income losses
from the pandemic, compared with 40 percent in the pre-pandemic era (IMF,
2022b). In the United States, the temporary expansion of income support was
large and progressive (Ganong et al., 2022). EMDEs also expanded transfers
and the coverage of social assistance to poor households during the pandemic,

but much more modestly than AEs, owing to limited fiscal space and less developed social safety nets (IMF, 2022b).

In response to rising food and fuel prices in the wake of the war in Ukraine, both advanced and developing countries have increased subsidies and reduced indirect taxes for these products. In most countries, announced measures (including additional cash transfers) have been costly (averaging more than a half point of GDP) and not well targeted to low-income groups (Amaglobeli et al., 2022; IMF, 2022b). As such, it is unlikely that this support has altered the redistributive effect of fiscal policy. As noted above, the impact of indirect taxes and subsidies on income inequality in developing countries is zero.

It is important to note that policies that reduce inequality (such as cuts in energy subsidies) may, in the short run, reduce the real incomes of households that are at or below the poverty level. In most cases, however, appropriate policy design can help avoid such a tradeoff between goals for inequality and poverty reduction by including compensatory measures for low-income groups that are adversely affected by reforms (see, for example, Banerji et al., 2017). In cases where adequate compensatory measures cannot be implemented in the near term, a more gradual reform of redistribution policies can attenuate this tradeoff. Over the longer term, there is no tradeoff between goals for redistribution and poverty reduction, provided that (1) governments can relocate government spending to progressive programs where the poor capture a sizeable share of benefits; (2) social benefit programs are designed to avoid adverse effects on labor market participation (thus avoiding harmful effects on growth and the pace of poverty reduction); (3) spending on health and education reaches the poor and helps build their human capital and productivity; and (4) redistributive policies are consistent with fiscal sustainability (Clements et al., 2015).

10.4   FISCAL CONSOLIDATIONS AND INEQUALITY

COVID-19 has led to the largest one-year increase in public debt since the Second World War, in 2020, although a massive debt build-up had been underway for a decade (Estevão and Essl, 2022, and Chapter 2). In the coming years, most economies will need to bring their fiscal house in order by reducing some of the spending instituted during the era of low interest rates. More worrisome, 60 percent of the world's poorest countries are currently in debt distress or at elevated risk of it, and some emerging market countries are considered at high risk as well.

There is considerable literature on the distributional effects of fiscal retrenchment. Fiscal retrenchment can exacerbate high and rising income and wealth disparities, with adverse consequences for long-term economic growth. There are two principal channels through which fiscal consolidation affects inequality: first, it may directly reduce spending for fiscal redistribution and increase regressive taxes, such as value added and excise taxes; second, inequality is affected through several indirect channels induced by the consolidation. These channels are a priori uncertain and difficult to pinpoint because the same policy instrument can induce different behavioral responses by economic agents, particularly in the context of labor supply decisions. Employers may hoard high-skilled workers, who usually have higher income levels, which could raise inequality at times of fiscal restraint. Fiscal consolidation can worsen inequality by increasing unemployment, thereby decreasing the wage share of national income. Empirical studies suggest that fiscal consolidation worsens income inequality (Agnello and Sousa, 2014; Woo et al., 2017).

An important aspect of fiscal consolidation is its composition. Fiscal consolidation can be tax-based and/or spending-based, where the former is defined as having tax increases larger than spending cuts, and vice versa for spending-based consolidations. Tax-based consolidations produce deeper and longer recessions than spending-based ones (Alesina et al., 2015). But existing evidence suggests that spending-based consolidations increase income inequality, while there is no consensus on the distributional impact of tax-based fiscal adjustments. The inclusion of certain fiscal measures (such as increased spending on social benefits and more progressive taxation) in the consolidation package can mitigate the impact of fiscal adjustment on income distribution. Indeed, this approach was followed by European adjustments in the aftermath of the global financial crisis (Fabrizio and Flamini in Clements et al., 2015).

10.5 AN AGENDA FOR REFORMING TAXATION AND SPENDING TO ACHIEVE BETTER REDISTRIBUTION

High levels of public debt and rising debt service costs will necessitate fiscal adjustment in both advanced and developing countries in the coming years. The fiscal challenge facing policymakers is acute considering new demands for military spending in response to the war in Ukraine (Clements and Gupta, 2022) and the transition to a green economy (see Chapter 13). The elevated levels of food and energy prices have led to demands to cut taxes on these products or subsidize them (IMF, 2022a). Over the longer term, projected increases in age-related spending (health and pensions) will put pressure on government budgets, as explained in Chapter 12. Thus, there is little room for higher levels of spending to achieve goals for redistribution, unless matched by cuts in other outlays or, in developing countries, increases in tax revenues. Nevertheless, there is scope to make government spending better support redistribution goals by changing its composition. There is also room in many countries to change the composition of taxation to make it more progressive.

For advanced economies, there is little scope to raise the overall tax effort, given its already elevated level. There are several reform options, however, to improve the tax composition. In this context, increases in more progressive taxes could be used to reduce the burden of other taxes that have more adverse effects on efficiency, such as taxes on labor income. These reform options include:

- *Raising top marginal rates for the personal income tax in countries where they are low.* The revenue maximizing rate (which considers the effect of higher tax rates on labor supply) is estimated at about 50–60 percent (IMF, 2013).
- *Reducing tax exemptions for income taxes.* They often favor upper-income groups and make the tax system less efficient.
- *Implementing the recently, globally agreed minimum corporate tax rate.* This can help safeguard these revenues and reduce the incentives for tax competition between countries.
- *Introducing or increasing taxes on net wealth.* These are useful when other capital incomes are difficult to tax. Recent increases in the wealth of high-income groups – since the onset of the COVID pandemic – have made this alternative more attractive with substantial potential for revenues (Chancel et al., 2021).
- *Raising property taxes.* These taxes are progressive and more efficient than other forms of taxing capital.
- *Instituting an appropriate carbon tax to incentivize the transition to cleaner energy.* This could generate substantial revenues (about 1–2 percent of GDP, on average) in G20 countries (Black et al., 2021), which could be used to finance reductions in labor taxes or finance progressive expenditures, including those needed to protect low-income groups adversely affected by higher energy costs.

With respect to *expenditures*, more efficient redistribution will involve improving the quality of public services that focus on ensuring greater equality of opportunity. This will entail the following:

- *Improving the quality of public education spending available for low-income households.* Considering the adverse effects of the pandemic on learning in poor households – which have less access to virtual learning tools – special attention needs to be paid to helping these students catch up (Agostinelli et al., 2022).
- *Improving the quality of public health services and making these services more accessible for low-income households.*

- *Raising social assistance payments to levels needed to eliminate poverty.*
  To avoid adverse effects on labor supply, benefits can be tied to work
  requirements and benefits phased out gradually as labor income rises.

Emerging and developing economies, unlike AEs, will need to raise revenues
as a share of GDP to finance higher levels of spending while making progress
on fiscal consolidation. The potential for raising additional revenues in developing countries is estimated at between 3 and 4 percent of GDP on average
(Gupta and Jalles, 2022). All revenue reforms for AEs are relevant for EMDEs,
although the administrative capacity to implement some of these (such as net
wealth and property taxes) could limit their feasibility. Additional priorities for
tax reform in EMDEs include:

- *Adjusting the threshold for the personal income tax.* In some countries,
  a relatively small number of workers pay income tax because the threshold
  is set high. It could be adjusted to the average wage (Abdol Kader and de
  Mooij, 2022).
- *Reducing exemptions and special tax rates for the VAT.* The revenues lost
  to these tax expenditures are considerable (Gupta and Jalles, 2023). In
  some cases, the exemptions are given for products consumed heavily by
  the poor, including food. In many countries, however, these exemptions
  have not reduced inequality, given the high levels of consumption of these
  products by middle- and upper-income groups (Granger et al., 2022). Even
  if the application of VAT to some exempted products makes the tax more
  regressive, this can be offset by raising pro-poor spending.
- *Setting an appropriately high threshold for the VAT.* One way to make
  the VAT more progressive is to establish a higher minimum threshold
  for filing. This will exclude many small sellers from the system and ease
  administration of the VAT.
- *Strengthening tax compliance and minimizing tax evasion.* In many countries, actual revenue collection is below tax potential because of poor tax
  compliance.

On the *expenditure* side, developing countries face an acute challenge from
weak global demand and economic growth, which will limit the growth of tax
revenues and their capacity to fund higher levels of spending while making
progress on restoring fiscal sustainability. The COVID-19 pandemic has also
left a legacy of increased poverty and greater inequality. In this context, some
priority reforms are:

- *Expanding coverage of the poor in social assistance in a durable manner.*
  These efforts can build on the improved coverage of the poor that many
  countries realized as they delivered pandemic relief. Some of the new

spending on COVID-19 programs could be replaced by better targeted instruments (IMF, 2022b).

- *Reducing food and energy subsidies.* Generalized food and energy subsidies should be phased out, as much of the benefit from these subsidies accrues to upper-income households. These should be replaced with cash assistance for low-income groups to prevent increases in poverty.
- *Moving toward universal health care coverage.* In many countries, spending levels will need to rise to achieve this objective, even with a modest package of benefits (Gaspar et al., 2019). Resources should be reallocated away from hospital-centric structures and toward primary care (Filmer et al., 2022). The mix of spending inputs (such as wages and medicines) could be improved to deliver better quality services. More system-wide reforms are needed in many countries, focusing on strengthening incentives for cost-effective care (Filmer et al., 2022).
- *Reallocating education spending.* Some countries will need to raise spending, but even more important is improving its composition and efficiency. Many countries need to reallocate spending away from public universities and toward primary and secondary schools to make these outlays more progressive. Raising fees and tuition at the tertiary level could be matched by an expansion of financial assistance for low-income students. There is room to improve the efficiency of these outlays, based on the large differences in the performance of education systems across countries with similar levels of spending. To improve efficiency, education systems need to better focus on learning outcomes and improve the quality of teaching (Filmer et al., 2022). Special attention needs to be given to raising the quality of education offered to students in low-income regions.
- *Improving the efficiency of spending outside the social sectors.* Governments will need to generate savings throughout the entire budget to generate fiscal space to boost redistributive spending. For those countries with adequate institutional capacity, spending reviews could be undertaken on a regular basis to identify low-priority outlays that could be cut.

REFERENCES

Abdel-Kader, K. and R. de Mooij (2022), "Tax policy", in V. Cerra, B. Eichengreen, A. El-Ganainy and M. Schindler (eds), *How to Achieve Inclusive Growth*. Oxford: Oxford University Press.

Agnello, L. and R. M. Sousa (2014), "How does fiscal consolidation impact on income inequality?", *Review of Income and Wealth*, 60(4).

Agostinelli, A., M. Doepke, G. Sorrent and F. Zilibotti (2022), "When the great equalizer shuts down: Schools, peers, and parents in pandemic times", *Journal of Public Economics*, 206, 104574.

Alesina, A., O. Barbiero, C. Favero, F. Giavazzi and M. Paradisi (2015), "Austerity in 2009–2013", *Economic Policy*, 30(83).

Amaglobeli, D., E. Hanedar, G. Hong and C. Thévenot (2022), "Fiscal policy for mitigating the social impact of high energy and food prices", *IMF* Note 2022/001, June.

Bachas, P., L. Gadenne and A. Jensen (2021), "Informality, consumption taxes, and redistribution", *HKS* Working Paper No. RWP21-006.

Banerji, A., V. Crispolti, E. Dabla-Norris, R. Duval, C. Ebeke, D. Furceri, T. Komatsuzaki and T. Poghosyan (2017), "Labor and product market reforms in advanced economies: Fiscal costs, gains, and support", *IMF* Staff Discussion Note 2017/003.

Berg, A. and J. Ostry (2017), "Inequality and unsustainable growth: Two sides of the same coin?", *IMF Economic Review*, 65(4).

Black, S., I. Parry, J. Roaf and K. Zhunussova (2021), "Not yet on track to net zero: The urgent need for greater ambition and policy action", *IMF* Staff Climate Note 2021/005.

Blofield, M., N. Lustig and M. Trasberg (2021), "Social protection during the pandemic. Argentina, Brazil, Columbia and Mexico", *Center for Global Development* Note, February 2021.

Causa, O. and M. Hermansen (2017), "Income redistribution through taxes and transfers across OECD countries", *OECD Economics Department* Working Papers No. 1453, OECD, Paris.

Chancel, L., T. Piketty, E. Saez and G. Zucman (2021), "World Inequality Report 2022", *World Inequality Lab* (wir2022.wid.world).

Clements, B., R. de Mooij, M. S. Gupta and M. M. Keen (2015), *Inequality and Fiscal Policy*. Washington, DC: IMF.

Clements, B. and S. Gupta (2022), "Global implications of the war on Ukraine on military and other spending", *Center for Global Development* blog, April 5. https://www.cgdev.org/blog/global-implications-ukraine-war-military-and-other-spending

Clements, B., S. Gupta and J. T. Jalles (2022), "Fiscal policy for inclusive growth in Asia", *CGD* Working Paper 611. Washington, DC: Center for Global Development.

Credit Suisse (2021), *Global Wealth Databook*. Credit Suisse.

Dabla-Norris, E., K. Kochhar, N. Suphaphiphat, F. Ricka and E. Tsounta (2015), "Causes and consequences of income inequality: A global perspective", *IMF* Staff Discussion Notes, 15(13), 1.

Duval, R., D. Furceri and J. Miethe (2021), "Robust political economy correlates of major product and labor market reforms in advanced economies: Evidence from BAMLE for logit models", *Journal of Applied Econometrics*, 36.

Estevão, M. and S. Essl (2022), "When the debt crises hit, don't simply blame the pandemic", *World Bank Blogs*, June 28, 2022. https://blogs.worldbank.org/voices/when-debt-crises-hit-dont-simply-blame-pandemic

Filmer, D., R. Gatti, H. Rogers, N. Spatafora and D. Emrullaha (2022), "Education and health", in V. Cerra, B. Eichengreen, A. El-Ganainy and M. Schindler (eds), *How to Achieve Inclusive Growth*. Oxford: Oxford University Press.

Ganong, P., F. Greig, P. Noel, D. Sullivan and J. Vavara (2022), "Unemployment insurance", in W. Edelberg, L. Sheiner and D. Wessel (eds), *Recession Remedies: Lessons Learned from the U.S. Economic Policy Response to COVID-19*. Washington, DC: Brookings Institution.

Gaspar, V., D. Amagobeli, M. Garcia-Escribano, D. Prady and M. Soto (2019), "Fiscal policy and development: Human, social, and physical investments for the SDGs", *IMF* Staff Discussion Note 2019/003.

Granger, H., L. Abramovsky and J. Pudessery (2022), "Fiscal policy and income inequality: The role of taxes and social spending", *ODI Report*, September.

Gupta, S. (2018), "Fiscal policy and inequality: An agenda for reform", Working Paper commissioned by the *Group of 24 and Friedrich-Ebert-Stiftung*. New York. https://www.g24.org/wp-content/uploads/2018/08/Income_Inequality_and_Fiscal_Policy_FINAL.pdf

Gupta, S. and J. Jalles (2022), "Do tax reforms affect income distribution? Evidence from developing countries", *Economic Modelling*, 110, 105804.

Gupta, S. and J. Jalles (2023), "Priorities for strengthening key revenue sources in Asia", *Asian Development Bank*, 40(2).

International Monetary Fund (2013), "Fiscal monitor: Taxing times". IMF.

International Monetary Fund (2021), "Fiscal monitor: A fair shot, April". IMF.

International Monetary Fund (2022a), "World economic outlook, April". IMF.

International Monetary Fund (2022b). "Fiscal monitor, October". IMF.

Jenkins, G., H. Jenkins and C. Y. Kuo (2006), "Is the value added tax naturally progressive?", *Queen's University*, Kingston, Working Paper 1059.

OECD (2014), *The Distributional Effects of Consumption Taxes*. OECD Publishing.

Ostry, J., A. Berg and C. Tsangarides (2014), "Redistribution, inequality, and growth", *IMF* Staff Discussion Notes, 14(02), 1.

Piketty, T. (2014), *Capital in the Twenty-First Century*. Cambridge, MA, USA: Harvard University Press.

Piketty, T. (2022), *A Brief History of Equality*. Cambridge, MA, USA: Belknap Press of Harvard University Press.

Solt, F. (2009), "The standardized world income inequality database", *Social Science Quarterly*, 90(2) (updated).

Woo, J., E. Bova, T. Kinda and Y. Zhang (2017), "Distributional consequences of fiscal consolidation and the role of fiscal policy: What do the data say", *IMF Economic Review*, 65(2).

11. Redistribution, automatic stabilizers and public debt

Enisse Kharroubi, Benoit Mojon and Luiz Pereira da Silva

11.1   INTRODUCTION

A wide range of factors accounts for the steady rise in inequality in both advanced economies (AEs) and emerging market and developing economies (EMDEs) over the last 40 years (see evidence reported in Chapter 10 of this book). These factors include secular forces such as globalization and technology outside the direct perimeter of macroeconomic stabilization policies. In addition, hysteresis over the business cycle has meant that income inequality has increased to new and higher levels following recessions (see Pereira da Silva et al., 2022). This has proved difficult to reverse in subsequent expansions, creating a ratchet effect and increasingly turning business cycle downturns into events that worsen inequality.

As discussed in the previous chapter, fiscal policy can deploy an array of instruments that can heavily affect inequality. Taxes and transfers redistribute income from high- to low-income households, thereby reducing inequality. However, fiscal policy reforms have limited the extent of redistribution in several OECD countries. Governments have generally reduced tax burdens while, at the same time, making personal income taxation less progressive. Taxes on high-income households have fallen more quickly than taxes on low-income households. Similarly, public insurance against unemployment risk has been weakened. This is mostly visible in the steady fall in replacement ratios (i.e. a person's income when unemployed relative to her last income when still on the job), particularly for longer unemployment durations. Income losses associated with unemployment have therefore increased, especially for longer unemployment spells.

Reduced redistribution through less progressive taxes and lower unemployment insurance (UI) replacement ratios has had important macroeconomic implications that we propose to investigate in this chapter. In a nutshell, this chapter makes two points. On the one hand, reduced redistribution has been a driving force behind the weakening of fiscal automatic stabilizers. This has made fiscal policy less countercyclical and hence less capable of cushioning fluctuations in economic activity. On the other hand, if weaker automatic stabilizers have meant lower fiscal surpluses during expansions, there is no evidence that governments have run lower deficits during recessions. As a result, weaker redistribution and automatic stabilizers have prevented governments from replenishing fiscal buffers during expansion phases, leading to higher public debt.

The rest of the chapter develops these points in more detail. It first sets out stylized facts about the evolution of taxation and UI in OECD economies over the last 20 years. Second, the chapter assesses the impact of tax progressivity and UI across different phases of the business cycle, highlighting the asymmetry between expansions and recessions. Then, via simulations, the chapter derives implications for the path of public debt under different tax progressivity and UI parameters. In conclusion, the chapter draws broader conclusions on the optimal policy mix for stabilization and growth.

11.2 STRUCTURAL CHANGES IN FISCAL POLICY: LESS PROGRESSIVE TAXES AND WEAKER INSURANCE AGAINST UNEMPLOYMENT RISK

Economists studying fiscal policy issues, in particular the question of public debt accumulation and fiscal sustainability, usually focus on a relatively narrow set of variables, e.g. fiscal deficits, the size of the government in the economy as proxied by fiscal revenues or expenditures in relation to GDP, or the public sector borrowing costs.[1] While these are all important elements to look at, as they can all affect the pace at which governments accumulate debt, this chapter proposes to expand this analysis. Specifically, we focus on the redistribution function of fiscal policy and how it affects public debt accumulation. We argue that the rapid pace of public debt accumulation in advanced economies over the last two decades is partly a reflection of a structural change in fiscal policies in these countries towards less fiscal redistribution. Hence, contrary to the popular view, weaker redistribution has been associated with a faster not a slower pace of public debt accumulation; in addition, the usual costs of lower redistribution have materialized, be it in terms of higher inequality or less stabilizing fiscal policy along the business cycle.

Governments redistribute income across their constituents in a variety of ways. Public expenditures for instance tend to have a large redistribution component.[2] There are, however, more visible, tangible and debated aspects of fiscal redistribution. One is taxation, in particular personal income taxation (PIT). Another is unemployment insurance. On taxation, the debate is usually focused on tax burdens, i.e. how much taxpayers pay to the government. Yet, a key measure of redistribution is rather the PIT progressivity, i.e. the sensitivity of the tax rate to personal income. Regarding unemployment insurance, replacement ratios provide a good gauge of the extent to which the system is redistributive, as UI essentially acts as a transfer from those with a job to those without one, with higher replacement ratios implying higher transfers. Let us in turn look to recent evolutions in these two systems.

In practice, PIT systems (average burden and progressivity) have changed considerably over the last two decades.[3] Across countries, personal income tax rates have dropped from the early 2000s for about a decade from 25 per cent to 21 per cent, on average, before starting a slow recovery in the wake of the European debt crisis that brought tax rates back to 23 per cent on average in 2019 (Figure 11.1, top panel, solid black line). In addition, household taxation has become steadily less progressive. To give a sense of the magnitudes involved, consider a high-income household earning five times the median income. Then the average tax rate applied to this household has dropped about 10 percentage points over the last two decades relative to the average tax rate applied to a median-earner household. Interestingly, the evolution of the tax progressivity distribution across countries shows that tax progressivity has fallen, particularly in countries where tax systems were highly progressive. The drop in tax progressivity therefore reflects a convergence of countries on the least progressive tax systems, not a broad shift with all countries cutting tax progressivity.[4]

In parallel to the changes in tax schemes, UI has also evolved significantly.[5] Comparing replacement rates in 2001 with those in 2019 shows a significant drop for unemployment durations of 18 months and above (Figure 11.1, bottom panel). While they have been broadly stable for shorter durations, replacement ratios for longer durations have fallen considerably. The average replacement rate (considering the main family statuses) dropped by about 10 percentage points across countries, from 40 to 30 percentage points, while the median replacement rate (also considering the main family statuses) dropped by 17 percentage points, from 42 per cent in 2001 to 25 per cent in 2019. This latter figure means that, for the most recent period, in half the countries we look at, people unemployed for more than a year and a half received unemployment benefits amounting to less than a quarter of their income in their last paid jobs.

Changes in tax progressivity and UI are the outcome of several forces. A key factor that has pushed governments to reduce tax progressivity and UI is the view that high progressivity and broad UI can erode work incentives, thereby harming the whole economy. In addition, when labour is mobile across countries, governments may want to reduce tax progressivity, hoping this will help attract or at least retain the most productive workers, expanding the overall tax base.

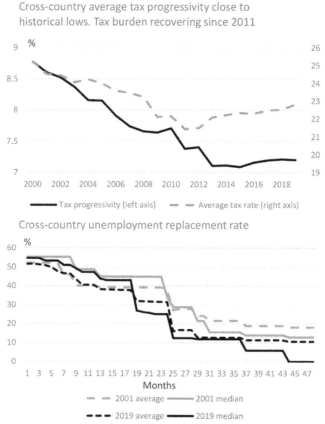

Notes: (Top) Country sample: 26 advanced economies. Tax progressivity is estimated for each country and year as the semi-elasticity of average personal income tax rate to personal income. Average personal income tax rates are computed based on marginal tax rates for different income brackets for 100 hypothetical personal incomes, from 4 per cent to 400 per cent of GDP per capita with a 4 percentage point increment. Average tax rate is the mean across countries of average personal income tax rates, averaged over the 100 hypothetical personal incomes. (Bottom) Average and median across family statuses and countries. Family statuses: single w/o children, couple without children and partner in/out of work, couple with children and partner in/out of work. Countries: 17 advanced economies.
Sources: OECD; authors' calculations.

Figure 11.1 Tax progressivity has been steadily falling in advanced economies

High as well as progressive taxes have indeed been shown to reduce the incentives to take better jobs (Gentry and Hubbard, 2004), while skills-biased technical change, i.e. technical change that preferentially benefits highly skilled

172 *Fiscal policy in a turbulent era*

workers, typically calls for lower tax progressivity (Heathcote et al., 2020). On the other hand, tax progressivity can usefully substitute for missing credit and insurance markets despite redistribution-induced distortions (Benabou, 2003). In addition, tax progressivity – as well as UI – can help to stabilize inefficient business cycles (McKay and Reis, 2016, 2021), with significant welfare benefits when monetary policy is constrained by the zero lower bound. Finally, Berg et al. (2018) show that lower levels of post-tax and transfer inequality are robustly correlated with faster and more durable growth.[6]

On unemployment insurance, there is a widely held view that high replacement ratios, particularly for longer unemployment durations, discourage the unemployed from taking jobs, thereby reducing the labour supply and possibly leading to adverse effects through unemployment hysteresis. For instance, Meyer (1990) provides evidence showing that higher UI benefits typically reduce the likelihood of recipients leaving unemployment. Likewise, the rise in the number of people exiting unemployment around the end of UI benefits (Moffit, 1985) has long been considered as evidence of the distortions that social insurance schemes introduce in labour supply decisions (Feldstein, 2005).[7] More recently, Johnston and Mas (2018) provide evidence that a cut in the duration of UI leads to a significant reduction in non-employment spells, even in periods of high unemployment. From a normative standpoint, Mitman and Rabinovich (2015) even argue that optimal UI should be procyclical over long time horizons, i.e. that a higher unemployment rate should lead to a cut in UI benefits.[8]

Finally, as described in the introductory chapter, there was a belief (up to the GFC) that, with limited aggregate fluctuations – the so-called Great Moderation – the focus of fiscal policy should not be macroeconomic stabilization, a task left to monetary policy, but rather reducing distortions in the economy, implementing pro-growth structural policies and ensuring that public debt remains safe and hence low.[9] The occurrence within a decade of two major recessions (the Great Recession and the Covid recession) has, however, prompted a major rethink of the respective role of fiscal and monetary policies in macroeconomic stabilization (Blanchard and Summers, 2020, and Chapter 4).

To wrap up, tax progressivity and UI replacement rates have declined on average across OECD countries in the last two decades. While reduced redistribution has probably contributed to rising inequality, the consequences may have been wider, notably for the macroeconomic stabilization properties of fiscal policy. This is what we investigate in the next section.

11.3 TAX PROGRESSIVITY, UNEMPLOYMENT INSURANCE AND FISCAL POLICY CYCLICALITY

11.3.1 Fiscal Policy Cyclicality

The steady increase in public debt in most AEs over the last 20 years has received considerable attention, with growing worries that current trends in the pace of public debt accumulation are simply not sustainable. In the meantime, other significant changes, especially in the stabilization properties of fiscal policies, have almost gone unnoticed. With monetary policy, fiscal policy is an important tool to stabilize the economy and smooth out business cycle fluctuations, as public expenditures usually tend to exceed fiscal revenues in recessions while revenues tend to exceed expenditures in expansions.

Empirical estimates reported in Pereira da Silva et al. (2022) indeed show that both total and primary fiscal balances – both expressed as a share of potential GDP – have gradually become less sensitive to the output gap. A trough was indeed reached after the GFC with only a very modest recovery since. In other words, governments have been running lower surpluses in expansions and lower deficits in recessions over the last two decades. To give an order of magnitude, in the early 2000s, a 1 percentage point increase in the output gap used to translate into a 0.5 percentage point of GDP increase in the total fiscal balance. Any increase in economic growth would therefore reduce fiscal deficits or increase the fiscal balance considerably. But more recently, a similar 1 percentage point increase in the output gap would increase fiscal balances only by 0.1 percentage point of GDP, an 80 per cent drop relative to the early 2000s.

There are obviously several reasons why lower fiscal redistribution – through less progressive PIT systems and/or less generous UI systems – could result in fiscal policy being less countercyclical. The next paragraphs provide some arguments that can guide intuition.

11.3.2 Tax Progressivity

When taxes are progressive, marginal tax rates increase with income so that higher-income households face higher average tax rates than lower-income households. Applying this logic to the business cycle, where household income is relatively high in expansions but relatively low in recessions, means that the government is imposing higher tax rates in expansions than in recessions, and the more so, the higher the progressivity of taxes. In other words, government tax revenues tend to increase faster with the pace of growth when taxes are more progressive. This is the so-called automatic stabilizer effect of progressive taxes. Everything else constant, fiscal policy is therefore more countercyclical when taxes are more progressive, because the fiscal surplus is larger in expansions and the fiscal deficit is larger in recessions.

Applying this intuition to the data, the fiscal balance should be more sensitive to the business cycle where taxes are more progressive. Based on a panel of OECD countries for the 2001–2019 period, the empirical evidence provides a clear confirmation. When tax progressivity is relatively low, the fiscal balance (total or primary) is basically a-cyclical as the sensitivity to the output gap is essentially zero. By contrast, when tax progressivity is relatively high, the fiscal balance is significantly countercyclical as the sensitivity to the output gap is positive and significant.

Interestingly, running a similar exercise with the average or median PIT rate shows no similar difference. The fiscal balance does not seem to be either more or less sensitive to the business cycle when the average (median) tax rate is relatively low or relatively high. In other words, the progressivity, not the level, of taxes is what affects the cyclical pattern of fiscal policy.

In addition, as would be expected, high progressivity raises the fiscal balance countercyclicality essentially by tightening the co-movement of fiscal revenues with the cycle (Figure 11.2, top panel). For instance, fiscal revenues are roughly twice as sensitive to the business cycle when tax progressivity is relatively high – looking at the fourth quartile of tax progressivity – than when it is relatively low. By contrast, and consistent with a simple intuition, tax progressivity does not seem to have any meaningful impact on the sensitivity of fiscal expenditures to the cycle.

11.3.3   Unemployment Insurance

UI consists of providing an income to those who have lost their jobs, funded by contributions raised on the income of those holding a job. This type of insurance has two aspects. One is cross-sectional: at any given point in time, contributions from the employed fund the benefits going to the unemployed. Another is intertemporal: in expansions, UI schemes tend to run surpluses as many people hold a job and therefore pay contributions while the pool of unemployed who receive benefits is limited. By contrast, in recessions, UI systems tend to run deficits as contributions from the pool of people on the job tend to shrink while the number of people unemployed who are eligible for unemployment benefits tends to expand.

The intertemporal dimension embedded in UI schemes suggests that, wherever UI coverage is broader and replacement ratios for those losing their jobs are higher, fiscal policy should be more countercyclical: the fiscal balance should display larger surpluses in expansions, and larger deficits in recessions.[10] Moreover, given that UI funds need to balance their budgets over the

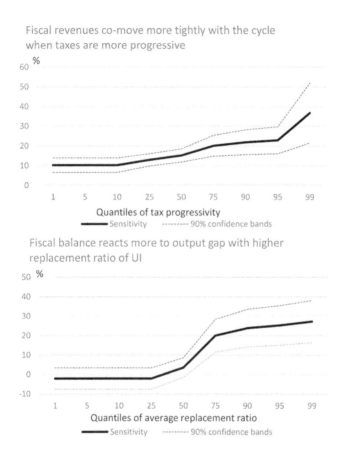

Fiscal revenues co-move more tightly with the cycle when taxes are more progressive

Quantiles of tax progressivity
——— Sensitivity   -------- 90% confidence bands

Fiscal balance reacts more to output gap with higher replacement ratio of UI

Quantiles of average replacement ratio
——— Sensitivity   -------- 90% confidence bands

Note: Sensitivity estimated in a cross-country panel regression for 22 countries in the period 2001–2019, where fiscal revenue (fiscal balance) to potential GDP is regressed on its one-year lagged value, the one-year lagged public debt to potential GDP, the one-year lagged tax progressivity (the one-year lagged unemployment replacement ratio), the current output gap and the interaction between the current output gap and the lagged tax progressivity (the lagged unemployment replacement ratio), controlling for country and time fixed effects. Sensitivities are evaluated at different values of tax progressivity (unemployment replacement ratio) using the estimated coefficients on the output gap and the interaction between the output gap and tax progressivity (and unemployment replacement ratio).
Sources: OECD; authors' calculations.

Figure 11.2   *Progressive taxes and strong unemployment insurance make fiscal policy countercyclical*

cycle, high replacement ratios must go hand in hand with high contributions. As a result, wider UI would affect not only fiscal expenditures, as higher replacement ratios imply higher disbursements, but also fiscal revenues, as higher replacement ratios imply higher contributions and hence higher receipts.

Empirical evidence based on the same sample of OECD countries shows that the (total or primary) fiscal balance is approximately acyclical when UI replacement ratios are low (Figure 11.2, bottom panel). By contrast, in countries where the average replacement ratio for the unemployed was relatively high, then fiscal policy was significantly countercyclical as the fiscal balance increases hand in hand with the output gap.

11.4   THE IMPACT OF REDISTRIBUTION ACROSS DIFFERENT PHASES OF THE BUSINESS CYCLE

Strong automatic stabilizers, in the form of progressive taxes and/or strong UI make fiscal policy more countercyclical. Yet this stronger countercyclical pattern could stem either from expansions or from recessions (or equally from both). In the first case, this would show up in governments running larger fiscal surpluses, while in the second case, strong automatic stabilizers would imply larger fiscal deficits. In this section, we examine this specific question and the possible implications, especially, for the pace of public debt accumulation.

Separating expansions, i.e. periods of positive output gaps from recessions, i.e. periods of negative output gaps, shows that while strong automatic stabilizers operate in both phases of the business cycle, they appear most relevant in expansions where the fiscal balance responds much more significantly to the output gap. Starting with the case of tax progressivity, the evidence shows that when taxes are barely progressive, the fiscal balance sensitivity to the business cycle is roughly comparable across expansions and recessions (Figure 11.3, top panel). Conversely, when taxes are strongly progressive, then the fiscal balance sensitivity to the output gap is significantly larger in expansions than in recessions (last two bars). Hence, while fiscal policy is broadly more countercyclical as taxes become more progressive, this effect is mainly due to expansion periods, where governments run particularly large surpluses. To give an order of magnitude, in recessions, fiscal deficits are roughly double in countries where taxes are highly progressive relative to the case of countries with low tax progressivity. However, in expansions the fiscal surplus is more than three times larger in countries where taxes are highly progressive relative to the case of countries with low tax progressivity.

A similar conclusion holds in the case of unemployment insurance: when UI replacement ratios are low, the fiscal balance is equally a-cyclical in expansions and recessions (Figure 11.3, bottom panel). In other words, fiscal policy does not contribute to attenuating business cycle fluctuations. However, with high UI replacement ratios, the fiscal balance appears to be very sensitive to the output gap, but mostly in expansions.

Progressive taxes raise fiscal balance sensitivity to
the output gap, particularly in expansions

High replacement ratio also raises fiscal balance
sensitivity to the output gap, driven by expansions

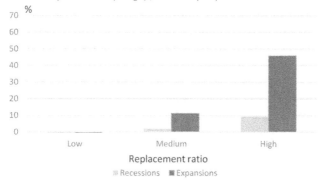

Note: See Figure 11.2 for the measurement of sensitivity. Low, medium and high respectively
correspond to the first, second and third quartile values of tax progressivity (unemployment
replacement ratio). Country sample: 22 advanced economies. Reference period: 2001–2019.
Sources: OECD; authors' calculations.

*Figure 11.3   Progressivity and replacement ratio make a larger difference
in expansions*

To wrap up, weaker redistribution in the form of less progressive taxes and/
or reduced UI has likely reduced governments' ability to stabilize the business
cycle, which has had two consequences. On the one hand, governments have
been left with few alternatives to discretionary policy to address major downturns, such as the GFC or the Covid-19 recession. The pitfalls of discretionary
fiscal policy being well documented, this has probably contributed to the
deterioration of the quality of public expenditures. On the other hand, rebuild-

ing fiscal buffers and drawing down public debt when the economy is rapidly expanding has proved more difficult, as the steady rise in public debt over the last 20 years testifies.

In economies with weaker redistribution and automatic stabilizers, governments therefore tend to expand fiscal policy in recessions through ad hoc expansionary measures, while they do not equally tighten fiscal policy in expansions, e.g. through discretionary tax hikes or expenditure cuts. The conclusion, arguably surprising, is that weak redistribution and automatic stabilizers prevent governments from running large enough surpluses in expansions. Absent such surpluses in expansions, governments fail to rebuild fiscal space and maintain public debt on a sustainable path. The next section illustrates these conjectures by simulating business cycle fluctuations for different degrees or redistribution by fiscal policy means.

11.5   REDISTRIBUTION AND THE PACE OF PUBLIC DEBT ACCUMULATION

Differences in the impact of tax progressivity and UI across different phases of the business cycle suggest that redistribution choices are likely to affect the pace of public debt accumulation. Over the long run, public debt would indeed increase more sharply in countries with weak automatic stabilizers, if governments do not run, in expansions, the large surpluses needed to replenish fiscal buffers. To be sure, this effect is likely to depend on the specific sequence of shocks that economies meet with. To the extent that strong redistribution implies a marginally stronger policy response in recessions, a succession of negative shocks could send public debt temporarily higher in economies with relatively strong automatic stabilizers. Moreover, a temporary increase in public debt could have long-lasting effects as public debt snowballs over time, something that could happen when the financial cost and the level of public debt are sufficiently high. Conversely, in such circumstances, a short sequence of positive shocks could also lead to persistently lower public debt if strong automatic stabilizers lead to large surpluses.

In practice, differences in tax progressivity and UI replacement ratio can have a significant impact on the path of public debt. To get a sense of this impact, we simulate the path for public debt under alternative assumptions for tax progressivity or UI replacement ratio and proceed in three steps. First, using random draws in the empirical distribution of output gap we compute corresponding primary balances, using relationships estimated above. In a second step, using simulated primary balances, we compute the path for public debt, equating changes in the public debt to GDP ratio to simulated fiscal balances.[11] Finally, we compute the median path for public debt over a large number of simulations, for each tax progressivity (UI replacement ratio) assumption, and consider the difference in these median paths between the case of high and low tax progressivity (UI replacement ratios).

Simulation results show that high tax progressivity can cut public debt-to-GDP levels by more than 2 percentage points after 20 years, relative to the case of low tax progressivity (Figure 11.4, top panel). In probabilistic terms, after 20 years, public debt ends up being lower under high tax progressivity in about 70 per cent of our simulations. As noted above, high tax progressivity, insofar as it prompts governments to run larger deficits in recessions, can indeed lead to higher public debt if the economy faces many or large recessions such as the 2008 GFC or the 2020 Covid-19 lockdowns.

For UI replacement ratios, the drop in public debt is more impressive: with high UI replacement ratios, public debt-to-GDP levels end up more than 6 percentage points lower after 20 years relative to the case of where UI replacement ratios are low (Figure 11.4, bottom panel). The likelihood that public debt ends up lower under a high UI replacement ratio is roughly similar, at 70 per cent, to the figure obtained for tax progressivity.

This exercise therefore suggests that redistribution and automatic stabilizers through more progressive taxation and/or a higher UI replacement ratio can improve fiscal sustainability and reduce the pace of public debt accumulation. This reflects the additional tightening that strong automatic stabilizers bring in expansions which translates, in most of our simulations, into lower public debt in the long run, despite stronger accommodation in recessions. In addition, UI appears to be a significantly more effective policy tool than tax progressivity in cutting public debt, about two to three times more so. Redistributive policies that strengthen automatic stabilizers can therefore help to slow the pace of public debt accumulation and improve fiscal sustainability.

11.6   CONCLUSIONS

Fiscal policies in AEs have changed in several dimensions over the last two decades. In this chapter, we have focused on the reduction in the progressivity of taxes and the reduction of unemployment benefits and analysed their impact on the cyclical properties of fiscal policy. We argue that lower tax progressivity and less generous unemployment benefits have weakened fiscal automatic stabilizers, likely accelerating the pace of public debt accumulation. In addition, as argued in Pereira da Silva et al. (2022) less redistribution has most likely contributed to rising inequality, which in turn has adversely affected other policies, e.g. monetary policy. As a result, the ability of both fiscal and monetary policy to stabilize the economy has suffered from the reduction in their redistribution capacity, probably forcing fiscal policymakers to rely more extensively on discretionary measures, particularly when dealing with large recessions.

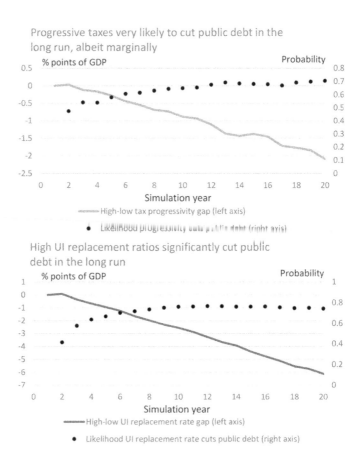

Note: Change in public debt-to-GDP 1 to 20 years ahead relative to public debt-to-GDP level in year 0. The public debt level d is simulated using the law of motion $d=(1+r-g)d_{-1}-b$; $r-g$, the interest-growth differential is set to zero, d_{-1} is the one-year lagged debt to GDP level, which starts at 100 per cent in year 0, and b, the primary fiscal balance to GDP, is simulated using estimated sensitivities to the output gap, the considered values for tax progressivity or UI replacement ratio and random draws of the output gap from its empirical distribution. Low and high tax progressivity (UI replacement rate) represent, respectively, the median change in public debt at the relevant horizon for the 10th and 90th percentile values. The gap is the difference between the two median public debt levels. The series likelihood UI replacement rates cut public debt, which shows the fraction of simulations for which public debt-to-GDP is lower under higher tax progressivity (UI replacement ratio) at any given horizon. See Figure 11.2 for the measurement of sensitivity. Low, medium and high respectively correspond to the first, second and third quartile values of tax progressivity (unemployment replacement ratio). Country sample: 22 advanced economies. Reference period: 2001–2019.
Sources: OECD; authors' calculations.

Figure 11.4   Redistribution and automatic stabilizers reduce public debt

This chapter shows that, contrary to widespread beliefs, the reduction in redistribution through fiscal policy has coincided with a faster not slower pace of public debt accumulation. Yet steadily rising public debt is not simply a fiscal problem. It can also act as a major constraint on monetary policy. High public debt and large financing needs can put pressure on central banks, forcing them to adopt a more accommodative stance, possibly above and beyond what output and inflation stabilization would prescribe.

More broadly, these changes in fiscal policy have implications for the policy mix. With fiscal policy being less countercyclical, monetary policy needs to bear a larger share of the macroeconomic stabilization burden. While this assignment may have been sensible during the "Great Moderation" period, where business cycle volatility was contained, large shocks such as the GFC or the Covid-19 recession exemplify the need to rethink the balance between fiscal and monetary policy.[12] If anything, this would rather call for strengthening, not weakening, automatic stabilizers. In this respect, bringing the focus back to more ambitious redistributive policies could benefit both the reduction of income inequality and enhance the effectiveness of macroeconomic stabilization policies.

NOTES

1. See for instance Blanchard and Perotti (2002) or Fatas and Mihov (2012).
2. Two clear-cut examples are public education or public health systems, which tend to benefit more those at the bottom of the income distribution.
3. We will use household and personal income taxation interchangeably in what follows.
4. See Piketty and Saez (2007) for historical and cross-country complementary evidence on the drop in tax progressivity.
5. UI shows up in both fiscal expenditures and revenues. Payments to the unemployed are typically counted as public expenditures while contributions that fund UI are counted as revenues from social contributions.
6. On the determinants of tax progressivity, Lyon and Waugh (2018) argue that tax progressivity should increase with openness to trade while Chunzan (2021) shows that an ageing population and high interest rates typically imply less progressive taxes.
7. Card et al. (2007) have challenged this evidence, claiming that the observed spike corresponds rather to people leaving unemployment for administrative reasons as exhausted benefits imply a mechanical exit from the category of the unemployed. Schmieder et al. (2012) also dispute the idea that UI creates moral hazard, using data from Germany over a 20-year period.
8. The intuition for this result is that a rise in unemployment raises the *social* not the *private* gains from posting vacancies. The generosity of UI therefore falls in the long run, in response to a rise in unemployment.
9. Kirsanova et al. (2009) provide a discussion of this consensus assignment and its possible limitations.

10. To be more specific, UI replacement ratios should affect how the fiscal balance responds to fluctuations in (un)employment. For simplicity, we overlook this difference and assume here that output and employment gaps are close to each other.
11. This boils down to assuming that the financial cost of public debt is equal to nominal GDP growth.
12. Kocherlakota (2021) shows, in the context of a Heterogenous Agents New Keynesian model, that stabilizing inflation or output using interest rates (monetary) is not possible when public debt is large.

REFERENCES

Benabou, R. (2003), "Tax and education policy in a heterogeneous-agent economy: what levels of redistribution maximize growth and efficiency?", *Econometrica*, 70.

Berg, A., J Ostry, C. Tsangarides and Y. Yakhshilikov (2018), "Redistribution, inequality and growth: new evidence", *Journal of Economic Growth*, 23.

Blanchard, O. and R. Perotti (2002), "An empirical characterization of the dynamic effects of changes in government spending and taxes on output", *The Quarterly Journal of Economics*, 117.

Blanchard, O. and L. Summers (2020), "Automatic stabilizers in a low-rate environment", *American Economic Association* papers and Proceedings, 110.

Card, D., R. Chetty and A. Weber (2007), "The spike at benefit exhaustion: leaving the unemployment system or starting a new job?", *American Economic Review*, 97.

Chunzan, W. (2021), "More unequal income but less progressive taxation", *Journal of Monetary Economics*, 117.

Fatas, A. and I. Mihov (2012), "Fiscal policy as a stabilization tool", *Journal of Macroeconomics*, 12.

Feldstein, M. (2005), "Rethinking social insurance", *American Economic Review*, 95(1).

Gentry, W. and G. Hubbard (2004), "The effects of progressive income taxation on job turnover", *Journal of Public Economics*, 88.

Heathcote, J., H. Storesletten and G. Violante (2020), "How should tax progressivity respond to rising income inequality?", *NBER* Working Papers, No. 28006.

Johnston, A. and A. Mas (2018), "Potential unemployment insurance duration and labor supply: the individual and market-level response to a benefit cut", *Journal of Political Economy*, 126(6).

Kirsanova, T., L. Campbell and S. Wren-Lewis (2009), "Monetary and fiscal policy interaction: the current consensus assignment in the light of recent developments", *The Economic Journal*, 119.

Kocherlakota, N. (2021), "Stabilization with fiscal policy", *NBER* Working Papers, No. 29226.

Lyon, S. and M. Waugh (2018), "Redistributing the gains from trade through progressive taxation", *Journal of International Economics*, 115.

McKay, A. and R. Reis (2016), "The role of automatic stabilizers in the U.S. business cycle", *Econometrica*, 24.

McKay, A. and R. Reis (2021), "Optimal automatic stabilizers", *Review of Economic Studies*, 88.

Meyer, B. (1990), "Unemployment insurance and unemployment spells", *Econometrica*, 58.

Mitman, K. and S. Rabinovich (2015), "Optimal unemployment insurance in an equilibrium business-cycle model", *Journal of Monetary Economics*, 71©.

Moffit, R. (1985), "Unemployment insurance and the distribution of unemployment spells", *Journal of Econometrics*, 28.

Pereira da Silva, L., E. Kharroubi, E. Kohlscheen, M. Lombardi and B. Mojon (2022), "Inequality hysteresis and the effectiveness of macroeconomic stabilisation policies", *BIS*, May.

Piketty, T. and E. Saez (2007), "How progressive is the U.S. federal tax system? A historical and international perspective", *Journal of Economic Perspectives*, 21.

Schmieder, J. F., T. von Wachter and S. Bender (2012), "The effects of extended unemployment insurance over the business cycle: evidence from regression discontinuity estimates over 20 years", *The Quarterly Journal of Economics*, 127.

12. Meeting the economic challenges of a greying world

Aida Caldera and Dorothée Rouzet

12.1 INTRODUCTION

The world is experiencing a staggering rise in the number of old people and they will live longer than ever before. Advanced economies are already ageing rapidly as life expectancy increases and fertility continues to decline. While most large emerging economies have a younger population, population ageing will nonetheless occur rapidly in the coming years – sometimes at a faster pace than among advanced economies. Yet, all major economies will experience significant increases in the number of people over 65 supported by each working-age person – and should prepare for it.

An ageing economy risks being a slower growing and more unequal one and will put pressure on public finances. For fiscal and social security systems, revenues will be eroded by slower economic dynamism and pension, health and long-term care costs will increase and could become unmanageable for many countries. Ageing-related expenditures would add to already high public debt in many countries in the next decades or require steep tax revenue increases or severe cuts in productive public expenditure. There is also a risk of slower growth, as there will be less working-age people in the population and older workers tend to be employed less and may be less productive and entrepreneurial (see Chapter 4 in this book). Those who are currently young may face higher inequality and poverty risk in their old age than older generations, as they are expected to spend more years on retirement income. The less privileged may also accumulate disadvantages over a longer life including more unstable labour market conditions and poorer earnings, as has been observed in many countries.

To deal with the challenges brought by ageing, governments need a whole-of-government approach across many policy areas. This chapter assesses the implication of ageing societies for the sustainability of public finances. It also discusses possible policy responses to address the challenges of demographic change.

12.2 CHALLENGES OF AGEING FOR FISCAL SUSTAINABILITY

Population ageing will put unprecedented stress on public finances to finance pension, health and long-term care expenditures. The ageing-related stress comes first and foremost from two drivers: the pace of increase in dependency ratios, and the declining growth in potential GDP. On the other hand, some authors emphasize that ageing might lead to more automation and higher productivity (Acemoglu and Restrepo, 2021). Countries with publicly financed pay-as-you-go (PAYG) pension, health and long-term care schemes may require adjusting spending or raising additional revenues to ensure long-term sustainability, as revenues from taxes and social security contributions will be levied on a shrinking share of the working-age people while they will need to finance the benefits of a rising share of retirees.

Public pension expenditures have risen by about 1.7 percentage points of GDP on average since 2000 in G20 countries, with Turkey and Japan recording the strongest increases. Past pension reforms have helped contain future pressures on pension expenditure, nonetheless, pension spending is projected to increase in the majority of G20 countries by 2050/60 (Rouzet et al., 2019). The projected increase is particularly pronounced in several emerging G20 countries such as Brazil, China, and Saudi Arabia, but from a low share of GDP.

Despite the gains in healthy life expectancy seen in recent years in all OECD countries, health systems and long-term care systems will need to adapt to meet the needs of an ageing population. In 2019, prior to the COVID-19 pandemic, OECD countries spent, on average, around 8.8 per cent of their GDP on health care – a figure unchanged since 2013 (OECD, 2021). Across OECD countries, more than 76 per cent of all health spending is financed through government or compulsory insurance schemes. Moreover, the COVID-19 pandemic has led to significant increases in health spending in most OECD countries. According to OECD health statistics, health expenditure grew on average 5 per cent in 2020 across OECD countries (OECD, 2021), as a result of the COVID-19 pandemic.

Data from most countries show that, on average, older people have higher health expenditures than younger people (OECD, 2021). This often leads to the assumption that health expenditure growth will accelerate as older people make up an increasing share of the population, potentially challenging the sustainability of health systems. Yet, while providing appropriate health care to an increasing number of older persons does place additional pressure on the health system, ageing is not the main driver of expenditure growth. Non-demographic factors such as organization of care, technology, price regulation, proximity to death and health status are more important drivers of the growth of health care spending than age (Marino et al., 2017; De la Maisonneuve et al., 2016;

Lorenzoni et al., 2019). In fact, income improvements and the associated demand for higher quality services have been the main reason behind increases in health spending over the last 20 to 30 years. Health spending has also been driven by higher costs. Productivity gains that would alleviate spending growth, whilst achievable, are made more challenging by the labour-intensive nature of the health care sector. The type of technological progress we have seen over past decades helps extend the scope, range, and quality of health care services, but can also increase the costs of treatments.

The extent to which ageing will play a larger role in future health spending than it did in the past depends largely on whether longevity gains will translate into additional years in good health without disabilities. Among demographic factors, time-to-death, particularly the final years of life, are a strong driver of health care expenditures (Marino et al., 2017). This suggests that policies to promote healthy ageing can help to reduce growth in health spending because of population ageing.

As populations are ageing rapidly, demand is increasing on the long-term care (LTC) sector to provide care for more, and older, people with complex conditions and heightened needs for expert care. This has already put strains on LTC systems, made evident by the rapid spread of COVID-19 among residents and health care workers in LTC (OECD, 2021). Compared with other areas of health care, spending on LTC has seen the highest growth in recent years and substantial further increases are expected in the coming years. In 2019, 1.5 per cent of GDP was allocated to LTC (including both the health and social component) across OECD countries. Spending on LTC greatly varies across countries, ranging from 3 to 4.1 per cent in the Netherlands and Scandinavian countries to between 0.1 per cent and 0.2 per cent of GDP in Mexico, Chile, Greece and Turkey, with four out of five dollars spent on LTC coming from public sources. This variation in spending partly mirrors differences in the population structure, but mostly reflects the stage of development of formal LTC systems.

Ageing will continue to exert pressure on long-term care (LTC) expenditure, especially owing to the rapid increase in the share of people over 80 in the population. While higher spending may be partially offset by better health, increased dependency due to chronic diseases such as dementia could exert additional cost pressure (OECD, 2017a). Between 2015 and 2030, the number of older people in need of care around the world is projected to increase by 100 million (ILO and OECD, 2019). Public LTC systems will need adequate resources to meet increased demand while maintaining access and quality. As populations continue to age, demand for LTC workers is likely to rise. Responding to increasing demand will require policies to improve recruitment and retention and increase productivity.

Public health and long-term care expenditure is projected to increase by 2.2 percentage points of GDP in the median country between 2021 and 2060 (Guillemette and Turner, 2021). These projections are based on a pre-pandemic spending baseline, so any permanent increase in health spending in response to COVID-19 (for instance to build more spare capacity in intensive care units or raise pay levels for workers in public care homes) would add to it. In major emerging economies, spending could increase much more rapidly but from a lower level.

Overall, the combined fiscal stress from ageing-related spending could lead to unsustainable public debts, require sharp cuts in other public spending, or large tax increases that could hinder economic growth (Crowe et al., 2022). Considering the increase in pension, health care costs and other primary expenditure together with the downward pressure on revenues, tax revenue would have to increase between 4.5 and 11.5 percentage points of GDP by 2060 to keep debt at current levels in G20 countries, without other policy changes (Guillemette and Turner, 2018).

If governments would not offset the ageing-related expenditure pressures through increases in tax revenues, cuts in other spending or improved efficiency of spending, public debt levels would increase significantly in both advanced and emerging G20 economies (Rouzet et al., 2019).

12.3   POLICIES TO PROMOTE FINANCIALLY SUSTAINABLE PENSIONS, HEALTH, AND LONG-TERM COSTS SYSTEMS

12.3.1   Improving the Design of Mandatory Pension Systems

The design of pension schemes needs to address the triple challenge of ensuring fiscal sustainability, providing adequate incomes in retirement, and ensuring intergenerational fairness. In most advanced countries, public pension systems, often financed on a pay-as-you-go basis and structured as a defined benefit system, are the main source of coverage. Policy responses will need to be adapted to each country's priorities, fiscal and demographic situation, risk tolerance and existing policy and institutional settings.

In response to rising pressures on public finances from ageing populations, many countries have reformed their pension systems in recent years. Reforms have included raising contribution rates (e.g. Canada, the United Kingdom), cutting initial benefits or limiting the indexation of pensions to inflation and wages (e.g. Argentina), indexation to life expectancy (e.g. Japan), raising retirement ages (e.g. Indonesia, Russia, the United Kingdom), and closing early pathways into retirement via reforms of the unemployment insurance or disability pension schemes. An important challenge for many countries is to fully implement legislated reforms to improve sustainability, and to withstand pressures to backtrack on reforms given that pension reforms are typically unpopular and the share of older voters keeps increasing.

Raising the retirement age can help both increase the labour force participation of older workers and maintain pension levels in the face of rising pressures. Normal retirement ages have increased over the last two decades in almost all OECD countries, and in G20 emerging economies (e.g. Indonesia, Russia). However, the increase in the statutory retirement age has so far not been high enough to keep pace with rising life expectancy in most countries and the share of adult life spent in retirement has increased. A few countries (e.g. Denmark, Finland, Italy, the Netherlands, and Portugal) have established an automatic link through which a given share of future increases in life expectancy will be reflected in the normal retirement age (OECD, 2017b). If all OECD countries adopted a similar approach it would help to alleviate the stress on public finances and would raise senior employment rates and GDP per capita in the long term (Geppert et al., 2019). However, such reforms are not easy to implement politically and require careful communication.

Unifying pension frameworks for all workers and phasing out special regimes is another way to help enhance both efficiency and equity in pension systems. Differences in contributions and pension rights among different categories of workers in pension schemes for civil servants can be substantial and fuel dissatisfaction with public pension systems. On the equity side, it is difficult to argue today that, for instance, civil servants and public sector workers require higher income replacement in retirement than private sector ones. On the efficiency side, there are significant economies of scale in managing unified pension systems, for example in contribution collection, record-keeping, and benefit payments.

However, policymakers should consider the potentially regressive effects of pension reforms when raising the statutory retirement age and phasing out special schemes. Lower socio-economic groups have shorter life expectancy and will see their pension wealth reduced relatively more if the retirement age increases without a corresponding gain in life expectancy, although the effect is relatively small (OECD, 2017c). Some countries have explored compensating higher inequality by introducing more granularity in retirement eligibility based on people's skills and the physical requirements of their jobs. However, these schemes also tend to introduce administrative complexity for firms and workers and may create distorted incentives.

To respond to both financing challenges and diverse wishes among workers, pension design should allow for flexible retirement options, such as the option to continue to work, often part-time, while drawing at least a partial pension, or to choose when to retire with pension rights adjusted in an actuarially neutral way.

Cutting benefits and limiting the full indexation of pensions to prices can improve fiscal sustainability but can jeopardize the adequacy of pension incomes and can make pensioners more vulnerable to old-age poverty. Moreover, funded defined contribution (DC) schemes and notional DC systems automatically adjust annuities to changes in longevity. These automatic links help lower the financial pressure but require efficient complementary measures to boost employment at older age so as not to result in consistently lower pension levels and heightened poverty risk among pensioners. Safety net pensions – means-tested, non-contributory basic pensions – as well as minimum pensions in contributory schemes, play a key role in preventing poverty at old age, especially for low earners, people with non-standard or incomplete careers and women who interrupted their careers to care for children. Countries combining low safety net benefits and high rates of old-age poverty may need to make space for higher spending on basic and minimum pensions, offsetting it by either cutting other categories of spending or by raising more revenue.

Finally, it needs to be considered that higher contributions may improve financial sustainability and/or pension adequacy but raise non-wage costs for employers, which may weigh on net wages and employment over time. Increasing contributions may also raise questions of intergenerational fairness by placing the burden on younger generations.

12.3.2 Incentivizing Savings and Managing Risks in Private Pension Schemes

With increased stress on public pensions, the reliance on private pensions is likely to rise in many countries. Within private systems, pensions are shifting away from employer-sponsored schemes towards personal retirement saving plans, raising the risk of insufficient contributions. Individuals will be increasingly responsible for building assets to finance their retirement; however, most people tend to underestimate how long they will stay in retirement and their financial needs at old age (Aegon, 2018). Policies should therefore encourage people to contribute more and for longer periods. Introducing automatic enrolment systems, where people are automatically signed up to a pension plan but are free to opt out at some point, tend to be an efficient alternative to increase participation. The evidence shows that enrolees usually continue to participate, however, it is important to make automatic enrolment mandatory for employers in parallel, to lower entry barriers to make it more accessible and to introduce financial incentives to minimize opt-out rates. Schemes that allow workers to opt for regular increases in contribution rates or to automatically allocate a portion of future salary increases towards their retirement savings are also effective in raising contributions gradually over time (Thaler and Benartzi, 2004).

Improving the structure of incentives can help expand coverage and increase contributions. Several countries have tax incentives in place. However, their effectiveness must be assessed against the substantial fiscal cost and potential regressive effect, as high earners de facto receive larger subsidies compared with tax-exempt low-income workers (OECD, 2018). Policymakers could consider reviewing and harmonizing tax treatments and simplifying them, especially in countries where financial literacy is low. There can be a case to pare back excessively generous tax concessions which are mainly benefiting the top of the income distribution. Matching contributions are increasingly used in OECD countries and are typically more effective than tax incentives at increasing participation in retirement savings plans by low-income earners, who may have insufficient tax liability to benefit from the tax relief.

Furthermore, policymakers should promote competition among private pension providers to reduce fees and improve efficiency. This needs to be complemented by more transparent and accessible information so that people can easily switch providers.

12.3.3 Containing Costs in the Health Sector

The effect of ageing on future health care expenditures will depend on whether gains in longevity will translate into further improvements in years in good health. Projections for OECD economies indicate that effective health promotion policies could dampen the increase in total (private and public) health care costs by around 0.3 percentage points of GDP by 2030 – from 8.8 per cent in 2015 to 9.7 per cent of GDP in 2030, instead of 10 per cent of GDP in 2030 (Lorenzoni et al., 2019).

Promoting healthier lifestyles requires action both within and beyond the health sector. Curbing the major risk factors of smoking, alcohol consumption and obesity can reduce associated treatment costs. For example, alcohol prevention policies – such as brief general practitioner interventions, taxation, and regulations on advertising and drink-driving – have been shown to reduce costs compared with treating associated illnesses when they appear. "Sin taxes" on alcohol and tobacco reduce consumption of products harmful to health while also raising revenue that can be earmarked for health care (OECD, 2015). More specific policies targeted at the elderly include promoting physical and cognitive exercise to prevent cognitive decline and physical frailty, addressing social isolation, and stopping infectious diseases among the elderly. Digitalization and new technologies (e.g. telemedicine) can also make life better for the elderly, lend a helping hand to those who care for them, and help prevent expensive health care and long-term care costs (Garcia Escribano et al., 2022).

At the same time, there is ample scope to improve the efficiency of health spending in most countries (Lorenzoni et al., 2018; OECD, 2017d; Garcia Escribano et al., 2022). Efficiency savings could help offset future spending pressures and help counteract the effect of ageing. Countries' experience shows that a number of policies can help to contain health care costs and improve efficiency.

• *Budgetary caps*, such as ceilings on overall or sector (e.g. inpatient care) health expenditures, have had some success in containing health costs for example in Germany and the United Kingdom. In Germany, the imposition of a budget cap on drugs prescribed at the individual physician level resulted in an upsurge in the number of referrals and hospital admissions, presumably due to physicians referring their patients to other physicians or hospitals for fear of exceeding the ceiling. However, the additional costs in other sectors seem outweighed by the savings generated by the cap policy (OECD, 2015).

• *Efforts to tackle wasteful spending*, including reduced spending on care that is at best ineffective or at worst harmful (e.g. over-prescription of antibiotics) as well as instances where the same benefits from care could be obtained at a lower cost – for instance by using generic rather than branded drugs. Changing the attitude and behaviours of patients and providers is often key to reducing wasteful spending, as well as improving coordination among providers and aligning financial incentives including provider payment methods (OECD, 2017d).

• *Moving away from volume-incentive payment methods* could help contain the rising demand for and supply of health care services associated with rising incomes. Newer payment methods are geared towards improving value for money (OECD, 2016). They include "add-on payments", including pay-for performance, whereby health care providers are rewarded for delivering more coordinated, safer and effective care (e.g. Portugal and Norway); "bundled payments", whereby payments for all services provided to a patient with a given medical problem are pooled together (e.g. England and Sweden); and "population-based payments", whereby the payment covers most care needs of patients (e.g. Germany and Spain).

• *More competition among health care providers, accompanied by strong and effective regulation*, can curb spending growth and improve the quality of care. Regulated competition can strengthen incentives to achieve efficiency gains, better align health care service characteristics with patient preferences and promote access to care (with, for instance, means-tested subsidized insurance premiums). Strict regulation, enforcing quality standards and promoting access to care is, however, paramount to achieve these outcomes, as unfettered market forces are likely to lead to low-quality services because of asymmetric information, and to under-provision for the most vulnerable segments of the population because of their inability to pay. The introduction of market-oriented reforms in the English National Health Service in 2006, for example, seems to have had some success. GPs were required to offer patients a choice of provider for inpatient care, and providers started to be remunerated based on fixed prices. Hence, the reforms encouraged providers to compete for patients through improvements in quality of care. Hospital efficiency was found to improve in that better health outcomes were achieved in hospitals more exposed to competitive pressure, with lower average length-of-stay and no general increases in hospital expenditures (OECD, 2015).

- *Paying more attention to primary and preventive health care and increasing the scope of goods and services covered by basic (primary) health care coverage can help achieve better value for money by increasing life expectancy and moderating health spending growth. Coverage expansion* significantly increases patients' access to and use of preventive care, whereas less generous insurance coverage and an increased cost-sharing can discourage low-income and high-risk populations from seeking health care, with adverse consequences for health status and potentially higher spending in the future (Lorenzoni et al., 2018).

12.3.4   Financing Long-term Care

As people get older, it becomes more likely that they will one day need long-term care. Public schemes play a crucial role in maintaining the costs of care for older people with LTC needs at affordable levels. Without public financial support, the total costs of LTC would be higher than median incomes among older people in most OECD countries and EU Member States (OECD, 2021).

In most OECD countries, the costs for LTC are covered to a great extent (four out of every five dollars spent on LTC on average) by either a government scheme (such as a National Health Service or regional health boards) or through compulsory insurance (mainly social insurance), with care in a residential facility generally less well covered than home care (OECD, 2020). However, the estimated level of public social protection against the total costs of LTC in old age varies widely both across and within countries and subnational areas in the OECD (Oliveira Hashiguchi and Llena-Nozal, 2020). Most public social protection systems provide lower levels of support to older people receiving informal care and in some cases out-of-pocket costs for home care can be very high, while institutional care for the same individuals is often more affordable.

Most advanced economies provide some form of public risk pooling to deal with the unpredictability and potentially large costs of LTC, however, the approaches differ across countries. For instance, the Nordics have universal, tax-funded social care systems, which provide comprehensive coverage of LTC costs. Other countries have dedicated social insurance schemes, which can provide relatively comprehensive (e.g. the Netherlands and Japan) or partial (e.g. Korea and Germany) coverage of costs. A third group of countries (e.g. Italy) relies largely on cash benefits to support people with LTC needs. The United Kingdom and the United States both have means-tested, safety net systems, under which the poorest are fully covered but the wealthiest get little or no support. In contrast, in emerging and lower income countries, public risk pooling is often lacking and care provided through informal arrangements largely relies on unpaid family members.

One of the main challenges in the future will be to strike the right balance between providing appropriate social protection to people with LTC needs and ensuring that this protection is fiscally sustainable. Reducing the burden on declining working-age populations and ensuring sustainable financing will require broadening contributions to LTC across revenue sources and inter-generationally. For example, Japan, the Netherlands, Belgium and Luxembourg complement payroll contributions with alternative revenues sources. In Japan and Germany, LTC premia are not only levied on the working-age population but also on retirees.

Given the ageing-related pressure on public finances, a stronger role of private LTC insurance may be desirable. If effectively regulated, private LTC insurance can help people manage more effectively the risk of facing significant out-of-pocket expenses. However, the private LTC insurance market is small in most countries due to well-known market failures (e.g. adverse selection) and consumer myopia, and remains focused on wealthier and higher income individuals. To encourage private insurance coverage, some countries provide tax incentives, but the evidence of their effectiveness is mixed (Colombo et al., 2011). In some countries, group insurance plays a significant role to supplement public coverage (e.g. France) and has the advantage of encouraging early subscription. Benefits for enrolees include the ability to negotiate better coverage solutions, as well as lower premia. However, countries relying on group insurance should pay attention to expanding coverage to the self-employed and workers in non-traditional forms of employment. In some advanced economies, innovative private financing instruments such as LTC insurance as part of life insurance policies and reverse mortgages to draw on illiquid assets have also been used and can help manage out-of-pocket costs.

Countries will also need to seek options to improve efficiency of LTC services. Some possible avenues include (Colombo et al., 2011):

- A better targeting of benefits towards those with lower income and/or higher needs. Means-testing – making the level of public support depend on the recipient's income and assets can help to promote equity and efficiency (Oliveira Hashiguchi and Llena-Nozal, 2020).
- Nearly all OECD countries have been encouraging home care, in order to limit institutional costs and satisfy people's preference for receiving care at home. They have done so through the direct expansion of home care supply, and the implementation of regulatory measures and financial incentives (e.g. cash benefits). However, some evidence suggests that home care may become more expensive than institutional care for severely disabled people. Another challenge is to ensure a sufficient supply of well-trained care workers (ILO and OECD, 2019).
- Efficiency gains might be achieved by enabling choice and hence competition among private LTC providers, such as in the case of vouchers used in the Nordic countries. Policies to increase competition should be flanked by improved monitoring of the quality of private services provided.
- The introduction of new technologies could improve the productivity of LTC workers, but there is a dearth of evaluation of cost-effectiveness of many "smart" technologies and often technology appears useful as a supplement rather than a substitute of labour. Some evidence from the Netherlands and Norway suggests that cameras and sensors have reduced the number of emergency visits, freeing professionals to provide care elsewhere and reducing costs.
- Inefficiencies may arise from the interactions of the LTC system with the health care system. Several OECD countries have targeted the inappropriate use of acute health care services for LTC needs via financial measures, changes in administrative responsibilities and the introduction of information technology. Many OECD countries have attempted to coordinate or integrate health care and LTC services, but the difficulties faced are not trivial. The use of case managers and more geriatric expertise among health care professionals can help improve coordination and reduce admissions to, and time spent in, hospitals.

12.3.5   Lifting Employment

Workers can be encouraged to stay employed longer by tackling barriers to older workers' employment and flexible retirement, within and outside the pension system. Many pension systems currently allow some form of flexible retirement, but take-up remains low. Nearly three in five workers globally envisage a transition to retirement where they either work part-time in retirement or continue working past retirement age (Aegon, 2018). However, only a minority of employers appear to offer older workers these options. Governments could consider abolishing the practice of mandatory retirement set by firms or collective agreements, while reforming employment rules to provide employers with greater flexibility to dismiss poorly performing workers. Another option is to grant firms more flexibility in reallocating older workers within the firm to improve the match between the skills of older workers and the tasks of the job. Given the deterioration of abilities along the lifetime, the possibility to change tasks as people age can be useful in extending the working life (Anghel and Lacuesta, 2020).

The public sector could lead the way by curtailing the use of mandatory retirement at a certain age for civil servants. Governments can encourage firms to hire and retain older workers through regulation, employer guidelines and information campaigns. Flexible working hours and workplaces can help respond to ageing, for instance through teleworking arrangements that make it easier for older workers to remain active.

In some instances, tackling objective barriers to retaining older workers may involve measures to better align the age productivity and wage profiles in collective bargaining agreements. For example, seniority wage-setting in collective bargaining agreements or insufficiently flexible wages can make older workers relatively costly to hire compared with how productive they are, as older workers' productivity may decline at old age for repetitive tasks or for health-related reasons. Overall, a package of placement, training and counselling measures targeted at disadvantaged older workers may be more effective than the wage subsidies some countries apply.

If people are to extend their working lives, they must have access to effective skills development throughout their life to enable them to update and upgrade their skills according to changing labour market needs. Lifelong learning programmes for older workers should be designed to strengthen the skills required to perform non-routine jobs and to address the skills needs of technology-intensive occupations in the digital economy.

Finally, expanding the labour supply of low-skilled workers, women and youth can help to mitigate the effects of ageing on dependency ratios. Promoting a good start for the youth in their working lives can yield the double benefit of increasing employment rates and fighting lifelong inequalities that build up early in life, resulting in old-age poverty decades later. Policies to enhance skills and labour market inclusion of the youth include providing sufficient employment orientation, especially to those who cannot draw on social support networks, strengthening vocational education, and designing effective labour market policies to connect youths not in employment, education, or training with jobs.

Female participation gaps remain high in many countries. A better provision of affordable childcare for children below three and child-friendly employment arrangements are key to closing gender gaps. Efforts to raise the supply of formal long-term care would help reduce the burden from taking care of the elderly, which disproportionately falls on women. Many countries also have scope to remove tax and benefit disincentives to work for second earners, such as tax allowances for non-working spouses and systems of joint taxation.

12.4   CONCLUSION

Rising old-age dependency ratios will put unprecedented stress on the financing of public pensions, health and long-term care, especially in a slow growth environment.

Pension reform should address the triple challenge of improving fiscal sustainability and reducing old-age poverty risks, while ensuring a fair sharing of the burden across generations. Advanced economies, where ageing is already well under way, typically face more pressing challenges to finance rising pension costs. Depending on each country's existing pension systems and policy objectives, options include linking the retirement age to life expectancy, allowing for flexible retirement with adequate financial incentives, expanding pension coverage of non-standard workers and improving the adequacy of safety net pensions.

Rising health and long-term care expenditure will exacerbate the pressure on public finances already strained by rising pension costs. Promoting healthy ageing, containing costs, and realizing efficiency gains in the health and long-term care sector is crucial to ensure sustainability.

In many emerging economies, ensuring sufficient coverage of pensions, health and long-term care is the main challenge. Reducing informality will be essential to improve the financing and adequacy of pension and social security systems. Policy action should rest on three pillars: reducing the costs of formalization, increasing the perceived benefits of formal employment, and strengthening compliance with regulations through better enforcement.

To increase employment, policies should tackle barriers to the employment of older workers, such as mandatory retirement, lack of flexible work arrangements and seniority wage-setting. Promoting lifelong skills development to enhance the employability and productivity of senior workers, through training in the use of digital technologies will help. Policies to improve the labour force inclusion of women, youth and migrants can counter the decline in the workforce and help mitigate the consequences of ageing on the financing of pensions and can reduce old-age inequality and poverty. Policies that help reconcile work and family commitments are key to encouraging female labour force participation and can also have a positive effect on fertility.

REFERENCES

Acemoglu, D. and Restrepo, P. (2021), "Demographics and automation". *Review of Economic Studies*, 89, 1–44.

Aegon (2018), "The new social contract: A blueprint for retirement in the 21st century". *The Aegon Retirement Readiness Survey 2018*, Center for Longevity and Retirement.

Anghel, B. and Lacuesta, A. (2020), "Ageing productivity and retirement status", *Bank of Spain Economic Bulletin*, 2020/1.

Colombo, F., Llena-Nozal, A., Mercier, J., and Tjadens, F. (2011), "Help wanted?: Providing and paying for long-term care", *OECD Health Policy Studies*. Paris: OECD Publishing.

Crowe, D., Haas, J., Millot, V., Rawdanowicz, Ł., and Turban, S. (2022), "Population ageing and government revenue: Expected trends and policy considerations to boost revenue", *Economics Department* Working Paper No. 1373.

De la Maisonneuve, C., Moreno-Serra, R., Murtin, F., and Oliveira Martins, J. (2016), "The drivers of public health spending: Integrating policies and institutions", *OECD Economics Department* Working Paper No. 1283. Paris: OECD Publishing.

Garcia Escribano, M., Juarros, P., and Mogues, T. (2022), "Patterns and drivers of health spending efficiency", *IMF* Working Paper No. 2022/048.

Geppert, C., Guillemette, Y., Morgavi, H., and Turner, D. (2019), "Labour supply of older people in advanced economies: The impact of changes to statutory retirement ages", *OECD Economics Department* Working Paper No. 1554. Paris: OECD Publishing.

Guillemette, Y. and Turner, D. (2018), "The long view: Scenarios for the world economy to 2060", *OECD Economic* Policy Paper No. 22. Paris: OECD Publishing.

Guillemette, Y. and Turner, D. (2021), "The long game: Fiscal outlooks to 2060 underline need for structural reform", *OECD Economic* Policy Paper No. 29. Paris: OECD Publishing.

ILO and OECD (2019), *New Job Opportunities in an Ageing Society*. Paris: OECD.

Lorenzoni, L., Murtin, F., Springare, L., Auraaen, A., and Daniel, F. (2018), "Which policies increase value for money in health care?", *OECD Health* Working Papers No. 104. Paris: OECD Publishing.

Lorenzoni, L., Marino, A., Morgan, D., and James, C. (2019), "Health spending projections to 2030: New results based on a revised OECD methodology", *OECD Health* Working Paper No. 110. Paris: OECD Publishing.

Marino, A., Morgan, D., Lorenzoni, L., and James, C. (2017), "Future trends in health care expenditure: A modelling framework for cross-country forecasts", *OECD Health* Working Paper No. 95. Paris: OECD Publishing.

OECD (2015), *Fiscal Sustainability of Health Systems: Bridging Health and Finance Perspectives*. Paris: OECD Publishing.

OECD (2016), "Better ways to pay for health care", *OECD Health Policy Studies*. Paris: OECD Publishing.

OECD (2017a), *Health at a Glance 2017: OECD Indicators*. Paris: OECD Publishing.

OECD (2017b), *Pensions at a Glance 2017: OECD and G20 Indicators*. Paris: OECD Publishing.

OECD (2017c), *Preventing Ageing Unequally*. Paris: OECD Publishing.

OECD (2017d), *Tackling Wasteful Spending on Health*. Paris: OECD Publishing.

OECD (2018), *Financial Incentives and Retirement Savings*. Paris: OECD Publishing.

OECD (2020), "Spending on long-term care", *OECD Policy Brief* Paris; OECD Publishing.

OECD (2021), *Health at a Glance 2021: OECD Indicators*. Paris: OECD Publishing.

Oliveira Hashiguchi, T. and Llena-Nozal, A. (2020), "The effectiveness of social protection for long-term care in old age: Is social protection reducing the risk of poverty associated with care needs?", *OECD Health* Working Papers No. 117. Paris: OECD Publishing.

Rouzet, D., Caldera Sánchez, A., Renault, T., and Roehn, O. (2019), "Fiscal challenges and inclusive growth in ageing societies", *OECD Economic* Policy Papers No. 27.

Thaler, R. and Benartzi, S. (2004), "Save more tomorrow: Using behavioral economics to increase employee saving", *Journal of Political Economy*, 112(S1), S164–S187.

13. Climate transition: implications for fiscal policies

Lorenzo Forni

13.1 INTRODUCTION

The fight against climate change has become a global policy priority in the last decades and particularly in recent years. Most countries have committed to reducing their emissions within the 2015 Paris Agreement. The goal is limiting the global temperature rise to below 2°C above pre-industrial levels and pursuing efforts to limit it to 1.5°C. For example, the European Union committed to reducing emissions by 55 per cent by 2030 compared with 1990 levels and achieving net zero emissions by 2050. These targets are enshrined in the European Climate Law of 29 July 2021 and are binding for all member countries.[1] Several countries increased their commitments in various ways at the COP26 meeting held in Glasgow in 2021 and afterwards. Prior to Glasgow, the Biden administration in the US announced a (non-binding) target to reduce net greenhouse gas emissions by between 50 per cent and 52 per cent by 2030, compared with 2005 levels; the UK adopted an emissions reduction target of 78 per cent by 2035 compared with 1990 levels. Thus, at least for advanced countries, there seems no lack of progress on commitments.

However, following up on all these commitments will not be easy. It will require not only formulation of a detailed strategy, including a range of measures defined at the sectoral level, but also the establishment of clear governance to manage the process. Not only will following through on these commitments be challenging but also, to date, they are insufficient to achieve the Intergovernmental Panel on Climate Change (IPCC) goal of containing global warming to 1.5°C by the end of this century. At present, the best estimates are that the current commitments are consistent with an end-of-century temperature increase of more than 2°C, rather than the 1.5°C deemed necessary to avoid significant climate change-related consequences (Climate Action Tracker, 2022). Of course, the situation differs among countries. Some have made significant progress in recent years, thanks largely to the substitution of coal with natural gas for power generation, and some have been able to meet the 2020 targets. However, further progress will be much more difficult.

In the European Union, the sharp increases in energy prices and the geo-political implications of Russia's invasion of Ukraine hindered investment in the green transition. Governments have prioritized reduction of their energy dependence on Russia, combined with accessing alternative affordable sources, which, in many cases, has implied a return to use of fossil fuels such as oil and coal. The need to reduce polluting emissions seems to have been relegated to some future yet to be identified. So extreme was the rise in energy prices that some European governments intervened to ease the increases. This is incon-sistent with climate needs that require a rise in the costs associated with CO_2 emissions and, thus, an increase in energy costs. What remains of European governments' ambitious commitments to reduce greenhouse gas emissions? The European Commission seems to be responding by implementing efforts to accelerate the green transition. In the RePowerEU plan, announced on 18 May 2022,[2] it reiterated the commitment to reducing emissions by 55 per cent by 2030 compared with 1990 levels, and achieving net zero emissions by 2050. The RePowerEU plan includes several measures to boost energy efficiency, diversify energy sources, accelerate adoption of renewables, reduce fossil fuel consumption in industry and transportation and increase public investment, but the challenges are significant.[3]

In addition, the strong growth in government spending because of the pandemic has not been directed toward "green" spending. The Covid-19 pandemic triggered the expansion of fiscal deficits, involving massive inter-ventions to rescue the economy. However, in many countries, the composition of these interventions caused emissions to increase further rather than to reduce. According to estimates from Vivideconomics (2021), only around $5 trillion out of a total announced or approved fiscal stimulus of $17.2 trillion, as of July 2021, had green features. As of July 2021, 15 of the G20 countries' announced stimulus measures that would have a negative environmental effect. According to Pigato et al. (2021), at the end of May 2021, the global announced fiscal stimulus totalled $19.8 trillion, with the 24 highest-income economies accounting for more than three-quarters of this amount. About 85 per cent of spending was aimed at "rescuing" the economy and can be classified, almost entirely, as "legacy" or "light brown" spending to support households, businesses and activities that would otherwise not have survived. Recovery spending accounted for only 15 per cent of the total stimulus. It included a relatively large share of green spending (19.4 per cent) and an even larger share of high-emitting activities (20.4 per cent). Thus, in general, the large sums invested in coping with the pandemic have not contributed to reducing emissions; on the contrary, they have probably contributed to their increase. Governments are now being faced with higher public debts, less time to implement climate measures and increased emissions compared with the pre-pandemic situation. Thus, governments are finding that they have less fiscal space, but greater urgency to reduce emissions.

To meet the emissions targets required to avoid the risk of severe and irreversible climate change, governments – and fiscal policies in particular – must rapidly increase the ambition of their interventions. This begs the question of how to build a public policy package that, on the one hand, makes emissions increasingly costly, and, on the other hand, contributes – through public investment and tax incentives – to the growth of low-emission energy production capacity and energy efficiency. These measures cannot be the same for the whole economy and will require adaptation to the specific characteristics and needs of different production sectors. Finance ministries and fiscal policies more generally, must bear responsibility for this process, based on their obligations to implement fiscal measures to enable achievement of the official goals in terms of emission reductions. However, currently, even the most virtuous countries are producing higher levels of emissions than is consistent with their announced targets. In short, despite announced commitments, we have yet to truly embark on the path to a green transition.

The road to achieving climate goals involves at least three obstacles for fiscal policies. The first is the further increase in public debt that will be needed to finance the expenditure associated with the green transition. The second is the political barriers related to the required increase in emissions costs, which will have inflationary and redistributive effects. The third relates to the political uncertainty stemming from alternating governments with different preferences and sensitivities regarding the green transition.

This chapter will first discuss the range of fiscal tools that policymakers can use to steer the transition (Section 13.2). Second, it will argue that a combination of diverse fiscal tools might be needed to support the transition and that accepting a higher level of public debt during the transition phase is probably the strategy that can better achieve debt sustainability in the long run (Section 13.3). Section 13.4 highlights the challenges that fiscal policy must face, even assuming a fiscal strategy to support the transition has been devised. Finally, the paper will offer some suggestions on how fiscal policy should address the green transition, making the point that general climate principles and targets should be enshrined in the law and that all measures implemented by governments and fiscal authorities should follow from these principles (Section 13.5).

13.2   SEVERAL FISCAL INSTRUMENTS CAN SUPPORT THE GREEN TRANSITION

Economists have long advocated for the use of a carbon tax or a cap-and-trade system as a fiscal policy tool to reduce emissions. These systems are built on the idea that emissions impose a cost on society, so companies must pay if they want to release greenhouse gases into the atmosphere. The underlying economic principle is externality: the emitting entity creates a negative externality that must be corrected by means of a Pigouvian tax. However, although a carbon tax is considered a fiscal policy pillar in relation to reducing the rise in emissions, global carbon tax levels remain low. Only about 20 per cent of global emissions are covered by a carbon pricing programme, and at a global average price – when taking account fossil fuel subsidies – is just a few dollars per ton. This is very far from the circa $75 per ton global carbon price that is estimated to be needed to reduce emissions to maintain global warming at below 2°C (Parry, 2021).

It must be said that, within the international community, a more nuanced position regarding carbon pricing seems to be developing. There is a recognition that in the short run the elasticity of demand for energy to its price is quite low and that even large price increases for CO_2 emissions and, therefore, energy prices, may not stimulate significant levels of substitution by lower-emission forms of production. This would occur were there to be insufficient green (low-emissions) energy production capacity or green energy production not technologically well integrated into traditional energy production and distribution systems, such that economic agents would be unable to replace easily high-emissions energy sources with green energy sources even were the price charged for emissions to increase. The energy crisis in Europe, related to the Russian invasion of Ukraine, has made this point quite clear: at the present time, European countries do not have sufficient installed green energy production capacity to significantly reduce their gas consumption, despite the still relatively high gas prices. So, in the short term, the chances of substitution are limited. This limited short-run substitutability might limit the effectiveness of carbon prices in the short run also in normal times. For example, increasing the carbon tax may not be effective for reducing the use of combustion engine vehicles and promoting purchases of electric vehicles. A carbon tax would raise the price of gasoline only to a limited extent and, in the absence of a widespread network of recharging stations, would not encourage the purchase and use of electric cars. Investment in recharging stations would be more effective (Stock and Stuart, 2021). A second limitation of the carbon tax is that, in the current context with limited alternatives to traditional energy sources, it leads to an increase in the cost of energy and, thus, weighs particularly heavily on lower-income households for whom energy-related expenditure accounts for a relatively higher share of their incomes. This acts as a strong barrier to policies that impose a cost on or raise the price of emissions.

Overall, there is a need to construct a public policy package that, on the one hand, recognizes the importance of carbon pricing as a policy tool by making emissions increasingly expensive, but, on the other hand, acknowledges its limitations and the need for other policies to complement carbon pricing. Fiscal policy can deploy other instruments to foster the climate transition, from incentives for private investments, to public green investments for mitigation, to direct regulation. The goal of these different measures would be to curb high-emissions activities while at the same time supporting the creation of higher production capacity of low-emissions energy. As I will argue in the next section, this process is likely to lead to higher public debt, not least because the transition will produce distributional effects that will need to be addressed.

13.3 THE FISCAL COST OF THE GREEN TRANSITION IS GOING TO BE SIGNIFICANT

There are three major areas of climate-related intervention that would affect public budgets: measures to support the "mitigation" process, that is, to reduce emissions; measures to support the "adaptation" process, that is, to both preventively and *ex post* manage the costs caused by extreme climate events (tornadoes, floods, fires, etc.); measures to address the distributive impact of the transition, be they the need to support workers in shrinking sectors, or measures to support households and firms to face the potentially high cost of energy during the transition.

There are several reasons why, within a package of measures – including carbon pricing or direct regulation – aimed at curbing emissions, an expansionary fiscal policy in the form of subsidies or direct public investment might be appropriate. First, as already mentioned, there is a need to increase green energy production capacity, both through public investment and private investment which may need to be subsidized. Second, an expansionary fiscal policy could help to support economic activity during the energy transition, when the high cost of energy is likely to have negative effects on economic activity. Specifically, fiscal policies aimed at fostering the expansion of green sectors would help to contain emissions and global warming in the medium term, and therefore reduce the associated negative impacts of climate change on the economy, while at the same time support economic activity in the short term. In turn, this would imply an expansionary effect on economic activity in both the short and medium-to-long runs and would therefore help to contain the long-run increase in government debt-to-GDP ratios.

In short, expansionary fiscal policy can raise green investments and so support economic activity to counteract the supply-side shock on brown sectors imposed by the rising cost of emissions. The latter will reduce activity in the high-emitting sectors, while subsidies and green public investment will foster production in low-emitting sectors. In this way, fiscal policy will accelerate the transition, by containing activity in brown sectors and expanding the one in green sectors. Estimates conducted with integrated macroeconomic and climate models – in which the public sector is assumed to rebate carbon tax revenues in green tax incentives and, also, to activate green public investments – show that such policies may indeed also be optimal for long-term public debt sustainability. Compared with alternative policies, an increase in public debt to GDP would be observed in the short run to finance subsidies and government public investment, but it would drop to lower levels in the medium to long runs (Catalano et al., 2021).[4]

At this point, we might wonder whether the public spending currently planned by countries will be sufficient to achieve the stated goals. We have seen that, at the global level, it would not. However, since the European Union embarked on the de-carbonization path earlier than some other world areas, it can give us an indication on how complicated the journey might be. The European Environmental Agency analyses show that, in order to meet the 2030 targets, all major eurozone countries would need to reduce their yearly emissions by 5 per cent, to 8 per cent, a faster pace than achieved, on average, in the past.[5] Also, the transport and construction sectors, which are not subject to the European Trading System (ETS), are particularly lagging.[6] It must be emphasized however, that the situation is quickly evolving. For example, the European National Recovery and Resilience Plan (NRRP) calls for increased green spending. It requires EU countries: (1) to allocate at least 37 per cent of their NRRP funds, to measures that contribute to the green transition; and (2) for the remaining initiatives to comply with the principle of "Do No Significant Harm" (DNSH), which means that any NRRP interventions should not be harmful to the environment.

In terms of costs, those related to adaptation expenditures are difficult to estimate because they require forecasts of the progress of adverse climate phenomena related to global warming. According to Barrage's (2021) analysis for the US, climate change might affect: (i) government intermediate consumption expenditures (e.g., health care); (ii) government transfers (e.g., income support); (iii) tax revenues; and (iv) expenditure on adaptations to climate change impacts (e.g., public funding for the construction of sea walls to protect against sea-level rises). Barrage estimates that, under a high-emissions scenario, climate change will increase total government consumption needs (and transfers) by about 1.45 per cent by 2050, with health care expenditures accounting for most of the cost increases. This low estimate should be considered a minimum level. It reflects the fact that, in the US, the federal government and states intervene relatively little in environmental disasters and a large portion of the costs are covered by private insurance companies.

Finally, the distributional effects of the green transition could be extremely significant. Some sectors may have to downsize considerably, which will raise the question of how to compensate displaced workers. This compensation would appear essential to prevent the formation of political blocs that oppose the transition. In fact, it would be realistic to expect that these blocs would form anyway and will have the power to obtain generous concessions. The fiscal cost of these compensations is, currently, difficult to quantify, but should not be underestimated.

13.4 FISCAL POLICIES MUST RAPIDLY INCREASE THE AMBITION OF THEIR INTERVENTIONS

Finance and budget policy ministries are key players in managing the energy transition. The task is complex, as policymakers will have to face several challenges: (i) a growing need to use the fiscal lever to support the transition, with the associated likely increase in public debts; (ii) the political economy and distributional hurdles related to the transition; (iii) the need for consistency and credibility in policies if these need to steer expectations and private sector behaviours. In consideration of these challenges, the ambition of fiscal policies in the climate space should be stepped up significantly.

A first challenge that budgetary policy will have to face, as already argued, is the further increase in public debt necessary to finance expenditure related to the green transition. An increase in the public debt to GDP related to financing green public investment and green incentives could lead to a surge in public debt in the short run, but to its containment (compared with a scenario with less public investment) in the long run. This is because this type of spending would help to limit the increase in emissions and, thus, temperatures and adverse weather events, which have negative effects on the economy. However, managing an increase in public debt – from the high level already reached – will be challenging.

The second issue is the political obstacles related to the need for an increase in the cost of emissions, which will have inflationary and redistributive effects. In fact, achieving the Paris goals will require strengthened measures on the emissions costs side. It will be unfeasible to curb emissions to the extent necessary based only on expenditure side interventions (public investment and incentives), since this would put at risk the sustainability of public budgets (Catalano et al., 2021). Recall that green public investments support the transition on the supply side, but also support overall consumer demand without necessarily directing it toward green consumption. Therefore, a large reliance on carbon pricing will be unavoidable, and with it the need to support the households and firms more exposed to its effects.

Third, fiscal policy needs to play a crucial role in establishing credible measures and criteria that will influence long-term expectations. Climate policies must persist beyond the terms of alternating governments and must not focus only on the expenditure side. The stability of climate policies beyond electoral cycles is necessary to create a stable set of long-term rules. Climate policies will be credible if, in addition to being predictable, they are consistent with climate goals and fiscally sustainable. Thus, it is important to acknowledge that emissions targets cannot be achieved just by leveraging budget incentives.[7] That is, we cannot construct a credible and lasting de-carbonization strategy based only on fiscal incentives. This would risk expenditure of substantial amounts of public resources with no coherent or plausible plan – something that is vital for the sustainable achievement of emissions reduction targets. To make the transition happen, clear and credible policies, able to direct private sector long-term expectations and help shift investment to lower-emitting sectors (G30 Working Group on Climate Change and Finance, 2020), are required. However, the formulation of long-term clear and credible policies, in a context of limited budget space, numerous other urgencies (e.g., military spending) and high levels of uncertainty about climate and technological developments, is far from straightforward. It involves the risk of suboptimal choices, such as over-investment in a technology that may not be the dominant one in the future. Governments should not focus on choosing among specific technologies, but rather should find ways to incentivize the adoption of low-emission technologies, while leaving it to the private sector to decide in which ones to invest.

13.5   HOW TO MOVE FORWARD

Many governments around the world, especially in advanced economies, have announced ambitious commitments in terms of emission reductions. However, they don't have the required policies ready to deliver on these commitments, or have a suitable governance process in place. Indeed, most governments around the world are only now beginning to incorporate climate goals in their budget processes. Green Public Finance Management (PFM), for example, is mostly embryonic even in the advanced economies; an OECD (2021) survey on green budgeting practices found that 60 per cent of OECD member countries do not use it. Only 14 countries in the world have implemented some form of green budgeting, mostly limited to *ex ante* or *ex post* environmental impact analyses to inform budget decisions. Implementation of green budgeting practices in Europe is scarce and, currently, is based on widely differing methodological approaches (Bova, 2021). Even the countries whose thinking is the most advanced in relation to the implementation of such policies tend to be at an early stage.

Moreover, emergencies able to push the green transition lower on the policy agenda often occur. Recently, it has been the rising prices of energy commodities resulting from Russia's invasion of Ukraine. This rise in gas prices so far had the effect, globally, of encouraging a renewal of fossil energy, by use of especially oil and coal which are relatively cheaper. In Europe, governments have also missed an opportunity to let rising energy prices exert a more decisive consumption-reducing effect. Several European governments have intervened to curb rising energy costs, while a policy consistent with the need to address the climate transition would allow energy prices to rise and provide targeted support only to the most affected households and threatened businesses. However, the interventions have instead helped a very wide range of taxpayers and resulted in public expenditure of significant amounts with aims that conflict with the objective of emissions reduction.

In this contribution I have argued that fiscal policy is essential to steer the green transition. Carbon pricing should be used more forcefully to contain production in high-emitting sectors, while fiscal incentives and direct green public investment should foster an increase in green capital. The limited time span that the world has to reach Net Zero and avoid significant increases in temperatures, mandates a credible and effective intervention from fiscal policies. To achieve this, countries should enshrine climate goals in their national laws (some countries have approved climate laws) which define the criteria that governments must adhere to. For example, "Do No Significant Harm" (DNSH) is a smart priority, which perhaps could have contributed to limiting recent government measures in Europe to cap energy prices. In addition, independent institutions, such as climate councils, should be entrusted with monitoring the achievement of the targets set in national laws. If climate targets are incorporated in the national laws, then it will be imperative for climate councils to have the expertise necessary to make the relevant assessments and the power to force policy changes. Nevertheless, any change in this direction would constitute only a first step. We need much bolder and speedier action on the part of governments.

NOTES

1. Even within the private sector, several companies have made net zero commitments by 2050. The Glasgow Financial Alliance for Net Zero (GFANZ) brings together a significant number of global financial institutions that have pledged to achieve the net zero goal by 2050.
2. https://ec.europa.eu/commission/presscorner/detail/en/ip_22_3131
3. In the EU, climate policy is included in the European Green Deal framework (European Commission, 2019). The European Green Deal or European Green Pact is a set of policy initiatives proposed by the European Commission, aimed at achieving climate neutrality in Europe by 2050. Within this framework, the "Fit for 55" package of measures to reduce net greenhouse gas emissions by at least 55% by 2030, compared to 1990 levels, has recently moved forward with the adoption of several proposals. The EU now has legally binding climate targets covering the main sectors of the economy.

Fiscal policy in a turbulent era

4. Also, green expenditures might have a higher multiplier than dirty expenditures and so might contribute more to supporting economic activity (Batini et al., 2021).
5. https://www.eea.europa.eu/data-and-maps/data/data-viewers/greenhouse-gases-viewer
6. The existing EU Emissions Trading System (ETS) encompasses sectors such as thermoelectric, refineries, metallurgical, petrochemical, chemical, and manufacturing (including cement, lime, ceramics, bricks, paper, etc.), as well as combustion plants with a power capacity exceeding 20 MW. However, following the legislation passed in April 2023, the ETS will be expanded to include the maritime sector. In addition, a distinct ETS will be established to regulate emissions originating from buildings, road transport, and fuels.
7. In addition, budget incentives typically tend to be transitory and target-specific sectors.

REFERENCES

Barrage, L. (2021), "The Fiscal Costs of Climate Change in the United States", *Mimeo* UCSD.
Batini, N., M. Di Serio, M. Fragetta, G. Melina and A. Waldron (2021), "Building Back Better: How Big are Green Spending Multipliers?", *Ecological Economics*, 193(C).
Bova, E. (2021), "Green Budgeting Practices in the EU: A First Review", *European Commission* Discussion Paper No 140.
Catalano M. and L. Forni (2021), "Fiscal Policies for a Sustainable Recovery and a Green Transformation", *Policy Research* Working Paper No. 9799. Washington, D.C., World Bank Group. http://documents.worldbank.org/curated/en/499301633704126369/Fiscal-Policies-for-a-Sustainable-Recovery-and-a-Green-Transformation.
Catalano, M., L. Forni and E. Pezzolla (2019), "Climate Change Adaptation – the Role of Fiscal Policy", *Resource and Energy Economics*, 59.
Climate Action Tracker (2022), "Glasgow's 2030 Credibility Gap: Net Zero's Lip Service to Climate Action", *Climate Action Tracker* 2022.
European Commission (2019), *The European Green Deal*, COM(2019) 640 final.
G30 Working Group on Climate Change and Finance (2020), "Mainstreaming the Transition to a Net-Zero Economy", *G30 Working Group on Climate Change and Finance*, https://group30.org/publications/detail/4791
OECD (2021), *Green Budgeting in OECD Countries*. Paris: OECD Publishing.
Parry, I. (2021), "Five Things to Know about Carbon Pricing, Finance and Development", *IMF*, September, https://www.imf.org/en/Publications/fandd/issues/2021/09/five-things-to-know-about-carbon-pricing-parry
Pigato, M., R. Rafaty, J. Kai and J. Kurle (2021), "The COVID-19 Crisis and the Road to Recovery: Green or Brown?", *The World Bank* Working Paper No. 166127.
Stock, J.H. and D. Stuart (2021), "Emissions and Electricity Price Effects of a Small Carbon Tax Combined with Renewable Tax Credit Extensions", *Harvard University* Working Paper.
Vivideconomics (2021), "Greenness of Stimulus Index", *Vivideconomics*, Finance for Biodiversity Initiative, https://www.vivideconomics.com/wp-content/uploads/2021/07/Green-Stimulus-Index-6th-Edition_final-report.pdf

PART IV

Conclusion

14. The future of fiscal policy

Vitor Gaspar, Sandra Lizarazo and Adrián Peralta-Alva

14.1   INTRODUCTION

Fiscal policy is as vast as public finance. The budget has a central role in determining who gets what. The budget lies at the heart of politics. But politics is also a fundamental means for fiscal policy. The primacy of liberal democracies' Parliament in budget matters is a fundamental pillar of the complex set of institutional arrangements that deliver the ability of the Treasury to credibly commit to repaying public debt. And public debt, in turn, constitutes, together with tax capacity, the distinctive characteristic of modern public finance. Fiscal policy is therefore a financial record of the relations between the state and civil society.

The focus of this chapter is much narrower. It is limited to fiscal policy in macroeconomics. The idea is to look at developments in fiscal policy in the last decades to identify important avenues to the future of fiscal policy in theory and practice. To do so, we will focus on the interaction between fiscal and monetary policy over time. Interest rates, debt levels, and fiscal policy space play a fundamental role in this interaction through the government's budget constraint. The chapter will look at growth, price stability, financial stability, and business cycle fluctuations only. It will largely abstract from international complications.[1]

The next section of the paper deals with government debt, capital accumulation, and growth. It asks the classical questions: Do government deficits absorb private savings? Does the accumulation of public debt diminish the stock of productive private capital?[2] It does so in a general equilibrium, overlapping generations model that reproduces a low interest rate environment. Specifically, the model is calibrated so that the interest rate is lower than the growth rate of the economy ($r<g$). We argue that even in such a benign situation, government deficits absorb private savings and public debt crowds out productive private sector assets, thereby diminishing output growth.

The third section changes the focus from real to nominal interest rates. It looks at the monetary and fiscal policy mix from 1965 to 2022. The link to the second section comes from the fact that low equilibrium real interest rates increase the likelihood of the zero or effective lower bound (ELB) becoming binding.[3] That, in turn, leads to strong Keynesian type complementarities between fiscal and monetary policies.

Section 14.4 zooms in to the last 15 years, that is, the turbulent era. It argues that the scope of fiscal policy has become broader as the government has increasingly taken the role of a financier of last resort.[4] While this expanded role has helped people and firms to bounce back from the pandemic and contributed to financial stability, the government can only perform this role efficiently if it has credibility and fiscal policy space.

The three main sections, in our view, provide a useful perspective on fiscal policy, interest rates and the accumulation of assets and liabilities over time. Some difficult questions for researchers, politicians, and policymakers about the future of fiscal policy are posed in our concluding section. Our main takeaway is that effective fiscal policy demands fiscal credibility, achieved through fiscal buffers or a predictable fiscal framework.

14.2   GOVERNMENT DEBT AND CAPITAL ACCUMULATION

Debt-to-GDP ratios, in advanced economies (AEs), reached record highs in 2020. According to the IMF Global Database, debt reached the highly symbolic level of 100 percent of GDP.[5] It increased by 16 percentage points (pp) of GDP, on the year, reflecting the very strong fiscal policy response to COVID-19 and the contraction in economic activity that accompanied the Great Lockdown. But, surprisingly, and almost paradoxically, these record high levels of public debt were accompanied by record low interest rates and debt servicing costs (see Figure 4.1 in Chapter 4). Low nominal interest rates can, in part, be explained by monetary policy interventions. But structural factors also pushed neutral real interest rates lower. Relevant factors include slowing productivity growth; the demographic transition; and the elevated savings relative to investment (the savings glut). The issue has been widely debated (see, for example, Bean et al., 2015; Blanchard, 2019, 2023; and Chapter 4 in this book).

In a series of recent works that have reinvigorated the literature about debt sustainability, Blanchard (2019, 2023) argues that the costs associated with the accumulation of public debt may be considerably less than traditionally believed. Blanchard's argument hinges on interest rates on public debt (r) being lower than GDP growth rates (g). r–g<0 became the focus of a very lively policy debate. It was claimed that r–g<0 turned the case for fiscal prudence upside down. r–g<0 restored the paradox of thrift: spending freely and boldly was the way to high levels of economic activity and employment now and to growth and prosperity in the future; under these conditions there was a free lunch available for wise politicians and policymakers to use.

Here we want to explore channels through which costs of public debt may be high.[6] One such channel comes from the possibility of fiscal crises. The theoretical literature shows that public debt above some threshold exposes countries to failures to meet their debt obligations due to their inability to pay in response to an unexpected shock or to multiple equilibria. In such an environment, attacks and market scares are possible (Cole and Kehoe, 2000; Aguiar and Amador, 2021). There is also an empirical literature on the determinants of fiscal crises (see Moreno Badia et al., 2022, for a recent example). The possibility of scares, crises and financial instability provides a very relevant case for fiscal prudence. Nevertheless, that is not the route that we will explore in this chapter. We will focus on a much simpler mechanism.

Reis (2021) emphasized that while the interest rate on public debt is frequently below growth rates of GDP, that is not sufficient for debt to be free. In fact, the marginal return on private capital is typically estimated to be much higher than both the return on public debt and the growth rate of GDP (see Figure 14.1). The accumulation of public debt may be costly because it may reduce the accumulation of productive private capital. The crucial issue here is whether government debt crowds out private capital accumulation. If Ricardian equivalence (Barro, 1979) holds there is no crowding out. But there is also no effect of deficit financing on aggregate demand. Deficit finance entails a perfect offset from taxpayers that save to compensate their future tax liabilities (see Tobin, 1980).

Cao et al. (2023) focus squarely on the consequences of public debt crowding out private capital. Crowding out works in the following way. Total savings are distributed in a portfolio with two assets, public debt, and private capital.[7] The mechanism is standard, but the relevant question now is how quantitatively relevant it may be. The issue is addressed by first considering a simplified economy that can be analytically solved. The quantitative experiment uses a standard calibration and considers an initial level of public debt of 60 percent of GDP.[8] Public debt jumps 60pp of GDP. According to the calibrated model, this translates into a decline in the capital stock of about 16 percent and a corresponding permanent loss of 7.7 percent of GDP per period. The economic cost of public debt is very large measured in terms of lost output.

The simple model has the advantage of being analytically tractable, but it is not obvious that the quantitative impacts it predicts will hold in a more realistic economy. Cao et al. (2023) build on the work of McGrattan et al. (2019), which includes many more realistic details on fiscal policies and demographics, which appear relevant to performing quantitative analysis. In the empirically

Note: Earning over capital is calculated by dividing Net Operating Surplus by Net Fixed Assets for the Non-financial corporate sector. The Euro Area aggregate is an unbalanced simple average. Period: 1995–2019, annual frequency. Ten-year bond yields are annual averages.
Source: OECD and IMF staff calculations.

Figure 14.1   *Interest rates have declined but the marginal product of capital is much higher*

calibrated model, the permanent annual loss of GDP is 8 percent, very close to what we found in the simplified economy.[9]

The point which is most interesting conceptually follows from the fact that $r–g<0$ in the initial steady-state. Nevertheless, the increase in debt financing was costly in terms of private capital accumulation and potential output. The interest rate is endogenous and a sufficiently large increase in public debt can generate a change in the sign of the difference. That is interesting. But the truly important point is that for dynamically efficient economies the accumulation of public debt will be costly irrespective of the relation between the return on public debt and the growth rate of the economy. This analysis focuses on the costs of public debt. An overall assessment of the impact of public debt, which goes beyond the scope of this chapter, would also consider the possible uses of the resources (e.g., public investment), which may positively impact the economy.

14.3   MONETARY–FISCAL POLICY MIX AND NOMINAL INTEREST RATES (1965–2022)

Monetary and fiscal policies always interact via the government's budget constraint. One fascinating example is the interaction between monetary and fiscal policy when monetary policy is constrained in its use of the policy interest rate. The constraint is binding when the neutral real rate – the rate that is compatible with price stability (and output at potential) – is *lower* than the real rate implied by setting the *nominal* policy rate at the ELB. At such a point, the monetary policy decision-maker cannot ease monetary policy through further reductions in the policy rate. Monetary policy has exhausted its (traditional) policy space.[10]

In a nutshell, the ELB comes from the existence of cash. Since households and firms can hold cash, they are reluctant to accept negative rates of return of their asset holdings. The ELB may not be zero as some assets provide convenience services (e.g., credit and debit cards) and carrying large amounts of cash is costly (e.g., storage, security, and insurance costs). Several authors have considered how the constraint can be removed altogether.[11] But, for the purpose of this section, we will take the constraint as a given.

There was a remarkable convergence between monetary policy practice and theory since the late 1990s, during the period of the "Great Moderation". The theory starts from a Real Business Cycle Model and adds three main ingredients: first, monopolistic competition to allow for price setting by individual firms; second, nominal frictions that prevent instantaneous price adjustment; third, money to pin down nominal variables. Abstracting from ELB leads to a clear division of labor between fiscal and monetary policy. Optimal fiscal policy offsets permanent distortions to the economy. For example, a wage subsidy can offset the effects of the average (monopolistic) mark-up. Such a perspective leads to thinking about fiscal policy as structural policy. Fiscal policy is crucial to promote investment in people and infrastructure, to provide incentives to save and invest; to work; to engage in research, accumulate knowledge and innovate. Fiscal policy is also crucial for distribution of income and wealth. Fiscal policy can also contribute to a resilient society. In a resilient society people and communities can bounce back from adversities. In contrast, monetary policy concentrates on preserving price stability. By doing so it keeps the economy close to potential over the business cycle.[12]

In the late 1990s and early 2000s there was a clear awareness that the zero lower bound (as the ELB was perceived back then) was a potential problem. But according to prevailing wisdom it was unlikely to be an actual problem. The world had just emerged from the Great Inflation of the late 1960s, 1970s and 1980s and inflation targeting promised an environment of low and stable inflation. Experience accumulated in the decades since the end of the Second World War, invited looking at floors on nominal interest rates as theoretical curiosities of no practical relevance. Second, the idea is that if the lower bound would bind, monetary policy could still resort to alternative instruments. The instruments include forward guidance (expectations management), asset purchases, long-term lending operations and yield curve control (see Bernanke, 2020, for an overview, and the discussion on unconventional monetary policy in Chapter 4 of this book).

Japan was the exception. For this country, the ELB was more than a theoretical curiosity. After the bursting of the bubble economy, inflation and nominal interest rates trended down. The struggle with too low inflation in Japan endured and is still ongoing (as of 2022). Since 1990, inflation in Japan has averaged around zero. In late 1999 the Bank of Japan introduced its zero-interest rate policy which has since followed. In 2013, it adopted an inflation target (at 2 percent). In 2016, it introduced yield curve control (YCC). But the general perception was that Japan was different. For example, savings rates were very high; the country was among the first in the world to experience the demographic transition into a declining labor force and declining population; and productivity growth was perceived to be low. Under such conditions it could be that the neutral real interest rate was particularly low in Japan. For a detailed, lucid, and well-informed review of the experience of Japan see Shirakawa (2021).

However, in the aftermath of the Global Financial Crisis (GFC) most AEs struggled to push inflation up to their 2 percent inflation target. Many were constrained by the ELB. Some looked stuck. Others temporarily exited just to be pushed back in the spring of 2020, when COVID-19 took the world economy by storm. For example, the ECB encountered the ELB during the 2010–2011 sovereign debt crises period and it took until 2022 to exit it.

The observations in the previous two paragraphs are impossible to reconcile with rational expectations under commitment. They open the way to notions such as management of expectations, earning credibility, inflation scares and much else. The truth is that we don't yet have a good model of credibility and expectations formation. Returning to Japan: on the one hand it is clear that the Bank of Japan (and the Japanese Government) has not been able to persuade the Japanese public (households and firms) that it is able to escape the "too low inflation trap". But, on the other hand, after more than 30 years, Japan has avoided a deflation spiral. Inflation expectations have been remarkably stable, suggesting some stickiness of inflation expectations near zero.[13]

The logic of the standard Neo-Keynesian model of policy analysis pushed for circumventing the effect of the ELB through persistence in policy. In practice, it led to forward guidance through lower for longer (i.e., keeping interest rates low for extended periods). In the case of the Fed, elements of average inflation targeting were introduced in the context of the review of its monetary policy strategy (Federal Reserve Board, 2020).

The latest reviews of monetary policy strategy by the Federal Reserve and by the ECB explicitly recognize the relevance of the ELB for monetary–fiscal interaction (see also European Central Bank, 2021). Specifically, when optimal policy rates are substantially lower than the ELB, monetary policy resorts to alternative instruments. Key among the instruments is forward guidance. "Low for long" meaning that interest rates will be kept low for an extended period. Under such conditions, fiscal multipliers are larger than in normal circumstances (see also Chapter 6). At the ELB there are considerable benefits associated with monetary–fiscal coordination. The limitations imposed on monetary policy space by the ELB are compensated by the fact that, by working together, monetary policy can empower fiscal policy by adding to the budget room to maneuver (Arbatli et al., 2016; Gaspar et al., 2016).[14]

Why has the ELB become a clear constraint on the conduct of monetary policy? We can identify three main reasons: first, the neutral real rate has been trending down for the majority of countries. Second, inflation trended down in most countries and converged to very low levels in several. Third, after 2007, overall economic volatility has considerably increased, which increases the frequency of events under which the zero lower bound may bind.

In recent years, central banks have used quantitative easing on top of forward guidance. Are there dangers associated with the use of non-conventional tools of monetary policy? Some channels have been mentioned in the literature. The first is the possibility of losses to the central bank balance sheet from holdings of long-term assets (e.g., government bonds). The second is the possibility of quantitative easing morphing into inflationary finance. On the first, central bank book losses do not impair the bank's ability to conduct monetary policy. The argument's relevance is, therefore, mostly political, and institutional. The second is most plausible if associated with reluctance to act quickly and decisively. That may be linked to financial stability considerations (see, Bernanke, 2022, for a review). Interestingly, forward guidance deliberately induces a delay in the response to inflation pressures, thereby heightening the danger of inflation financing.

In March 2020, under the threat from the COVID-19 pandemic, financial markets collapsed, and the world economy seemed about to enter an enduring tailspin. Unprecedented monetary and fiscal support was mobilized. Hall and Sargent (2022) liken the monetary–fiscal response to COVID-19 as war finance. Once the analogy is accepted, inflation is not surprising. In the same vein, given the evidence above on large multipliers, it is again not surprising that unprecedented stimulus eventually leads to considerable inflation.

With hindsight, the transition out of the ELB proved more turbulent than anticipated. The issue was well-understood (Gaspar et al., 2016) but its difficulty was underestimated. So, we are back to inflation fighting. Credibility is imperfect and inflation has already become a very salient macroeconomic policy problem in the perceptions of the public.

The experience of the 1960s and the 1970s is instructive. It was the epoch of stop-and-go policies. Monetary policy would tighten but, despite high inflation, would fail to keep policy tight in the face of economic slowdown. That implied that monetary policy did not stay tight long enough to end inflation. It looked like an endless and hopeless struggle.

The central banker's perspective is well captured in Arthur Burns' 1979 Per Jacobsson Lecture "The Anguish of Central Banking" (Burns, 1987). He recalls that monetary brakes were applied in 1966, 1969 and 1974 just to be eased as the economy slowed while inflation remained elevated. Imperfect credibility also plagued Paul Volcker's mandate (especially at the beginning). After aggressive tightening in October 1979, there was an equally dramatic drop in rates in 1980. At the time, the move was justified by a sharp drop in money growth (Volcker, 2018). With hindsight it was a mistake. Eventually the Volcker disinflation was successful. But the repetition of the stop-and-go pattern at the beginning made credibility harder to attain and increased the persistence of inflation. Long bond yields very significantly lagged the decline in headline inflation.

But the most spectacular challenges to credibility come from inconsistencies in the monetary–fiscal policy mix. The interaction between monetary and fiscal policy is always highly political. Tom Sargent (2022) tells the story of an episode, back from June 1976, at the Federal Reserve Board, in Washington, DC. It was a meeting with "academic consultants" presided by Fed Chairman Arthur Burns. Arthur Okun was the representative of the Keynesian perspective. When concluding, Okun warned Burns and other Governors that the Fed should not persist on its crusade to eliminate inflation quickly, against the preferences of the public. If they did so, they would only have themselves to blame if Congress were to legislate away the Fed's independence. Burns' concern with politics and fiscal policy pervades *The Anguish of Central Banking.*

14.4   WIDENING SCOPE OF FISCAL POLICY – CRISES IN ALL FORMS AND SHAPES

In the last 15 years the world economy has experienced profound crises, including the Global Financial Crisis, the European Sovereign Debt Crisis, the COVID-19 Pandemic, and the current Cost-of-Living Crisis. In response to these crises, the idea that stabilization policy should be the exclusive realm of monetary policy has been slowly abandoned (Furman, 2016).[15] The magnitude of the fiscal responses during these recent periods of extreme economic volatility has been massive.[16] Even more, under this broader scope, fiscal policy measures have been widely diverse, novel, increasingly flexible, and immediately impactful. It has helped economies to bounce back and bolster their resilience.

Key fiscal policy measures taken during deep crises focus on providing financial support to the corporate and financial sectors (e.g., credit guarantees, loan programs, liquidity injections) and in supporting households and firms (e.g., direct transfers, unemployment benefits, wage subsidies). There is evidence that these measures have been effective at mitigating the effects of significant crises.

For example, regarding support to households, Cunha et al. (2022) estimate at 1.5 the GDP fiscal multiplier of Brazil's emergency cash transfer program implemented during the COVID-19 crisis.[17] Similarly, the fourth bi-annual report of the European Commission on the temporary *Support to Mitigate Unemployment Risks in an Emergency* (SURE) asserts that the instrument protected 1.5 million people from unemployment in 2020 during the COVID-19 crisis.[18] Battersby et al. (2022) report that by acting as the financier of last resort through large financial support measures, including loans and guarantee programs, governments were able to avert a deeper economic contraction during the COVID-19 crisis, reducing its initial impact by about 3 percentage points of GDP.[19]

Yet the trade-offs imposed by using these measures cannot be ignored. For example, providing large-scale employment or consumption support might forfeit the ability to target the response, increasing its costs. Similarly, acting as a financier of last resort to distressed sectors in the economy exposes the public sector to contingent losses elevating the risks to fiscal stability (Battersby et al., 2022).[20]

To safely play an active policy role during a deep crisis and count with fiscal room to maneuver requires taking a longer-term perspective towards public finances (October 2022, IMF Fiscal Monitor). It requires accumulating fiscal buffers during good times and gaining or maintaining credibility. To accumulate fiscal buffers and gain or maintain credibility, governments must consistently exhibit fiscal prudence. One of the clearest lessons of the COVID-19 pandemic crises is that countries that could not deploy a large fiscal response experienced, before the cost-of-living crises broke out, a much slower recovery. Advanced economies recovered much faster than other economies and were able to increase their deficits by much more. At the onset of the crisis, AEs counted on average with higher buffers or higher credibility than other countries.[21]

Ways in which the governments can exercise fiscal prudence include embarking in structural reforms that facilitate the management of fiscal risks (e.g., pension reform or subsidies reform) and preparing and communicating response strategies and course of action under likely scenarios.

Committing to fiscal rules is one of the ways in which governments prepare and communicate their longer-term strategies (for more on fiscal rules see Chapter 7). As a communication tool, fiscal rules become a signaling device that provides an anchor for expectations on countries' fiscal responsibility even during periods in which a decisive fiscal response is required (Leeper, 2009).

In addition, rules can allow governments to reduce their fiscal balances and debt levels. For a group of 142 countries over the period 1985–2015, Caselli and Reynaud (2019) find that well-designed fiscal rules have a statistically significant impact on fiscal balances. But not all rules are created equally, Caselli et al. (2022) find that countries with more flexible rules are able to have more countercyclical policies; also, countries with rules suffer a more minor contraction during recessions than countries without those rules.

During the pandemic, fiscal rules around the world were suspended. In the current juncture of high inflation and a politically salient cost-of-living crisis created by the surge in food and energy prices, countries face difficult trade-offs: debt levels reached record levels during the pandemic and remain elevated, climate action is urgent, and many are facing important demographic changes. As Caselli et al. (2022) argue, the time seems right to return to fiscal rules to effectively communicate their fiscal plans.

Going back to rules has not only the benefit of helping reduce debt and deficits faster and making their budgets more credible and therefore improving their access to credit but can also grant governments a greater ability to respond to a crisis in real time, allowing fiscal policy to act not only as an engine of growth but as a source of economic resilience and strength.

14.5   CONCLUSION

This chapter has looked at central themes in fiscal policymaking in the last half century. After the Great Inflation, we have seen the surprising combination of unprecedented levels of public debt with unprecedented low levels of nominal interest rates. After COVID-19, inflation surged, and with it, nominal interest rates. This flipped the logic of the interaction between monetary and fiscal policy on its head. At the ELB, monetary policy benefits from fiscal support to bring inflation to target in a timely way. At the same time, monetary policy, by keeping interest rates low for long and by buying Treasuries, creates policy space that facilitates the ability of fiscal policy to respond to. Conversely, when inflation surges well above target after the onset of a temporary emergency, monetary policy, in its effort to bring inflation back to target in a timely manner, benefits from fiscal adjustment.

But these two examples are unusual. In normal times, monetary policy concentrates on price stability and financial stability, while fiscal policy focuses on growth, distribution, efficiency and sustainability.

The practical challenge is how to make all these bits and pieces fit together. They must do so over time as circumstances evolve.

We want to set two difficult challenges for researchers, policymakers, and politicians. Beforehand, we want to go back to Keynes who famously wrote: "But the long run is a misleading guide to current affairs. In the long run we are all dead." This amazing punchline is often interpreted as supporting the primacy of the short run. That is certainly true in an existential emergency. But, we think, is an incomplete account of Keynes' meaning. Because he continues "Economists set themselves too easy, too useless a task if in tempestuous seasons they can only tell us that when the storm is long past the ocean is flat again." This is a call for an explicit modeling of the dynamics of adjustment over time.

In recent years, new Keynesian models have delivered on this ambition. Their results and approaches were recognized and used in the monetary policy strategy reviews by both the Federal Reserve and the ECB. Such work should certainly continue.

But referring to a sentence from Keynes, one hundred years ago, is not good enough. What kind of questions seem most promising right now? We would like to suggest two.

First, how do individual perceptions, beliefs and expectations react to policy actions and announcements together with economic and financial outcomes? How can policy rules, procedures, and frameworks be designed so that private sector behavior helps the achievement of policy objectives?

Second, how should the rules of the political and policy games be designed so that policies are conducted over time in such a way as to promote stable, inclusive, sustainable and resilient growth?

NOTES

1. The field of macroeconomics is vast enough. Among macroeconomic objectives one may list growth, stability, stabilization, efficiency, and distribution. In today's world, global spillovers, of which pandemics and climate change are very salient examples, make the international dimension central to fiscal policy and macroeconomics. That adds an additional layer of complexity.
2. Ball and Mankiw (1995), Aiyagari and McGrattan (1998), and Blanchard (2019) are examples of papers that discuss the impact of debt accumulation on private savings and private capital accumulation.
3. Christiano et al. (2011) is an example of a study that looks at the interaction of fiscal and monetary policy when the ELB is binding. In other chapters of the book the ELB is referred to as zero lower bound (ZLB).
4. Furman (2016) and Furman and Summers (2020) discuss recent views on the role of fiscal policy in economic stabilization.
5. See the IMF's Global Debt Database: https://www.imf.org/external/datamapper/datasets/GDD
6. For a discussion of the drivers of debt cycles see Chapter 2 of this book.
7. Aguiar et al. (2022) show how to generate a wedge between the returns on private capital and public debt. Instead, Gaspar and Peralta-Alva take the spread as given and work out some consequences. To do so they use a standard closed economy, overlapping generations model in the spirit of McCandless and Wallace (1991). The only departure from standard assumptions is the distinction between the returns on the two assets.
8. The model is a simple two-period overlapping generation model with a neoclassical production function. To reproduce a reasonable life span with a two-period model we assume that each period lasts 40 years, and a standard share of income for capital of 0.4.

9. The main modification of the model is assuming a fixed wedge between public debt and private capital (perhaps driven by a convenience yield). The model is also simplified by dropping the disaggregation between the corporate and non-corporate sectors, which are not critical for the question at hand, and by assuming a stationary population. The model is calibrated for the United States. Population dynamics could be brought into the simulation, but we abstract from it to focus squarely on crowding out.
10. For more on the interaction between fiscal and monetary policies see Chapter 4.
11. See, for example, Goodfriend (2000, 2016), Rogoff (2016) and Bernanke (2022). In a cashless economy (Woodford, 2003), corresponding to Wicksell's pure credit economy (Wicksell, 1935), interest rates can as easily be positive as they can be negative.
12. Rotemberg and Woodford (1997), Goodfriend and King (1997, 2001), Clarida et al., (1999), Woodford (2003), Christiano et al., (2005) and Gali (2015).
13. One possibility is the Volcker–Greenspan curse. Both Fed chairs defined price stability as prevailing when inflation is no longer a relevant consideration in economic and financial decisions of households and firms. But when such a situation prevails, people act *as if* inflation and inflation expectations were at zero. If this perspective is taken seriously, defining operational price stability through an inflation target of 2 percent would be contradictory.
14. Ramey and Zubairy (2018) find empirical evidence for a government spending multiplier of 1.5, for the US, at the ZLB. Model-based arguments for very large multipliers at the ZLB include Christiano et al. (2011), Eggertsson (2011) and Woodford (2011). On the other side of the debate, Boneva et al. (2016) show that the effect may be smaller but still come out with a multiplier above 1.
15. See for example Barro (1974), Ball and Mankiw (1995), Blinder and Yellen (2001) and Blinder (2016) for arguments about the comparative ineffectiveness of fiscal policy as stabilization policy.
16. The October 2022 IMF Fiscal Monitor estimates the response of the deficit to GDP ratio to GDP growth to be at least 1.6 and 2 times larger during the GFC and COVID-19 than during typical recessions.
17. The program cost approximately 4 percent of GDP and covered almost 1/3 of the population.
18. The SURE instrument cost €100. Giupponi et al. (2022) state that in 2020 the uptake of those job retention programs had a median of 13 percent of the working population. Results from microsimulations in the October 2022 Fiscal Monitor suggest that these programs absorbed around 40 percent of the market income shock at the European Union level at a fiscal cost of about 2 percent of GDP.
19. The large financial measures prevented firms' bankruptcies and attenuated the recession by increasing corporate liquidity, reducing risk premiums and boosting confidence.
20. However, Gourinchas et al. (2021) do not find evidence that fiscal support to SMEs in 2020 increases the risk of corporate bankruptcy in 2021.
21. Similarly, Romer and Romer (2018) find that the decline on output after a financial crisis is much smaller for countries that count with fiscal and monetary space (about 10 percent decline in GDP for countries without space vs less than 1 percent for those with space). Also, the October 2016 Fiscal Monitor reports that entering a financial crisis with a weak fiscal position worsens the depth and duration of the ensuing recession.

REFERENCES

Aguiar, M. and M. Amador (2021), *The Economics of Sovereign Debt and Default*, Princeton University Press.

Aguiar, M., M. Amador and C. Arellano (2022), "Micro Risks and (Robust) Pareto Improving Policies." *NBER* Working Paper 28996.

Aiyagari, S. and E. McGrattan (1998), "The Optimum Quantity of Debt." *Journal of Monetary Economics* 42(3).

Arbatli, E., D. Botman, K. Clinton, P. Cova, V. Gaspar, Z. Jakab, D. Laxton, C. Lonkeng Ngouana, J. Mongardini and H. Wang (2016), "Reflating Japan: Time to Get Unconventional?" *IMF* Working Paper No. 16/157. International Monetary Fund.

Ball, L. and G. Mankiw (1995), "What Do Budget Deficits Do?" *Proceedings – Economic Policy Symposium – Jackson Hole*, Federal Reserve Bank of Kansas City, pp. 95–119.

Barro, R. (1974), "Are Government Bonds Net Wealth?" *Journal of Political Economy* 82(6).

Barro, R. (1979), "On the Determination of the Public Debt." *Journal of Political Economy* 87(5).

Battersby, B., R. Espinoza, J. Harris, G.H. Hong, S. Lizarazo, P. Mauro and M. Sayegh. (2022), "The State as Financier of Last Resort." *IMF* Staff Discussion Note SDN/2022/003.

Bean, C., C. Broda, T. Ito and R. Kroszner (2015), *Low for Long? Causes and Consequences of Persistently Low Interest Rates*. London, UK: International Center for Monetary and Banking Studies, Centre for Economic Policy Research.

Bernanke, B. (2020), "The New Tools of Monetary Policy." *American Economic Review* 110(4).

Bernanke, B. (2022), *21st Century Monetary Policy: The Federal Reserve from the Great Inflation to Covid-19*. W.W. Norton & Company.

Blanchard, O. (2019), "Public Debt and Low Interest Rates." *American Economic Review* 109(4).

Blanchard, O. (2023), *Fiscal Policy Under Low Interest Rates*. MIT Press.

Blinder, A. (2016), "Fiscal Policy Reconsidered." *The Hamilton Project Policy Proposal 2016-05*, Washington, DC: Brookings Institution.

Blinder, A. and J. Yellen (2001), *The Fabulous Decade: Macroeconomic Lessons From the 1990s*. Century Foundation Press.

Boneva, L., R. Braun and Y. Waki (2016), "Some Unpleasant Properties of Loglinearized Solutions when the Nominal Rate is Zero." *Journal of Monetary Economics* 84.

Burns, A. (1987), "The Anguish of Central Banking." *Money and the Economy: Central Bankers' Views*. Federal Reserve Bulletin, September.

Cao, Y., V. Gaspar and A. Peralta-Alva (2023), "Costly Increases in Public Debt when $r^* < g$." *IMF* Working Paper (forthcoming).

Caselli, F., H. Davoodi, C. Goncalves, G.H. Hong, A. Lagerborg, P. Medas, A.D.M. Nguyen and J. Yoo (2022), "The Return to Fiscal Rules." *IMF* Staff Discussion Note SDN/2022/002.

Caselli, F. and J. Reynaud (2019), "Do Fiscal Rules Cause Better Fiscal Balances? A New Instrumental Variable Strategy." *IMF* Working Paper WP/19/49.

Christiano, L., M. Eichembaum and C. Evans (2005), "Nominal Rigidities and the Dynamic Effects of a Shock to Monetary Policy." *Journal of Political Economy* 113(1).

Christiano, L., M. Eichembaum and S. Rebelo (2011), "When is the Government Spending Multiplier Large?" *Journal of Political Economy* 119(1).

Clarida, R., J. Gali and M. Gertler (1999), "The Science of Monetary Policy: A New Keynesian Perspective." *Journal of Economic Literature* 37(4).

Cole, H. and T. Kehoe (2000), "Self-fulfilling Debt Crises." *Review of Economic Studies* 67(1).

Cunha, D., J. Pereira, R. Perrelli and F. Toscani (2022), "Estimating the Employment and GDP Multiplier of Emergency Cash Transfers in Brazil." *IMF* Working Paper 22/55.

Eggertsson, G. (2011), "What Fiscal Policy is Effective at Zero Interest Rates?" *NBER Macroeconomics Annual* 25 (2011).

European Central Bank (2021), "The ECB's Monetary Policy Strategy Statement." *ECB* July 8, 2021.

Federal Reserve Board (2020), "Review of Monetary Policy Strategy, Tools, and Communications." August 27, 2020.

Furman, J. (2016), "The New View of Fiscal Policy and its Application." VoxEU.org, October 5, 2016, 2.

Furman, J. and L. Summers (2020), "A Reconsideration of Fiscal Policy in the Era of Low Interest Rates." Harvard Kennedy School, November 30, 2020, Working Paper.

Gali, J. (2015), *Monetary Policy, Inflation, and the Business Cycle: An Introduction to the New Keynesian Framework and its Applications.* Princeton University Press.

Gaspar, V., M. Obstfeld, R. Sahay and D. Laxton (2016), "Macroeconomic Management When Policy Space is Constrained: A Comprehensive, Consistent and Coordinated Approach to Economic Policy." *IMF* Staff Discussion Notes 2016/01/01.

Giupponi, G., C. Landais and A. Lapeyre (2022), "Should we Insure Workers or Jobs during Recessions?" *Journal of Economic Perspectives* 36(2).

Goodfriend, M. (2000), "Overcoming the Zero Bound on Interest Rate Policy." *Journal of Money, Credit and Banking* 32.

Goodfriend, M. (2016), "The Case for Unencumbering Interest Rate Policy." *Jackson Hole Economic Policy Symposium* 26.

Goodfriend, M. and R. King (1997), "The New Neoclassical Synthesis and the Role of Monetary Policy." *NBER Macroeconomic Annual* 12 (1997).

Goodfriend, M. and R. King (2001), "The Case for Price Stability." *NBER* Working Paper 8423.

Gourinchas, P.O., S. Kalemli-Özcan, V. Penciakova and N. Sander (2021), "COVID-19 and Small- and Medium-Sized Enterprises: A 2021 'Time Bomb'?" *AEA Papers and Proceedings* 2021, https://doi.org/10.1257/pandp.20211109

Hall, G. and T. Sargent (2022), "Three World Wars: Fiscal–Monetary Consequences." *Proceedings of the National Academy of Sciences.*

Leeper, E. (2009), "Anchoring Fiscal Expectations." *NBER* Working Paper 15269.

McCandless, G. and N. Wallace (1991), *Introduction to Dynamic Macroeconomic Theory: An Overlapping Generations Approach.* Harvard University Press.

McGrattan, E.R., M. Kazuaki and A. Peralta-Alva (2019), "On Financing Retirement, Health Care, and Long-Term Care in Japan." Staff Report 586, Federal Reserve Bank of Minneapolis.

Moreno Badia, M., P. Medas, P. Gupta and Y. Xiang (2022), "Debt is Not Free." *Journal of International Money and Finance* 127, October 2022, 102654.

Ramey, V. and S. Zubairy (2018), "Government Spending Multipliers in Good Times and in Bad: Evidence from US Historical Data." *Journal of Political Economy* 126(2).

Reis, R. (2021), "The Constraint on Public Debt when *r*<*g* but *g*<*m*." *BIS* Working Paper 939.

Rogoff, K. (2016), *The Curse of Cash*. Princeton University Press.

Romer, C. and D. Romer (2018), "Phillips Lecture – Why Some Times are Different: Macroeconomic Policy and the Aftermath of Financial Crises." *Economica* 85(337).

Rotemberg, J. and M. Woodford (1997), "An Optimization-Based Econometric Framework for the Evaluation of Monetary Policy." *NBER Macroeconomics Annual* 12.

Sargent, T. (2022), "Rational Expectations and Volcker's Disinflation." *Essays in Honor of Marvin Goodfriend: Economist and Central Banker*. Federal Reserve Bank of Richmond.

Shirakawa, M. (2021), *Tumultuous Times: Central Banking in an Era of Crisis*. Yale University Press.

Tobin, J. (1980), "Stabilization Policy Ten Years After." *Brooking Papers on Economic Activity*, 11(1), Tenth Anniversary Issue.

Volcker, P. (2018), *Keeping at It: The Quest for Sound Money and Good Government*. Public Affairs.

Wicksell, K. (1935), *Lectures on Political Economy V2: Money*. Kessinger Publishing, LLC (September 10, 2010).

Woodford, M. (2003), *Interest and Prices: Foundations of a Theory of Monetary Policy*. Princeton University Press.

Woodford, M. (2011), "Simple Analytics of the Government Expenditure Multiplier." *American Economic Journal: Macroeconomics* 3(1).

Index

Lane, P. R. 80
Lebanon 39
Leeper, E. 89–90
lender of last resort 143
life expectancy 10–11, 61–2, 184–5,
    187–8, 196
life insurance 193
liquidity 6, 44, 48, 63, 66, 69, 88, 93,
    145, 147–50, 217
litigation 40, 45, 47–8, 50–51
London Club 45–6
long-term care 10–11, 14, 184–7, 190,
    192–4, 196
low interest rates 3–5, 12–17, 58–72, 91,
    97, 135, 161, 210–11
low-income countries 34–5, 39, 43, 48,
    81, 104–5, 112, 160, *see also*
    individual countries
low-income groups 157, 161, 163, 165,
    168, 188, 192
Luxembourg 193

Maastricht Treaty 121, 124, 132
Malaysia 107
maturities 44–5
Mauritius 107
McGrattan, E. R. 212
medium-term fiscal frameworks 113
Mertens, K. 89
Mexico 186
Mian, A. 92
middle-income countries 25, 43, *see also*
    individual countries
migration 133
monetary policy 2–3, 5–6, 8, 12–13, 15,
    44, 58–72, 87, 90–92, 94–6, 98,
    132, 134, 139, 148, 150, 172–3,
    179, 181, 210–11, 213–16,
    219–20
moral hazard 46, 126, 134, 150
Mozambique 45
multilateral development banks 25, 39
multinationals 6–7, 10, 15–16, 73–81,
    163
Musgrave, R. 3

narrative approach 86, 88–9
National Recovery and Resilience Plan
    204

natural interest rate 5, 13, 58, 60–65, 68,
    70, 99
neo-classicalism 1–2
Netherlands 158, 186, 188, 193–4
non-bank financial intermediation
    150–51
Norway 75, 194

official creditors 39, 42–4, 46–51
Okun, A. 217
Organisation for Economic Co-operation
    and Development 87–90, 123,
    131, 145, 158–9, 168–9, 174, 176,
    185–6, 188, 190, 192, 194, 206
    Inclusive Framework 6, 74

Pandemic Crisis *see* Covid-19 pandemic
Panizza, U. 25, 40
paradox of thrift 12, 212
Paris Agreement 199, 205
Paris Club 39, 45–8, 50
    Common Framework for Debt
        Treatments 5, 44–52
    Evian Approach 47, 51
patents 73, 75
pensions 9–11, 14, 16, 30, 48, 62, 103,
    106, 121, 156, 158, 162, 184–5,
    187–90, 194, 196, 218
Pereira da Silva, L. 173, 179
Perotti, R. 88–9
personal income tax 10, 75, 81, 157–8,
    160, 163–4, 169–70, 173–4
Peru 107, 115
Philippon, T. 62
Piketty, T. 158
Poland 107
policy mix 90, 96, 136, 169, 181, 211,
    213–17
population ageing *see* ageing
populism 155
Portugal 188
poverty 44–5, 53, 155, 157, 161, 164–5,
    189, 195–6
price stability 2, 12, 64–5, 68, 124,
    134–5, 210, 213–14, 219
private debt 26, 86, 91–3
productivity growth 13, 60, 62, 64, 80,
    211, 215
profit shifting 6, 73–4, 76–81